AAT

Technician Unit 18

Preparing Business Taxation Computations (FA 2003)

For assessments in June 2004 and December 2004

Interactive Text

In this August 2003 first edition

- Material rewritten for assessments under the new standards
- Layout designed to be easier on the eye – and easy to use
- Clear language and presentation
- Activities checklist to tie in each activity to specific knowledge and understanding, performance criteria and/or range statement
- Thorough reliable updating of material to FA 2003

FOR EXAM BASED ASSESSMENTS IN JUNE 2004 AND DECEMBER 2004 UNDER THE FINANCE ACT 2003 TAX LEGISLATION

BPP PROFESSIONAL EDUCATION

First edition August 2003

ISBN 07517 1229 9

British Library Cataloguing-in-Publication Data
A catalogue record for this book
is available from the British Library

Published by

BPP Professional Education
Aldine House, Aldine Place
London W12 8AW

www.bpp.com

Printed in Great Britain by W M Print
45-47 Frederick Street
Walsall, West Midlands
WS2 9NE

We are grateful to the Lead Body for Accounting for permission to reproduce extracts from the Standards of Competence for Accounting, and to the AAT for permission to reproduce extracts from the mapping and Guidance Notes.

Contents

Introduction

PART D National insurance

PART E Administration

Introduction

How to use this Interactive Text

Aims of this Interactive Text

To provide the knowledge and practice to help you succeed in the assessment for Technician Unit 18 *Preparing Business Tax Computations.*

To pass the assessment successfully you need a thorough understanding in all areas covered by the standards of competence.

To tie in with the other components of the BPP Effective Study Package to ensure you have the best possible chance of success.

Interactive Text

This covers all you need to know for the exam based assessment for Unit 18 *Preparing Business Tax Computations.* Numerous activities throughout the text help you practise what you have just learnt.

Assessment Kit

When you have understood and practised the material in the Interactive Text, you will have the knowledge and experience to tackle the Assessment Kit for Unit 18 *Preparing Business Tax Computations.* This aims to get you through the exam by providing you with plenty of activities to practise

Passcards

These short memorable notes are focused on key topics for the technician units, designed to remind you of what the Interactive Text has taught you.

Recommended approach to this Interactive Text

(a) To achieve competence in Unit 18 (and all the other units) you need to be able to do **everything** specified by the standards. Study the Interactive Text carefully and do not skip any of it.

(b) Learning is an **active** process. Do **all** the activities as you work through the Interactive Text so you can be sure you really understand what you have read.

(c) After you have covered the material in the Interactive Text, work through the **Assessment Kit**.

(d) Before you take the examination, check that you still remember the material using the following quick revision plan for each chapter.

  (i) Read and learn the **key learning points**, which are a summary of the chapter. This includes key terms and shows the sort of things likely to come up in an assessment. Are there any gaps in your knowledge? If so, study the section again.

  (ii) Do the **quick quiz** again. If you know what you're doing, it shouldn't take long.

  (iii) Go through the **Passcards** as often as you can in the weeks leading up to your examination.

This approach is only a suggestion. Your college may well adapt it to suit your needs.

Quick quizzes

These include multiple choice questions, true/false and other formats not used by the AAT. However, these types of questions are usually very familiar to students and are used to help students adjust to otherwise unfamiliar material.

Remember this is a **practical** course.

(a) Try to relate the material to your experience in the workplace or any other work experience you may have had.

(b) Try to make as many links as you can to your study of the other Units at Technician level.

(c) Keep this text, (hopefully) you will find it invaluable in your everyday work too!

Inland Revenue forms

In your Assessment you are likely to have to either complete or take information from Inland Revenue Forms. We have included the applicable forms within an appendix to this text for illustrative purposes. You will practice using these forms when you try the Assessments in BPP's Unit 19 Assessment Kit.

Please note that at the time this Text was printed 2003/04 versions of the Inland Revenue forms were not available. We have therefore updated the 2002/03 versions of the forms and amended them where necessary to fit in with Finance Act 2003 tax legislation. This necessarily involves us in making 'guesses' about how the 2003/04 forms will change. Although, it is unlikely that the 2003/04 versions of the forms will differ significantly from what we have included here, it is important that you contact the Inland Revenue for updated copies before you take your assessment.

If you have internet access you should be able to find the 2003/04 forms on the Inland Revenue's website (www.inlandrevenue.gov.UK).

Technician qualification structure

The competence-based Education and Training Scheme of the Association of Accounting Technicians is based on an analysis of the work of accounting staff in a wide range of industries and types of organisation. The Standards of Competence for Accounting which students are expected to meet are based on this analysis.

The AAT issued new standards of competence in 2002, which take effect from 1 July 2003. This Text reflects the **new standards.**

The Standards identify the key purpose of the accounting occupation, which is to operate, maintain and improve systems to record, plan, monitor and report on the financial activities of an organisation, and a number of key roles of the occupation. Each key role is subdivided into units of competence, which are further divided into elements of competences. By successfully completing assessments in specified units of competence, students can gain qualifications at NVQ/SVQ levels 2, 3 and 4, which correspond to the AAT Foundation, Intermediate and Technician stages of competence respectively.

Whether you are competent in a Unit is demonstrated by means of:

- *Either* an Exam Based Assessment (set and marked by AAT assessors)
- *Or* a Skills Based Assessment (where competence is judged by an Approved Assessment Centre to whom responsibility for this is devolved)
- Or *both* Exam *and* Skills Based Assessment

Below we set out the overall structure of the Technician (NVQ/SVQ Level 4) stage, indicating how competence in each Unit is assessed. In the next section there is more detail about the Exam Based Assessments for Unit 18.

NVQ/SVQ Level 4

Group 1 Core Units – All units are mandatory.

Unit 8 Contributing to the Management of Performance and the Enhancement of Value	Element 8.1	Collect, analyse and disseminate information about costs
	Element 8.2	Make recommendations and make recommendations to enhance value
Unit 9 Contributing to the Planning and Control of Resources	Element 9.1	Prepare forecasts of income and expenditure
	Element 9.2	Produce draft budget proposals
	Element 9.3	Monitor the performance of responsibility centres against budgets
Unit 10 Managing Systems and People in the Accounting Environment	Element 10.1	Manage people within the accounting environment
	Element 10.2	Identify opportunities for improving the effectiveness of an accounting system
Unit 22 Contribute to the Maintenance of a Healthy, Safe and Productive Working Environment	Element 22.1	Contribute to the maintenance of a healthy, safe and productive working environment
	Element 22.2	Monitor and maintain an effective and efficient working environment

NVQ/SVQ Level 4, continued

Group 2 Optional Units – Choose **one** of the following **four** units.

Unit 11 Drafting Financial Statements (Accounting Practice, Industry and Commerce)	Element 11.1 Draft limited company financial statements Element 11.2 Interpret limited company financial statements
Unit 12 Drafting Financial Statements (Central Government)	Element 12.1 Draft Central Government financial statements Element 12.2 Interpret Central Government financial statements
Unit 13 Drafting Financial Statements (Local Government)	Element 13.1 Draft Local Authority financial statements Element 13.2 Interpret Local Authority financial statements
Unit 14 Drafting Financial Statements (National Health Service)	Element 14.1 Draft NHS accounting statements and returns Element 14.2 Interpret NHS accounting statements and returns

NVQ/SVQ Level 4, continued

Group 3 Optional Units – Choose **two** of the following **four** units.

Unit 15 Operating a Cash Management and Credit Control System	Element 15.1 Monitor and control cash receipts and payments Element 15.2 Manage cash balances Element 15.3 Grant credit Element 15.4 Monitor and control the collection of debts
Unit 17 Implementing Audit Procedures	Element 17.1 Contribute to the planning of an audit assignment Element 17.2 Contribute to the conduct of an audit assignment Element 17.3 Prepare related draft reports
Unit 18 Preparing Business Taxation Computations	Element 18.1 Prepare capital allowances computations Element 18.2 Compute assessable business income Element 18.3 Prepare capital gains computations Element 18.4 Prepare Corporation Tax computations
Unit 19 Preparing Personal Taxation Computations	Element 19.1 Calculate income from employment Element 19.2 Calculate property and investment income Element 19.3 Prepare Income Tax computations Element 19.4 Prepare Capital Gains Tax computations

Unit 18 Standards of competence

The structure of the Standards for Unit 18

The Unit commences with a statement of the **knowledge and understanding** which underpin competence in the Unit's elements.

The Unit of Competence is then divided into **elements of competence** describing activities which the individual should be able to perform.

Each element includes:

(a) A set of **performance criteria.** This defines what constitutes competent performance.

(b) A **range statement.** This defines the situations, contexts, methods etc in which competence should be displayed.

The elements of competence for Unit 18: *Preparing Business Taxation Computations* are set out below. Knowledge and understanding required for the Unit as a whole are listed first, followed by the performance criteria and range statements for each element.

Unit 18: Preparing Business Taxation Computations

What is the Unit about?

This unit is about preparing tax computations for businesses and completing the relevant tax returns. There are four elements.

The first element requires you to prepare capital allowances computations, including adjustments for private use by the owners of a business.

In the second element you must prepare assessable business income computations for partnerships and self-employed individuals. This includes identifying the National Insurance Contributions payable.

The third element is concerned with preparing capital gains computations for companies and unincorporated businesses.

The final element requires you to prepare Corporation Tax computations for UK resident companies.

Throughout the unit you must show that you take account of current tax law and Inland Revenue practice and make submissions within statutory timescales. You also need to show that you consult with the Inland Revenue in an open and constructive manner, give timely and constructive advice to business clients and maintain client confidentiality.

Knowledge and understanding

To perform this unit effectively you will need to know and understand:

The business environment

1 The duties and responsibilities of the tax practitioner (Elements 18.1, 18.2, 18.3 & 18.4)

2 The issues of taxation liability (Elements 18.1, 18.2, 18.3 & 18.4)

3 Relevant legislation and guidance from the Inland Revenue (Elements 18.1, 18.2, 18.3 & 18.4)

Taxation principles and theory

4 Basic law and practice relating to all issues covered in the range and referred to in the performance criteria (Elements 18.1, 18.2, 18.3 & 18.4)

5 Availability and types of capital allowance:
- first year allowance
- writing down allowance
- balancing allowance and charge (relevant to industrial buildings and plant and machinery including computers, motor vehicles and short life assets) (Element 18.1)

6 Treatment of capital allowances for unincorporated businesses including private use adjustments (Element 18.1)

7 Adjustment of trading profits and losses for tax purposes (Element 18.2)

8 Regulations relating to disallowed expenditure such as business entertaining, bad debt write-offs and provisions, private expenditure and capital expenditure (Element 18.2)

9 Basis of assessment of unincorporated businesses (Element 18.2)

10 Basic allocation of income between partners (Element 18.3)

11 Identification of business assets disposed of including part disposals (Element 18.3)

12 Calculation of gains and losses on disposals of business assets including indexation allowance (Element 18.3)

13 Capital gains exemptions and reliefs on business assets including rollover relief and taper relief but excluding retirement relief ((Element 18.3)

14 Rates of tax payable on gains on business assets disposed of by individuals (Element 18.3)

15 The computation of profit for Corporation Tax purposes including income, capital gains and charges (Element 18.4)

16 Calculation of Corporation Tax payable by starting, small, large and marginal companies including those with associated companies (Element 18.4)

17 Set-off of trading losses incurred by companies (Element 18.4)

18 Calculation of National Insurance Contributions payable by self-employed persons and employers of not contracted-out employees (Element 18.2 & 18.4)

19 Self assessment including payment of tax and filing of returns for unincorporated businesses and companies (Element 18.2 & 18.4)

The organisation

20 How the taxation liabilities of an organisation are affected by its legal structure and the nature of its business transactions (Elements 18.1, 18.2, 18.3 & 18.4)

21 The organisation's legal structure and its business transactions (Elements 18.1, 18.2, 18.3 & 18.4)

Element 18.1 Prepare capital allowances computations

Performance criteria

In order to perform this element successfully you need to:

A Classify expenditure on capital assets in accordance with the statutory distinction between capital and revenue expenditure

B Ensure that entries and calculations relating to the computation of capital allowances for a company are correct

C Make adjustments for private use by business owners

D Ensure that computations and submissions are made in accordance with current tax law and take account of current Inland Revenue practice

E Consult with Inland Revenue staff in an open and constructive manner

F Give timely and constructive advice to clients on the maintenance of accounts and the recording of information relevant to tax returns

G Maintain client confidentiality at all times

Range statement

Performance in this element relates to the following contexts:

- Self-employed individuals – Partnerships

Element 18.2 Compute assessable business income

Performance criteria

In order to perform this element successfully you need to:

A Adjust trading profits and losses for tax purposes

B Make adjustments for private use by business owners

C Divide profits and losses of partnerships amongst partners

D Apply the basis of assessment for unincorporated businesses in the opening and closing years

E Identify the due dates of payment of Income Tax by unincorporated businesses, including payments on account

F Identify the National Insurance Contributions payable by self-employed individuals

G Complete correctly the self-employed and partnership supplementary pages to the Tax Return for individuals, together with relevant claims and elections, and submit them within statutory time limits

H Consult with Inland Revenue staff in an open and constructive manner

I Give timely and constructive advice to clients on the maintenance of accounts and the recording of information relevant to tax returns

J Maintain client confidentiality at all times

Range statement

Performance in this element relates to the following contexts:

- Sole traders – Partnerships

Element 18.3 Prepare capital gains computations

Performance criteria

In order to perform this element successfully you need to:

A Identify and value correctly any chargeable assets that have been disposed of

B Identify shares disposed of by companies

C Calculate chargeable gains and allowable losses

D Apply reliefs, deferrals and exemptions correctly

E Ensure that computations and submissions are made in accordance with current tax law and take account of current Inland Revenue practice

F Consult with Inland Revenue staff in an open and constructive manner

G Give timely and constructive advice to clients on the maintenance of accounts and the recording of information relevant to tax returns

H Maintain client confidentiality at all times

Range statement

Performance in this element relates to the following contexts:

- Chargeable assets that have been:

  Sold
  Gifted
  Lost
  Destroyed

- Reliefs:

  Rollover relief
  Relief for gifts

Element 18.4 Prepare Corporation Tax computations

Performance criteria

In order to perform this element successfully you need to:

A Enter adjusted trading profits and losses, capital allowances, investment income and capital gains in the Corporation Tax computation

B Set-off and deduct loss reliefs and charges correctly

C Calculate Corporation Tax due, taking account of marginal relief

D Identify and set-off Income Tax deductions and credits

E Identify the National Insurance Contributions payable by employers

F Identify the amount of Corporation Tax payable and the due dates of payment, including payments on account

G Complete Corporation Tax returns correctly and submit them, together with relevant claims and elections, within statutory time limits

H Consult with Inland Revenue staff in an open and constructive manner

I Give timely and constructive advice to clients on the maintenance of accounts and the recording of information relevant to tax returns

J Maintain client confidentiality at all times

Range statement

Performance in this element relates to the following contexts:

- Loss reliefs relating to:

  Trade losses – Non-trade losses

Assessment strategy

This Unit is assessed by **exam based assessment** only.

Exam based assessment

An exam based assessment is a means of collecting evidence that you have the **essential knowledge and understanding** which underpins competence. It is also a means of collecting evidence across the **range of contexts** for the standards, and of your ability to **transfer skills**, knowledge and understanding to different situations. Thus, although central assessments contain practical tests linked to the performance criteria, they also focus on the underpinning knowledge and understanding. You should, in addition, expect each central assessment to contain tasks taken from across a broad range of the standards.

Format of exam

There will be a three hour exam in two sections.

Section 1:	Element 18.2 (taxation of sole traders and partnerships)
Section 2:	Element 18.4 (taxation of limited companies)

Elements 18.1 and 18.3 can appear in either section.

There will be an additional 15 minutes reading time.

Further guidance

The Standard is divided into four elements. Element 18.1 is called Prepare capital allowances computations, Element 18.2 is called Compute assessable business income, Element 18.3 is called Prepare capital gains computations and Element 18.4 is called Prepare Corporation Tax computations.

Element 18.1 is not to be seen in isolation. It has an impact on both Element 18.2 and 18.4. This is because both 18.2 and 18.4 require the calculation of Schedule D Case I/II profits or losses, and capital allowances need to be deducted as an allowable expense.

Specific areas that need to be covered are:

1. Awareness of the kind of expenditure on which capital allowances will be available: What is plant and machinery? What is an industrial building? When is expenditure for capital purposes and when is it for revenue purposes?
2. The ability to calculate capital allowances on: Plant and machinery. This includes special rules on: Motor vehicles; Short life assets; Computers; First year allowances; Private use assets (unincorporated businesses only); Industrial buildings allowance (this only includes buildings that have continuously been used for industrial purposes).

These calculations need to be made for both unincorporated and incorporated businesses. The rules governing opening, continuing and ceasing organisations need to be considered.

Writing down allowances, balancing allowances and balancing charges are required.

Students must consider the rationale behind these calculations, so that they can provide a written explanation of the calculations, for instance, when dealing with client queries.

The purpose of **Element 18.2** is to demonstrate the ability to calculate Schedule D Case I/II profits or losses.

Firstly, students should be able to determine whether trading is taking place, for instance, through the use of the badges of trade.

In calculating the adjusted Schedule D Case I/II profit or loss of the business, a sound knowledge is required of how to adjust the accounting profit or loss. Only a few of the adjustments required are specifically mentioned in the Knowledge and Understanding. This list should be viewed as being indicative, rather than exhaustive. Part of these adjustments is the ability to correctly identify, and adjust for, private usage of expenditure as shown in the accounting profit and loss account.

If the trade is being carried on by a partnership, students need to be able to determine how profits are to be split between the partners according to the rules laid down by the Inland Revenue. This includes changes in the profit-sharing agreement or a change in the composition of the partnership, such as when a partner joins or leaves the business.

For both a sole trader and a partnership, a sound knowledge is required of the rules for opening, continuing and closing years of trade. This includes overlap profits. However, the rules for the change of accounting date are excluded. Such calculations will be expected in round tax months, not in days.

Once determined, students need to demonstrate understanding of the use of the profit or loss in the inclusion of the income tax return. The dates for submission of the return and payment of income tax must be considered, together with the implications of making a late filing of the return. However, the completion of the actual income tax return and completion of the income tax computation is assessable under Unit 19.

If the Schedule D Case I/II figure results in a loss, students must have knowledge of the ways in which such a loss can be relieved. S.385, S.380, S.381 and S. 388 ICTA 1988 should all be covered, but detailed and complex loss relief provisions will not be assessed. Excluded from this are losses for partnerships.

For National Insurance Contributions, knowledge of both Class 2 and Class 4 is required.

Element 18.3 deals with the calculation of capital gains for businesses only. This includes chargeable disposals by individuals and companies of business assets, and of the business itself. Disposal of private assets held by individuals is assessable under Unit 19. Taper relief is therefore included where an individual disposes of a business asset, but the treatment of capital gains for a partnership is excluded.

Capital gains computations may include:

Shares and securities, including rights issues and bonus issues, FA 1985 pool and matching rules
Chattels
Part disposal of assets
Improvement expenditure
Indexation allowance
Tapering relief as appropriate to individuals

A capital gain computation will not be required on any assets acquired before 31 March 1982.

In addition, students should have an understanding of business reliefs, including rollover relief and relief for gifts. Students should be able to demonstrate knowledge about the conditions for such reliefs and be able to complete basic calculations. Complex calculations will not be required, for example assets with non-business use, depreciating assets or partial reinvestment or gift. Also, retirement relief is now excluded from the standards.

The capital tax implications for leases are also excluded.

Under **Element 18.4**, the student must be able to compute the Schedule D Case I profit or loss of a company using the same rules for capital allowances and adjustment of profit as detailed in Elements 18.1 and 18.2 respectively. A capital gains computation from Element 18.3 may also be included in a full Corporation Tax computation. For periods of accounts, students should be able to understand how those shorter or longer than twelve months affect the CT computation.

If the company has made a loss, knowledge is expected of how to deal with that loss under S.393 (1) and S393A (1) ICTA 1988. This includes computational aspects of loss relief, together with the ability to provide clients with advice on the best option to take for the most tax effective way of handling the loss, albeit in a simple way. The impact of charges on loss relief is restricted to non-trade charges only, given the change in classification of patent royalties from 1 April

2002. Students should be able to deal with company losses other than Schedule D Case I, such as capital losses and Schedule A.

When determining the amount of Corporation Tax payable, the following knowledge is required: the impact of the starting rate, the use of upper and lower limits for small company rate purposes, the use of the marginal relief calculation, together with the impact of associated companies on the limits for the marginal relief, the deduction of income tax and the calculation of Mainstream Corporation Tax payable.

Students should also be able to state the due date of payment and be able to explain the self-assessment rules. Translation of these figures to the short version of Form CT600 may also be required.

For National Insurance Contributions, students should be able to compute the NIC payable by companies for their employees who are not contracted out. This includes an understanding of the definition of earnings, on which the NIC will be based.

Excluded topics from this element are: close companies and close investment holding companies, investment companies, groups and consortium structures, group capital gains tax, overseas aspects, including double tax relief, calculation of Schedule A rental income (assessable under Unit 19).

Typical tasks in the first section

- Schedule D Case I/II computation, leading to either a profit or a loss. This could be for either a sole trader or a partnership
- Set-off of income tax losses for individuals
- Capital allowances computation for industrial buildings and/or plant and machinery
- Capital gains computation for business asset disposals for an individual
- National Insurance Contributions for the self-employed
- Opening and closing rules for unincorporated businesses, including overlap profits
- Completion of the supplementary pages to the Tax Return for individuals

Typical tasks in the second section

- Schedule D Case I computation, leading to either a profit or a loss
- Set-off of Schedule D Case I losses, restricted to a scenario involving four years
- Capital allowances computation for industrial buildings and/or plant and machinery
- Capital gains computation for limited companies
- Calculation of the Corporation Tax payable, including small company marginal relief, MCT and the dates of payment
- National Insurance Contributions for the employees of companies
- Completion of the Corporation Tax returns

It is not anticipated that students will be required to compute certain topics more than once during the examination. For instance, capital allowances for industrial buildings and plant and machinery will only be assessed once in either Section 1 or Section 2. The same principle applies for capital gains, although it may be appropriate to assess the disposal of a business in Section 1 and the disposal of shares in Section 2.

Finance Act 2003

Note that at the time of printing this Text the AAT had not issued any further guidance on how any of the Finance Act 2003 provisions will be examined. You are advised to check for this guidance before you sit your examination. BPP Professional Education will post any relevant information received into their internet site www.bpp.com/aat.

Building your portfolio

What is a portfolio?

A portfolio is a collection of work that demonstrates what the owner can do. In AAT language the portfolio demonstrates **competence**.

A painter will have a collection of his paintings to exhibit in a gallery, an advertising executive will have a range of advertisements and ideas that she has produced to show to a prospective client. Both the collection of paintings and the advertisements form the portfolio of that artist or advertising executive.

Your portfolio will be unique to you just as the portfolio of the artist will be unique because no one will paint the same range of pictures in the same way. It is a very personal collection of your work and should be treated as a **confidential** record.

What evidence should a portfolio include?

No two portfolios will be the same but by following some simple guidelines you can decide which of the following suggestions will be appropriate in your case.

(a) **Your current CV**

This should be at the front. It will give your personal details as well as brief descriptions of posts you have held with the most recent one shown first.

(b) **References and testimonials**

References from previous employers may be included especially those of which you are particularly proud.

(c) **Your current job description**

You should emphasise financial **responsibilities and duties**.

(d) **Your student record sheets**

These should be supplied by AAT when you begin your studies, and your training provider should also have some if necessary.

(e) **Evidence from your current workplace**

This could take many forms including **letters, memos, reports** you have written, **copies of accounts** or **reconciliations** you have prepared, **discrepancies** you have investigated etc. Remember to obtain permission to include the evidence from your line manager because some records may be sensitive. Discuss the performance criteria that are listed in your Student Record Sheets with your training provider and employer, and think of other evidence that could be appropriate to you.

(f) **Evidence from your social activities**

For example you may be the treasurer of a club in which case examples of your cash and banking records could be appropriate.

(g) **Evidence from your studies**

Few students are able to satisfy all the requirements of competence by workplace evidence alone. They therefore rely on simulations to provide the remaining evidence to complete a unit. If you are not working or not working in a relevant post, then you may need to rely more heavily on simulations as a source of evidence.

(h) **Additional work**

Your training provider may give you work that specifically targets one or a group of performance criteria in order to complete a unit. It could take the form of questions, presentations or demonstrations. Each training provider will approach this in a different way.

(i) **Evidence from a previous workplace**

This evidence may be difficult to obtain and should be used with caution because it must satisfy the 'rules' of evidence, that is it must be current. Only rely on this as evidence if you have changed jobs recently.

(j) **Prior achievements**

For example you may have already completed the health and safety unit during a previous course of study, and therefore there is no need to repeat this work. Advise your training provider who will check to ensure that it is the same unit and record it as complete if appropriate.

How should it be presented?

As you assemble the evidence remember to **make a note** of it on your Student Record Sheet in the space provided and **cross reference** it. In this way it is easy to check to see if your evidence is **appropriate**. Remember one piece of evidence may satisfy a number of performance criteria so remember to check this thoroughly and discuss it with your training provider if in doubt.

To keep all your evidence together a ring binder or lever arch file is a good means of storage.

When should evidence be assembled?

You should begin to assemble evidence **as soon as you have registered as a student**. **Don't leave it all** until the last few weeks of your studies, because you may miss vital deadlines and your resulting certificate sent by the AAT may not include all the units you have completed. Give yourself and your training provider time to examine your portfolio and report your results to AAT at regular intervals. In this way the task of assembling the portfolio will be spread out over a longer period of time and will be presented in a more professional manner.

What are the key criteria that the portfolio must fulfil?

As you assemble your evidence bear in mind that it must be:

- **Valid**. It must relate to the Standards.
- **Authentic**. It must be your own work.
- **Current**. It must refer to your current or most recent job.
- **Sufficient**. It must meet all the performance criteria by the time you have completed your portfolio.

What are the most important elements in a portfolio that covers Unit 18?

You should remember that the unit is about preparing **business tax computations**. Therefore you need to produce evidence demonstrating that you can compute the taxable profits of sole traders, partners and companies. You also need to produce evidence demonstrating that you can compute the tax on these taxable profits.

To satisfy *Element 18.1 prepare capital allowances computations* you can produce any capital allowance or industrial buildings allowance computation that you have prepared in practice.

For *Element 18.2 compute assessable business income* you need to demonstrate that you can adjust the profits/losses in a set of accounts to arrive at Schedule D Case I profit. Keep copies of any adjustments that you have prepared in practice.

To fulfil the requirements of *Element 18.3 prepare capital gains tax computations* you need to demonstrate that you can calculate chargeable gains for both companies and individuals. You also need to demonstrate that you can identify chargeable and exempt items.

Element 18.4 requires you to *prepare corporation tax computations and returns*. Suitable evidence will be an actual computation you have prepared or checked or any element of a company's profits chargeable to corporation tax that you have computed, or checked.

Finally

Remember that the portfolio is **your property** and **your responsibility**. Not only could it be presented to the external verifier before your award can be confirmed; it could be used when you are seeking **promotion** or applying for a more senior and better paid post elsewhere. How your portfolio is presented can say as much about you as the evidence inside.

For further information on portfolio building, see the BPP Text *Building Your Portfolio.* This can be ordered using the form at the back of this Text or via the Internet: www.bpp.com/aat

Tax rates and allowances

A Income tax

1 **Rates**

	2002/03		2003/04	
	£	%	£	%
Starting rate	1 – 1,920	10	1 – 1,960	10
Basic rate	1,921 – 29,900	22	1,961 – 30,500	22
Higher rate	29,901 and above	40	30,501 and above	40

Savings (excl. Dividend) income is taxed at 20% if it falls in the basic rate band. Dividend income in both the starting rate and the basic rate bands is taxed at 10%. Dividend income within the higher rate band is taxed at 32.5%.

2 **Allowances**

	2002/03	2003/04
	£	£
Personal allowance	4,615	4,615

3 **Authorised mileage rates (AMR) 2003/04 rates**

The rates for the maximum tax free mileage allowances for 2003/04 are as follows:

*Car mileage rates**

First 10,000 miles	40p per mile
Over 10,000 miles	25p per mile

Bicycles	*Motor cycles*
20p per mile	24p per mile
Passenger payments	5p per mile

* For NIC purposes, a rate of 40p applies irrespective of mileage.

4 **Capital allowances**

	%
Plant and machinery	
Writing down allowance	25
First year allowance (acquisitions after 2.7.98)	40
First year allowance (information and communication technology equipment – period 1.4.00 – 31.3.04, energy/water saving equipment)	100
Industrial buildings allowance	
Writing down allowance:	4

B Corporation tax

1 Rates

Financial year	Full rate %	Small companies rate %	Starting rate	Starting rate marginal relief fraction	Lower limit for starting rate £	Upper limit for starting rate £	Small companies' rate marginal relief	Upper limit for SCR £	Lower Limit for SCR £
1999	30	20	-	1/40	-	-	1/40	1,500,000	300,000
2000	30	20	10	1/40	10,000	50,000	1/40	1,500,000	300,000
2001	30	20	10	1/40	10,000	50,000	1/40	1,500,000	300,000
2002	30	19	0	19/400	10,000	50,000	11/400	1,500,000	300,000
2003	30	19	0	19/400	10,000	50,000	11/400	1,500,000	300,000

2 Marginal relief

$(M - P) \times I/P \times$ Marginal relief fraction

C Rates of interest

Official rate of interest: 5% (assumed)
Rate of interest on unpaid tax: 6.5% (assumed)
Rate of interest on overpaid tax: 2.5% (assumed)

D Capital gains tax

1 Annual exemption (individuals)

	£
2001/02	7,500
2002/03	7,700
2003/04	7,900

2 Taper relief

Number of complete years after 5.4.98 for which asset held	*Business assets % of gain chargeable*
0	100
1	50
2	25
3	25
4	25
5	25
6	25

E National insurance (not contracted out rates) 2003/04

Class 1 contributions

Employer	
Earnings threshold	£4,615 (£89 pw)
Employer contributions	12.8% on earnings above earnings threshold

Class 1A contributions

Rate 12.8%

Class 2 contributions

Rate	£2.00 pw
Small earnings exception	£4,095 pa

Class 4 contributions

Main rate between LEL and UEL	8%
Additional rate above UEL	1%
Lower earnings limit	£4,615
Upper earnings limit	£30,940

PART A

Business taxation

chapter 1

The taxation of business income on individuals

Contents

Performance criteria

This is an introductory chapter and there are no specific performance criteria applicable to it.

Range statement

18.2 Clients: sole traders, partnerships

Knowledge and understanding

1 The duties and responsibilities of the tax practitioner (Elements 18.1, 18.2, 18.3 & 18.4)
2 The issues of taxation liability (Elements 18.1, 18.2, 18.3, 18.4)
3 Relevant legislation and guidance from the Inland Revenue (Elements 18.1, 18.2, 18.3, 18.4)
4 Basic law and practice (Elements 18.1, 18.2, 18.3, 18.4)

1 Taxes in the UK

Central government raises revenue through a wide range of taxes. Tax law is made by **statute** and as this can be notoriously ambiguous and difficult to understand, there is a project to rewrite it in simpler more user-friendly language. The first Act to result from the tax law rewrite project was the Capital Allowances Act 2001. This has been followed by the Income Tax (Earnings and Pensions) Act 2003.

Statute is interpreted and amplified by **case law**. The Inland Revenue also issue:

(a) **statements of practice**, setting out how they intend to apply the law

(b) **extra-statutory concessions**, setting out circumstances in which they will not apply the strict letter of the law

(c) a wide range of **explanatory leaflets**

(d) **business economic notes**. These are notes on particular types of business, which are used as background information by the Inland Revenue and are also published

(e) the **Tax Bulletin**. This is a newsletter giving the Inland Revenue's view on specific points. It is published every two months

(f) the **Internal Guidance**, a series of manuals used by Inland Revenue staff

However, none of these Inland Revenue publications has the force of law.

A great deal of information and the Inland Revenue publications can now be found on the Revenue's internet site.

The main taxes suffered by individuals in business are income tax and capital gains tax. You will study these taxes in this unit. Companies suffer corporation tax. You will also study corporation tax in this unit, but we will leave our study of corporation tax until later in this Text.

As a general rule, income tax is charged on receipts which an individual might expect to recur (such as business profits) **whereas capital gains tax is charged on one-off gains** (for example from selling a factory owned for 20 years). Both taxes are charged for tax years.

The **tax year**, or **fiscal year**, or **year of assessment** runs from 6 April to 5 April. For example, the tax year 2003/04 runs from 6 April 2003 to 5 April 2004.

Finance Acts are passed each year, incorporating proposals set out in the **Budget**. They make changes which apply mainly to the tax year ahead. **This text includes the provisions of the Finance Act 2003. The Finance Act 2003 will be examined in June 2004 and December 2004.**

2 Various types of income

2.1 Gross and net income

Some income is received in full, with no tax deducted in advance. An example of such income is gilt interest (interest paid on government securities) which is normally received gross. National Savings Bank interest is also received gross.

Other income is received after deduction of tax. This is income taxed at source. The taxable income for a tax year is the **gross** amount (that is, adding back any tax deducted at source). For example, bank interest is normally received after the deduction of 20% tax at source. This means that if £80 interest is received you must gross it up by multiplying by 100/80. The gross amount of £100 (£80 × 100/80) is included in the individual's income tax computation.

Dividends on UK shares are received net of a 10% tax credit. The taxable income for a tax year is the gross dividend (the dividends received multiplied by 100/90). For example if a dividend of £180 is received, include the gross dividend of £200 (£180 × 100/90) in the income tax computation.

Activity 1.1

Harriet receives dividends of £2,250 and building society interest (net of 20% tax) of £2,400 in 2003/04. What are the gross amounts of dividends and interest to be included in her income tax computation for 2003/04?

2.2 The schedular system

Each type of income is taxed under a set of rules known as a schedule. Schedule D is divided into cases.

Schedule A	Income from land and buildings (rents and so on) in the UK
Schedules B and C	Abolished
Schedule D	
Case I	Profits of trades
Case II	Profits of professions or vocations
Case III	Interest
Case VI	Income not falling under any other schedule or case
Schedule F	UK dividends

Foreign income may be taxed under Schedule D Cases IV and V but this is not assessable in Unit 18.

The schedules and cases are important because each has its own set of rules. Once we have decided that income is taxed under, say, Schedule A, the rules of Schedule A determine the amount of income taxed in any year. Each type of income examinable at Unit 18 is considered in detail later in this text.

The schedular system arose for historical administrative reasons and is likely to become less important in the future as tax law is rewritten. For example, **Schedule E (which taxed employment income and pensions) has been abolished and replaced by the provisions of the Income Tax (Earnings and Pensions) Act 2003.**

Although the assessment for Unit 18 is concerned with business taxation, you may need to know broadly how to compute an individual's income tax liability in order to give advice on, for example, utilising business losses. The remainder of this chapter, therefore, gives some details of this computation. If you study Unit 19 *Preparing Personal Tax Computations* you will deal with the personal tax computations in more detail.

3 The aggregation of income

3.1 Introduction

An individual's income from all sources is brought together in a personal tax computation. We split income into dividend income, savings (excl. dividend) income and non-savings income.

Interest and dividends are **'savings income'** All other income is non-savings income.

3.2 Interest received net of 20% tax

The following interest income is received by **individuals** net of 20% tax.

(a) Interest paid by UK companies on debentures and loan stocks
(b) Bank and building society interest (but not National Savings Bank interest)

The amount received must be grossed up by multiplying by 100/80 and it must be included gross in the income tax computation.

In the exam you may be given either the net or the gross amount of such income: read the question carefully. If you are given the net amount (the amount received or credited), you should gross up the figure at the rate of 20%. However, if you are given the gross amount include the figure you are given in the income tax computation.

Although building society and bank deposit interest are generally paid net of 20% tax a recipient who is not liable to tax can recover the tax suffered For example, net building society interest of £160 is equivalent to gross income of £160 × 100/80 = £200 on which tax of £40 (20% of £200) has been suffered and a non-taxpayer can get the £40 tax suffered repaid to him. Alternatively, he can certify in advance that he is a non-taxpayer and get the interest paid gross.

3.3 Dividends on UK shares

Dividends received on UK shares are received net of a 10% tax credit. This means a dividend received of £90 has a £10 tax credit, giving gross income of £100 to be included in the tax computation. The tax credit attached to dividends **cannot be repaid to non-taxpayers but it is offsettable and can be set against a taxpayer's tax liability.**

3.4 Taxable income

Once income from all sources has been aggregated, charges and the personal allowance are deducted to arrive at taxable income. We will look at these items in more detail later in this chapter but now let us see an example of the layout of the computation of taxable income.

RICHARD: INCOME TAX COMPUTATION 2003/04

	Non-savings income	*Savings (excl dividend) income*	*Dividend income*	*Total*
	£	£	£	£
Business profits	38,000			
Building society interest		1,000		
National savings bank interest		320		
UK dividends			1,000	
	38,000	1,320	1,000	
Less charges on income	(2,000)			
Statutory total income (STI)	36,000	1,320	1,000	38,320
Less: personal allowance	(4,615)			
Taxable income	31,385	1,320	1,000	33,705

Now follow the above layout to try the next activity for yourself.

Activity 1.2

An individual has the following income in 2003/04.

	£
Business profits	16,000
Building society interest received	4,800
Dividends received	7,875

His personal allowance is £4,615. What is his taxable income?

3.5 Calculation of income tax

Income tax is charged on the figures of **'taxable income'. There is only one set of income tax bands to be used for all three types of income**. Non-savings income is dealt with first, then savings (excl. dividend) income and then dividend income.

Non-savings income of up to £1,960 is taxed at 10%. Next any non-savings income in the basic rate band is taxed at 22%, and finally non-savings income above the basic rate is taxed at 40%.

Savings (excl dividend) income is dealt with after non-savings income. If any of the starting or basic rate bands remain **after taxing non-savings income** they can be used here. Savings (excl dividend) income is taxed at 10% in the starting rate band. If savings (excl dividend) income falls within the basic rate band it is taxed at 20% (not 22%). Once income is above the higher rate threshold, it is taxed at 40%.

Lastly, tax dividend income. If dividend income falls within the starting or basic rate bands, it is taxed at 10% (never 20% or 22%). If, however, the dividend income exceeds the basic rate threshold of £30,500, it is taxed at 32.5%

Continuing Richard's income tax computation above, the tax liability is:

Income tax	£
Non savings income	
£1,960 × 10%	196
£28,540 × 22%	6,279
£885 × 40%	354
	6,829
Savings (excl. dividend) income	
£1,320 × 40%	528
Dividend income	
£1,000 × 32.5%	325
Tax liabilities	7,682

Savings (excl. dividend) and the dividend income are both above the higher rate threshold of £30,500 so they are taxed at 40% and 32.5% respectively.

Activity 1.3

An individual has total taxable income of £50,000 for 2003/04. All of his income is non-savings income. What is the total income tax liability?

Once the tax liability has been calculated, any tax suffered or deducted at source (for example, tax on building society interest) and the tax credit on dividend income are deducted to arrive at tax payable. Tax suffered on savings (excl. dividend) income is repayable if it exceeds the individual's tax liability. The tax credit on UK dividends is never repayable.

Activity 1.4

Kate, who is single and entitled to a personal allowance of £4,615, has business profits of £10,430 and building society interest received of £4,000. Calculate Kate's tax payable for 2003/04.

Activity 1.5

Doris received dividend income of £32,400 in 2003/04. She has no other income. Her personal allowance to deduct from dividend income is £4,615. Calculate the tax payable.

4 Charges on income

Charges on income are deducted in computing taxable income.

A **charge on income** is a payment by the taxpayer which income tax law allows as a deduction.

Examples of charges on income are:

(a) patent royalties
(b) copyright royalties

Any charge is deducted from the taxpayer's income to arrive at Statutory Total Income (STI).

Deduct charges from non-savings income then from savings (excl. dividend income) and lastly from dividend income.

If a charge is paid for business purposes it is known as a trade charge on income. Other charges are known as non-trade charges on income.

Activity 1.6

John, who is single and entitled to a personal allowance of £4,615, has Schedule D Case I profits of £8,000 in 2003/04. He also received building society interest of £14,000 and dividends of £450. He had charges on income of £12,000 to deduct in computing his taxable income. Show John's taxable income for 2003/04.

5 Personal allowance

All persons are entitled to the personal allowance of £4,615.

Once taxable income from all sources has been aggregated and any charges on income deducted, the remainder is the taxpayer's **statutory total income** (STI). The personal allowance is then deducted from STI. Like charges, it comes off non-savings income first, then savings (excl. dividend) income and then dividend income.

6 The layout of personal tax computations

Now let us work through some complete computations of income tax payable.

(a) Kathe has business profits of £10,000 and receives dividends of £4,500.

	Non-savings	*Dividends*	*Total*
	£	£	£
Schedule D Case I	10,000		
Dividends £4,500 × 100/90		5,000	
STI	10,000	5,000	15,000
Less personal allowance	(4,615)		
Taxable income	5,385	5,000	10,385

	£
Income tax	
Non savings income	
£1,960 × 10%	196
£3,425 × 22%	753
Dividend income	
£5,000 × 10%	500
Tax liability	1,449
Less tax credit on dividend	(500)
Tax payable	949

The dividend income falls within the basic rate band so it is taxed at 10% (*not* 22%).

(b) Jules has business profits of £50,000, net dividends of £6,750 and building society interest of £3,000 net. He has charges of £2,000 to deduct in computing taxable income.

	Non-savings	*Savings (excluding) dividend)*	*Dividends*	*Total*
	£	£		£
Schedule D Case I	50,000			
Dividends £6,750 × 100/90			7,500	
Building society interest £3,000 × 100/80		3,750		
	50,000	3,750	7,500	
Less charges	(2,000)			
STI	48,000	3,750	7,500	59,250
Less personal allowance	(4,615)			
Taxable income	43,385	3,750	7,500	54,635

Income tax	£
Non savings income	
£1,960 × 10%	196
£28,540 × 22%	6,279
£12,885 × 40%	5,154
	11,629
Savings (excl. dividend) income	
£3,750 × 40%	1,500
Dividend income	
£7,500 × 32.5%	2,438
Less tax credit on dividend income	(750)
Less tax suffered on building society interest	(750)
Tax payable	14,067

Savings (excl. dividend) income and dividend income fall above the basic rate threshold so they are taxed at 40% and 32.5% respectively.

The complete proforma

Here is a complete proforma computation of taxable income. We include it here as you might find it useful to refer back to later.

	Non-savings	*Savings (excluding dividend)*	*Dividend*	*Total*
	£	£	£	£
Business profits	X			
Less losses set against business profits	(X)			
	X			
Other non-savings (as many lines as necessary)	X			
Building society interest (gross)		X		
Other savings (excluding dividends) (gross) (as many lines as necessary)		X		
Dividends (gross)			X	
	X	X	X	
Less charges	(X)	(X)	(X)	
	X	X	X	
Less losses set against general income	(X)	(X)	(X)	
STI	X	X	X	X
Less personal allowance	(X)	(X)	(X)	
Taxable income	X	X	X	X

Key learning points

- ☑ Individuals suffer **income tax** and **capital gains tax**.
- ☑ Companies suffer **corporation tax**.
- ☑ Some income is **received in full** with no tax deducted, some income has **tax deducted** at source.
- ☑ All sources of income are **aggregated** in a **personal tax computation.**
- ☑ Income is divided into **non-savings** income, **savings (excluding dividend)** income and **dividend** income.
- ☑ **Charges** are deducted from the taxpayer's income to arrive at Statutory Total Income.
- ☑ The **personal allowance** is deducted from Statutory Total Income.
- ☑ There is one set of **income tax bands** which applies to all the income.
- ☑ The **non-savings income is taxed first**, then the **savings (excluding dividends) income** and **finally dividend income**.

Quick quiz

1 What are the main UK taxes suffered by businesses?

2 At what rates is income tax charged on non-savings income?

3 Under what schedule and case are the profits of a trade taxed?

Answers to quick quiz

1 Income tax and capital gains tax by individuals, corporation tax by companies.

2 10%, 22% and 40%

3 Schedule D Case I

Activity checklist

This checklist shows which knowledge and understanding point is covered by each activity in this chapter. Tick off each activity as you complete it.

Activity		
1.1	☐	This activity deals with Knowledge and Understanding point 4: basic law and practice.
1.2	☐	This activity deals with Knowledge and Understanding point 2: the issues of tax liability.
1.3	☐	This activity deals with Knowledge and Understanding point 2: the issues of tax liability.
1.4	☐	This activity deals with Knowledge and Understanding point 2: the issues of tax liability.
1.5	☐	This activity deals with Knowledge and Understanding point 2: the issues of tax liability.
1.6	☐	This activity deals with Knowledge and Understanding point 4: basic law and practice.

chapter 2

Schedule D Cases I and II

Contents

Performance criteria

18.1A Classify expenditure on capital assets in accordance with the statutory distinction between capital and revenue expenditure

18.2 A Adjust trading profits and losses for tax purposes

18.2.B Make adjustments for private use by business owners

18.2 D Apply the basis of assessment for unincorporated businesses in the opening and closing years

Range statement

18.2 Clients: sole traders, partnerships

Knowledge and understanding

7 Adjustment of trading profits and losses for tax purposes (Element 18.2)

8 Regulations relating to disallowed expenditure such as business entertaining, bad debt write-offs and provisions, private expenditure and capital expenditure (Element 18.2)

9 Basis of assessment of unincorporated businesses (Element 18.2)

1 The badges of trade

1.1 Nature of 'trade'

A trade is defined in the legislation only in an unhelpful manner as including every trade, manufacture, adventure or concern in the nature of a trade. It has therefore been left to the courts to provide guidance. This guidance is often summarised in a collection of principles known as the **'badges of trade'**. These are set out below.

Trading income is subject to tax under Schedule D Case I.

1.2 Traditional badges of trade

1.2.1 The subject matter

Whether a person is trading or not may sometimes be decided by examining the subject matter of the transaction. Some assets are commonly held as investments for their intrinsic value: an individual buying some shares or a painting may do so in order to enjoy the income from the shares or to enjoy the work of art. Any subsequent disposal, even at a profit, may produce a gain of a capital nature rather than a trading profit. But **where the subject matter of a transaction is such as would not be held as an investment** (for example 34,000,000 yards of aircraft linen (*Martin v Lowry 1927*) or 1,000,000 rolls of toilet paper (*Rutledge v CIR 1929*)), **it is to be presumed that any profit on resale is a trading profit.**

1.2.2 The frequency of transactions

Transactions which may be treated in isolation as being of a capital nature will be interpreted as trading transactions where their **frequency indicates the carrying on of a trade**. It was decided that whereas normally the purchase of a mill-owning company and the subsequent stripping of its assets might be a capital transaction, where the taxpayer was embarking on the same exercise for the fourth time he must be carrying on a trade (*Pickford v Quirke 1927*).

1.2.3 The length of ownership

The courts may infer adventures in the nature of **trade where items purchased are sold soon afterwards.**

1.2.4 Supplementary work and marketing

When work is done to make an asset more marketable, or steps are taken to find purchasers, the courts will be more ready to ascribe a trading motive. When a group of accountants bought, blended and recasked a quantity of brandy they were held to be taxable on a trading profit when the brandy was later sold (*Cape Brandy Syndicate v CIR 1921*).

1.2.5 A profit motive

The absence of a profit motive will not necessarily preclude a Schedule D Case I assessment, but its presence is a strong indication that a person is trading. The purchase and resale of £20,000 worth of silver bullion by the comedian Norman Wisdom, as a hedge against devaluation, was held to be a trading transaction (*Wisdom v Chamberlain 1969*).

1.2.6 The way in which the asset sold was acquired

If goods are acquired deliberately, trading may be indicated. If goods are acquired unintentionally, for example by gift or inheritance, their later sale is unlikely to constitute trading.

1.3 The taxpayer's intentions

Where a transaction clearly amounts to trading on objective criteria, **the taxpayer's intentions are irrelevant**. If, however, a transaction has (objectively) a dual purpose, the taxpayer's intentions may be taken into account. An example of a transaction with a dual purpose is the acquisition of a site partly as premises from which to conduct another trade, and partly with a view to the possible development and resale of the site.

This intentions test is not one of the traditional badges of trade, but it may be just as important.

Activity 2.1

Gareth inherited some land. He then bought some adjoining land, drained the combined plot, applied for planning permission and sold the combined plot at a profit. Which badges of trade would indicate that he was trading?

1.4 Alternative charges to income tax

If income is received by an individual and on applying the badges of trade the Inland Revenue do not conclude that the income is 'trading income' then they can potentially treat it as Schedule D Case VI income or a capital gain.

2 The computation of trading income

2.1 The adjustment of profits

Although the net profit before taxation shown in the accounts provides the starting point in computing the taxable trading profit, many adjustments may be required to find the profit taxable under the rules of Schedule D Case I. The same rules apply to Case II (profits of a profession or vocation), and we will just refer to Case I from now on.

Here is an illustrative adjustment.

	£	£
Net profit per accounts		140,000
Add: expenditure charged in the accounts which is not deductible under Schedule D Case I	50,000	
income taxable under Schedule D Case I which has not been included in the accounts	30,000	
		80,000
		220,000
Less: profits included in the accounts but which are not taxable under Schedule D Case I	40,000	
expenditure which is deductible under Schedule D Case I but has not been charged in the accounts	20,000	
		60,000
Profit adjusted for tax purposes		160,000

You may refer to deductible and non-deductible expenditure as allowable and disallowable expenditure respectively. The two sets of terms are interchangeable.

Individuals and companies are taxed on Schedule D Case I income. However, the computation of Schedule D Case I Income for companies differs slightly to the computation for individuals. We mention this at relevant points in this chapter. Companies are dealt with in more detail later in this text.

2.2 Accounting policies

As a rule, accounts drawn up on normal accepted accounting principles are acceptable for tax purposes. Two special points are worth noting.

(a) If there is a legal action in progress, the best estimate of the cost should be debited, not the most prudent estimate.

(b) Under SSAP 9, a loss on a long-term contract is recognised as soon as it is foreseen. Anticipating a loss in this way is not acceptable for tax purposes, so the debit to profit and loss must be added back.

The profits of a trade, profession or vocation must normally be computed for tax purposes on a basis which gives a true and fair view, subject to any adjustments permitted or required by tax law.

2.3 Deductible and non-deductible expenditure

2.3.1 Payments contrary to public policy and illegal payments

Fines and penalties are not deductible. However, the Inland Revenue usually allow employees' parking fines incurred in parking their employer's cars while on their employer's business. Fines relating to proprietors, however, are never allowed. (Similarly, a company would not be able to deduct fines relating to directors – companies are covered later in this text.)

A payment is (by statute) not deductible if making it constitutes an offence by the payer. This covers protection money paid to terrorists, and also bribes. Statute law also prevents any deduction for payments made in response to blackmail or extortion.

2.3.2 Capital expenditure

Income tax is a tax solely on income and so capital expenditure is not deductible. The most contentious items of expenditure will often be repairs (revenue expenditure) **and improvements** (capital expenditure).

- The cost of restoration of an asset by, for instance, replacing a subsidiary part of the asset will be treated as revenue expenditure. It was held that expenditure on a new factory chimney replacement was allowable since the chimney was a subsidiary part of the factory (*Samuel Jones & Co (Devondale) Ltd v CIR 1951*). However, in another case a football club demolished a spectators' stand and replaced it with a modern equivalent. This was held not to be repair, since repair is the restoration by renewal or replacement of subsidiary parts of a larger entity, and the stand formed a distinct and *separate* part of the club (*Brown v Burnley Football and Athletic Co Ltd 1980*).
- The cost of initial repairs to improve an asset recently acquired to make it fit to earn profits is disallowable capital expenditure. In *Law Shipping Co Ltd v CIR 1923* the taxpayer failed to obtain relief for expenditure on making a newly bought ship seaworthy prior to using it.
- The cost of initial repairs to remedy normal wear and tear of recently acquired assets will be treated as allowable. *Odeon Associated Theatres Ltd v Jones 1971* can be contrasted with the *Law Shipping* judgement. Odeon were allowed to charge expenditure incurred on improving the state of recently acquired cinemas.

Other examples to note include:

- A one-off payment made by a hotel owner to terminate an agreement for the management of a hotel was held to be revenue rather than capital expenditure in *Croydon Hotel & Leisure Co v Bowen 1996.* The payment did not affect the whole structure of the taxpayer's business; it merely enabled it to be run more efficiently.
- A one-off payment to remove a threat to the taxpayer's business was also held to be revenue rather than capital expenditure in *Lawson v Johnson Matthey plc 1992.*
- An initial payment for a franchise (as opposed to regular fees) is capital and not deductible.

Two exceptions to the 'capital' rule are worth noting.

(a) The costs of **registering patents and trade marks** are deductible.

(b) **Incidental costs of obtaining loan finance**, or of attempting to obtain or redeeming it, are deductible other than a discount on issue or a premium on redemption (which are really alternatives to paying interest). This deduction for incidental costs does not apply to companies because they get a deduction for the costs of borrowing in a different way. We will look at companies later in this text.

2.3.3 Appropriations

Salary or interest on capital paid to a proprietor, and also depreciation, amortisation and general provisions are not deductible. A specific provision against a particular trade debt is deductible if it is a reasonable estimate of the likely loss.

The private proportion of payments for motoring expenses, rent, heat and light and telephone expenses of a proprietor is not deductible. Where the payments are to or on behalf of employees, the full amounts are deductible but the employees are taxed on the benefits.

In specific circumstances a company may deduct depreciation or amortisation. Companies are covered in more detail later in this text.

2.3.4 Charges

Charges (such as royalties) are dealt with in the personal tax computation, so they cannot also be deducted in computing trading profits. Any charges deducted in the accounts must be added back in computing Schedule D Case I profit.

2.3.5 Entertaining and gifts

Entertaining for and gifts to employees are normally deductible although where gifts are made, or the entertainment is excessive, a charge to tax may arise on the employee under the benefits legislation.

Gifts to customers not costing more than £50 per donee per year are allowed if they carry a conspicuous advertisement for the business and are not food, drink, tobacco or vouchers exchangeable for goods.

Gifts to charities may also be allowed although many will fall foul of the 'wholly and exclusively' rule below.

Tax relief is available for certain donations of trading stock and equipment (see below).

There is a scheme for giving known as the 'gift aid' scheme. If a gift aid declaration is made in respect of a gift, income tax relief will be given under the gift aid scheme, **not as a Schedule D Case I deduction**. You will learn how this relief is given for gift aid donations if you study Unit 19. You do not need to study it at Unit 18. However, you may need to add the gift aid donations back to accounts profit in computing Schedule D Case I profits.

All other expenditure on entertaining and gifts is non-deductible.

Activity 2.2

The entertainment account of Green and Co showed:

	£
Staff tennis outing for 30 employees	1,800
2,000 tee shirts with firm's logo given to race runners	4,500
Advertising and sponsorship of an athletic event	2,000
Entertaining customers	7,300
Staff Christmas party (30 employees)	2,400

What amount must be added back in arriving at Schedule D Case I profits?

2.3.6 Expenditure not wholly and exclusively for the purposes of the trade

Expenditure is not deductible if it is not for the purposes of the trade (the remoteness test), or if it reflects more than one purpose (the duality test). If an exact apportionment is possible (as with motor expenses) relief is given on the business element.

The remoteness test is illustrated by the following cases.

- *Strong & Co of Romsey Ltd v Woodifield 1906*

  A customer injured by a falling chimney when sleeping in an inn owned by a brewery claimed compensation from the company. The compensation was not deductible: 'the loss sustained by the appellant was not really incidental to their trade as innkeepers and fell upon them in their character not of innkeepers but of householders'.

- *Bamford v ATA Advertising Ltd 1972*

  A director misappropriated £15,000. The loss was not allowable: 'the loss is not, as in the case of a dishonest shop assistant, an incident of the company's trading activities. It arises altogether outside such activities'.

- Expenditure which is wholly and exclusively to benefit the trades of several companies (for example in a group) but is not wholly and exclusively to benefit the trade of one specific company is not deductible *(Vodafone Cellular Ltd and others v Shaw 1995).*

- *McKnight (HMIT) v Sheppard (1999)* concerned expenses incurred by a stockbroker in defending allegations of infringements of Stock Exchange regulations. It was found that the expenditure was incurred to prevent the destruction of the taxpayer's business and that as the expenditure was incurred for business purposes it was deductible. It was also found that although the expenditure had the effect of preserving the taxpayer's reputation, that was not its purpose, so there was no duality of purpose.

The **duality test** is illustrated by the following cases.

- *Caillebotte v Quinn 1975*

  A self-employed carpenter spent an average of 40p per day when obliged to buy lunch away from home but just 10p when he lunched at home. He claimed the excess 30p. It was decided that the payment had a dual purpose and was not deductible: 'a Schedule D taxpayer must eat to live not eat to work'.

- *Mallalieu v Drummond 1983*

  Expenditure by a lady barrister on black clothing to be worn in court (and on its cleaning and repair) was not deductible. The expenditure was for the dual purpose of enabling the barrister to be warmly and properly clad as well as meeting her professional requirements.

- *McLaren v Mumford 1996*

  A publican, traded from a public house which had residential accommodation above it. He was obliged to live at the public house but he also had another house which he visited regularly. It was held that the private element of the expenditure incurred at the public house on electricity, rent, gas, etc was not incurred for the purpose of earning profits, but for serving the non-business purpose of satisfying the publican's ordinary human needs. The expenditure, therefore had a dual purpose and was disallowed.

However, the cost of overnight accommodation when on a business trip may be deductible and reasonable expenditure on an evening meal and breakfast in conjunction with such accommodation is then also deductible.

Activity 2.3

Why might a barrister not obtain a deduction for the cost of cleaning his or her gown and wig?

2.3.7 Subscriptions and donations

There is a general 'wholly and exclusively' rule which determines the deductibility of expenses. Subscriptions and donations are not deductible unless the expenditure is for the benefit of the trade. The following are the main types of subscriptions and donations you may meet and their correct treatments.

(a) Trade subscriptions (such as to a professional or trade association) are generally deductible.

(b) Charitable donations are deductible only if they are small and to local charities. Tax relief may be available for donations under the gift aid scheme (see above). In this case they are not a deductible Schedule D Case I expense.

(c) Political subscriptions and donations are generally not deductible. However, if it can be shown that political expenditure is incurred for the survival of the trade then it may be deducted. This follows a case in which it was held that expenditure incurred in resisting nationalisation was allowable on the grounds that it affected the survival of the business (*Morgan v Tate and Lyle Ltd 1954*).

(d) When a business makes a gift of equipment manufactured, sold or used in the course of its trade to an educational establishment or for a charitable purpose, nothing need be brought into account as a trading receipt or (if capital allowances had been obtained on the asset) as disposal proceeds, so full relief is obtained for the cost. The value of any benefit to the donor from the gift is taxable on him.

(e) Where a donation represents the most effective commercial way of disposing of stock (for example, where it would not be commercially effective to sell surplus perishable food), the donation can be treated as for the benefit of the trade and the disposal proceeds taken as £Nil. In other cases, the amount credited to the accounts in respect of a donation of stock should be its market value.

2.3.8 Legal and professional charges

Legal and professional charges relating to capital or non-trading items are not deductible. These include charges incurred in acquiring new capital assets or legal rights, issuing shares, drawing up partnership agreements and litigating disputes over the terms of a partnership agreement.

Charges incurred are deductible when they relate directly to trading. Deductible items include:

- legal and professional charges incurred defending the taxpayer's title to fixed assets
- charges connected with an action for breach of contract
- expenses of the **renewal** (not the original grant) of a lease for less than 50 years;
- charges for trade debt collection
- normal charges for preparing accounts and assisting with the self assessment of tax liabilities

Accountancy expenses arising out of an enquiry into the accounts information in a particular year's return are not allowed where the enquiry reveals discrepancies and additional liabilities for the year of enquiry, or any earlier year, which arise as a result of negligent or fraudulent conduct.

Where, however, the enquiry results in no addition to profits, or an adjustment to the profits for the year of enquiry only and that assessment does not arise as a result of negligent or fraudulent conduct, the additional accountancy expenses are allowable.

Activity 2.4

A manufacturing business spends the following amounts on legal and professional services.

		£
Debt collection:	trade debts	500
	loan to former employee	230
Defending action for faulty goods		1,900
Preparing accounts		450
Specialist tax consultancy		700
		3,780

How much must be added back in computing the taxable profits?

2.3.9 Bad and doubtful debts

Only bad debts incurred in the course of a business are deductible for taxation purposes. Thus loans to employees written off are not deductible unless the business is that of making loans, or it can be shown that the writing-off of the loan was an emolument laid out for the benefit of the trade. If a trade debt is released as part of a voluntary arrangement under the Insolvency Act 1986, or a compromise or arrangement under s 425 Companies Act 1985, the amount released is deductible as a bad debt.

General doubtful debt provisions are not deductible, but specific provisions and write-offs against individual debts are deductible. The only adjustment needed to the accounts profit is to add back an increase (or deduct a decrease) in the general provision.

Activity 2.5

The bad and doubtful debts account of a sole trader was as follows:

	£		£
Debts written off		Balances brought forward	
Trade	9,300	General provision	15,300
Loan to customer	1,400	Specific provision	7,800
Balances carried forward		Bad debts recovered (previously allowed)	5,400
General provision	12,200	Profit and loss account	1,600
Specific provision	7,200		
	30,100		30,100

What adjustment must be made to the accounts profit for tax purposes?

2.3.10 Interest

Interest paid by an individual on borrowings for trade purposes is deductible as a trading expense on an accruals basis, so no adjustment to the accounts figure is needed.

Companies have different rules for the cost of borrowing. We will look at these later in this text.

Individuals cannot deduct interest on overdue tax.

2.3.11 Miscellaneous deductions

The **costs of seconding employees to charities or educational establishments are deductible.**

Expenditure incurred before the commencement of trade *(***pre-trading expenditure***)* is deductible, if **it is incurred within seven years of the start of trade and it is of a type that would have been deductible had the trade already started.** It is treated as a trading expense incurred on the first day of trading.

Where earnings for employees are charged in the accounts but have still not been paid to the employees nine months after the end of the period of account, the cost is only deductible for the period of account in which the earnings are paid. When a tax computation is made within the nine month period, it is initially assumed that unpaid earnings will not be paid within that period. The computation is adjusted if they are so paid.

Earnings are treated as paid at the same time as they are treated as received for the purposes of calculating the employee's taxable earnings.

Redundancy payments made when a trade ends are deductible on the earlier of the day of payment and the last day of trading. If the trade does not end, they can be deducted as soon as they are provided for, so long as the redundancy was decided on within the period of account, the provision is accurately calculated and the payments are made within nine months of the end of the period of account.

Here is a list of various other items that you may meet.

Item	Treatment	Comment
Educational courses for staff	Allow	
Educational courses for proprietor	Allow	If to update existing knowledge or skills, not if to acquire new knowledge or skills
Removal expenses (to new business premises)	Allow	Only if not an expansionary move
Travelling expenses to the trader's place of business	Disallow	*Ricketts v Colquhoun 1925*: unless an itinerant trader (*Horton v Young 1971*)
Redundancy pay in excess of the statutory amount	Allow	If the trade ceases, the limit on allowability is 3 × the statutory amount (in addition to the statutory amount)
Compensation for loss of office and ex gratia payments	Allow	If for benefit of trade: *Mitchell v B W Noble Ltd 1927*
Counselling services for employees leaving employment	Allow	If qualify for exemption from tax charge on employees
Contributions to any of: local enterprise agencies; training and enterprise councils; local enterprise companies; business link organisations	Allow	
Pension contributions (to schemes for employees and company directors)	Allow	If paid, not if only provided for; special contributions may be spread over the year of payment and future years
Premiums for insurance: against an employee's death or illness to cover locum costs or fixed overheads whilst the policyholder is ill	Allow	Receipts are taxable
Payments to employees for restrictive undertakings	Allow	Taxable on employee
Damages paid	Allow	If not too remote from trade: *Strong and Co v Woodifield 1906*
Preparation and restoration of waste disposal sites	Allow	Spread preparation expenditure over period of use of site. Pre-trading expenditure is treated as incurred on the first day of trading. Allow restoration expenditure in period of expenditure
Improving an individual's personal security	Allow	Trader must be an individual or a partnership (not a company). Provision of a car, ship or dwelling is excluded

In the exam you could be given a copy of a business's profit and loss account and asked to calculate 'taxable profit'. You will have to look at every expense charged in the accounts to decide if it is (or isn't) a 'tax deductible expense'. To help you to achieve this you must become familiar with the many expenses you are likely to see and the correct tax treatment. Look at the above paragraphs again noting what expenses are (and are not) allowable for tax purposes.

2.4 Income taxable under Schedule D Case I but excluded from the accounts

The usual example is when a proprietor takes goods for his own use. In such circumstances the normal selling price of the goods is added to the accounting profit. In other words, the proprietor is treated for tax purposes as having made a sale to himself. This rule does not apply to supplies of services, which are treated as sold for the amount (if any) actually paid (but the cost of services to the trader or his household is not deductible).

2.5 Accounting profits not taxable under Schedule D Case I

There are three types of receipts which may be found in the accounting profits but which must be excluded from the Schedule D Case I computation. These are:

(a) **capital receipts**
(b) **income taxed in another way** (at source or under another case or schedule)
(c) **income specifically exempt from tax**

However, compensation received in one lump sum for the loss of income is likely to be treated as income.

Activity 2.6

Here is the profit and loss account of S Pring, a trader.

	£	£
Gross operating profit		30,000
Taxed interest received		860
		30,860
Wages and salaries	7,000	
Rent and rates	2,000	
Depreciation	1,500	
Bad debts written off	150	
Provision against a fall in the price of raw materials	5,000	
Entertainment expenses	750	
Patent royalties	1,200	
Bank interest	300	
Legal expenses on acquisition of new factory	250	
		(18,150)
Net profit		12,710

(a) Salaries include £500 paid to Mrs Pring who works full time in the business.
(b) No staff were entertained.
(c) The provision of £5,000 is charged because of an anticipated trade recession.

Compute the profit taxable under Schedule D Case I.

2.6 Deductible expenditure not charged in the accounts

Capital allowances (see the following chapter) **are deductible expenditure not charged in the accounts.**

2.7 Rounding

Where an individual, a partnership or a single company has an annual turnover of at least £5,000,000, and prepares its accounts with figures rounded to at least the nearest £1,000, figures in computations of adjusted profits (including, for companies, non-trading profits but excluding capital gains) may generally be rounded to the nearest £1,000.

2.8 The cessation of trades

2.8.1 Post cessation receipts and expenses

Post-cessation receipts (including any releases of debts incurred by the trader) **are taxable under Schedule D Case VI**. If they are received in the tax year of cessation or the next six tax years, the trader can elect that they be treated as received on the day of cessation. The time limit for electing is the 31 January which is 22 months after the end of the tax year of receipt.

An individual trader or a partner (not a company) can claim **post-cessation expenses in respect of payments made within seven years of a discontinuance** which are incurred wholly and exclusively:

(a) in remedying defective work done, goods supplied or services rendered

(b) in paying legal or other professional costs and expenses relating to a claim that the work done, etc was defective

(c) in insuring against liabilities arising out of any such claim or against such costs and expenses

(d) for the purpose of collecting debts taken into account in computing the profits or the former trade etc

Relief is also allowed for debts owed to the former business which were taken into account in computing the profits of the trade prior to discontinuance but which have subsequently proved to be bad.

Relief for allowable post-cessation expenses is given against income and gains in the year in which each allowable payment is made, or in which a debt is proved to be bad. The relief must be claimed by 31 January following the year of assessment concerned.

If there is insufficient income and gains to cover allowable expenditure in a given year, the unrelieved expenditure for that year cannot be carried forward except against any future post cessation receipts.

3 Basis periods

3.1 Introduction

A tax year runs from 6 April to 5 April, but most businesses do not have periods of account ending on 5 April. **Thus there must be a link between a period of account of a business and a tax year.** The procedure is to **find a period to act as the basis period for a tax year. The profits for a basis period are taxed in the corresponding tax year**. If a basis period is not identical to a period of account, the profits of periods of account are time-apportioned as required. We will assume that profits accrue evenly over a period of account. We will also apportion to the nearest month.

We will now look at the basis period rules that apply in the opening, continuing and closing years of a business when there is no change of accounting date. Special rules are needed when a trader changes his accounting date but you will not be assessed on these in Unit 18 so they are not considered here.

The first tax year is the year during which the trade commences. For example, if a trade commences on 1 June 2003 the first tax year is 2003/04.

3.2 The first tax year

The **basis period for the first tax year runs from the date the trade starts to the next 5 April** (or to the date of cessation if the trade does not last until the end of the tax year).

3.3 The second tax year

If the accounting date falling in the second tax year is at least 12 months after the start of trading, the basis period is the 12 months down to that accounting date.

If the accounting date falling in the second tax year is less than 12 months after the start of trading, the basis period is the first 12 months of trading.

If there is no accounting date falling in the second tax year, because the first period of account is a very long one which does not end until a date in the third tax year, **the basis period for the second tax year is the year itself (from 6 April to 5 April).**

Yr 1 commencement of trade — 5th April

The following flowchart may help you determine the basis period for the second tax year.

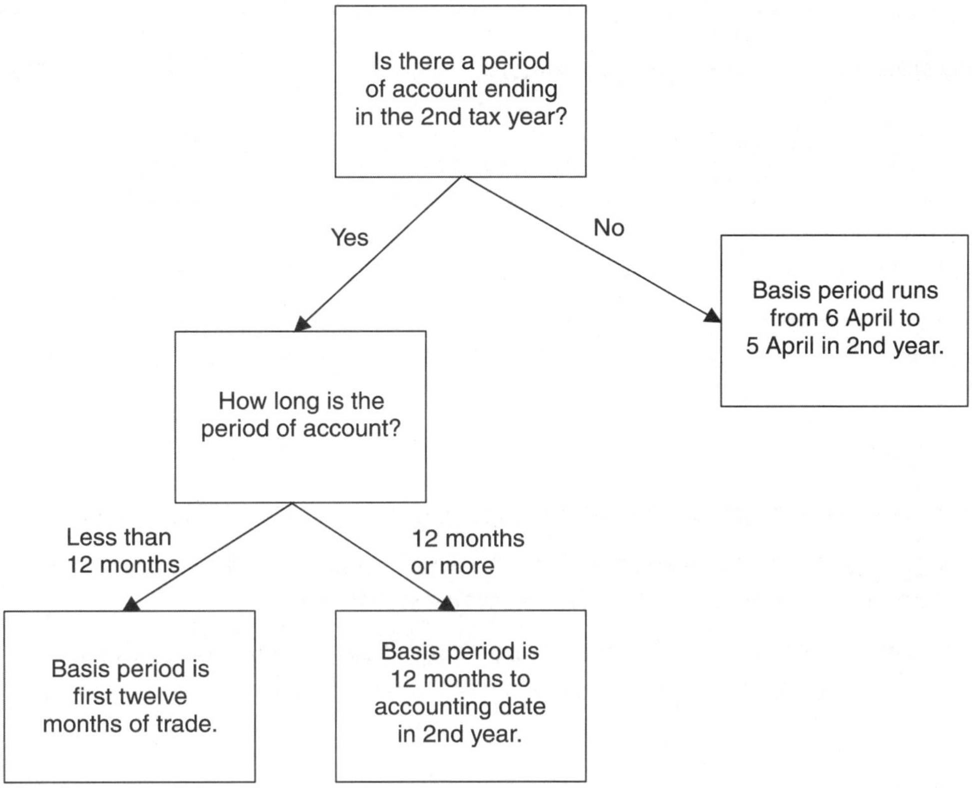

3.4 The third tax year

If there is an accounting date falling in the second tax year, the basis period for the third tax year is the period of account ending in the third tax year.

If there is no accounting date falling in the second tax year, the basis period for the third tax year is the 12 months down to the accounting date falling in the third tax year.

3.5 Later tax years

For later tax years, except the year in which the trade ceases, **the basis period is the period of account ending in the tax year**. This is known as the **current year basis of assessment**.

Activity 2.7

Mavis started in business as a newsagent on 1 July 2003. She made up accounts to 30 June and had the following results.

y/e 30.6.04	£10,000
y/e 30.6.05	£15,000
y/e 30.6.06	£18,000

Show the taxable profits for the year 2003/04 to 2006/07.

3.6 The final year

If a trade starts and ceases in the same tax year, the basis period for that year is the whole lifespan of the trade.

If the final year is the second year, the basis period runs from 6 April at the start of the second year to the date of cessation. This rule overrides the rules that normally apply for the second year.

If the final year is the third year or a later year, **the basis period runs from the end of the basis period for the previous year to the date of cessation**. This rule overrides the rules that normally apply in the third and later years.

Activity 2.8

Maud was in business as a dressmaker for many years. The business had the following results to closure on 31.12.04:

y/e 30.9.02	£10,000
y/e 30.9.03	£7,000
y/e 30.9.04	£6,000
p/e 31.12.04	£2,000

Show the taxable profits for the years 2002/03 to 2004/05 inclusive before considering any overlap relief (see below).

3.7 Overlap profits

Profits which have been taxed more than once are called **overlap profits**.

When a business starts, some profits may be taxed twice because the basis period for the second year includes some or all of the period of trading in the first year or because the basis period for the third year overlaps with that for the second year.

When the trade ceases overlap profits are deducted from the final year's taxable profits. Any deduction of overlap profits may create or increase a loss. The usual loss reliefs (covered later in this text) are then available.

3.8 Example: accounting date in 2nd year at least 12 months

Jenny trades from 1 July 1998 to 31 December 2003, with the following results.

Period	*Profit* £
1.7.98 – 31.8.99	7,000
1.9.99 – 31.8.00	12,000
1.9.00 – 31.8.01	15,000
1.9.01 – 31.8.02	21,000
1.9.02 – 31.8.03	18,000
1.9.03 – 31.12.03	5,600
	78,600

The profits to be taxed in each tax year from 1998/99 to 2003/04, and the total of these taxable profits are calculated as follows.

Year	*Basis period*	*Working*	*Taxable profit* £
1998/99	1.7.98 – 5.4.99	£7,000 × 9/14	4,500
1999/00	1.9.98 – 31.8.99	£7,000 × 12/14	6,000
2000/01	1.9.99 – 31.8.00		12,000
2001/02	1.9.00 – 31.8.01		15,000
2002/03	1.9.01 – 31.8.02		21,000
2003/04	1.9.02 – 31.12.03	£(18,000 + 5,600 – 3,500)	20,100
			78,600

The overlap profits are those in the period 1 September 1998 to 5 April 1999, a period of seven months. They are £7,000 × 7/14 = £3,500. Overlap profits are deducted from the final year's taxable profit when the business ceases. In this case the overlap profits are deducted when the business ceases. Over the life of the business, the total taxable profits equal the total actual profits.

Activity 2.9

Peter trades from 1 September 1998 to 30 June 2003, with the following results.

Period	*Profit*
	£
1.9.98 – 30.4.99	8,000
1.5.99 – 30.4.00	15,000
1.5.00 – 30.4.01	9,000
1.5.01 – 30.4.02	10,500
1.5.02 – 30.4.03	16,000
1.5.03 – 30.6.03	950
	59,450

Show the profits to be taxed in each year from 1998/99 to 2003/04, the total of these taxable profits and the overlap profits.

3.9 Example: no accounting date in the second year

Thelma starts to trade on 1 March 2002. Her first accounts, covering the 16 months to 30 June 2003, show a profit of £36,000. The taxable profits for the first three tax years and the overlap profits are as follows.

Year	Basis period	Working	*Taxable profits*
			£
2001/02	1.3.02 – 5.4.02	£36,000 × 1/16	2,250
2002/03	6.4.02 – 5.4.03	£36,000 × 12/16	27,000
2003/04	1.7.02 – 30.6.03	£36,000 × 12/16	27,000

The overlap profits are the profits from 1 July 2002 to 5 April 2003: £36,000 × 9/16 = £20,250.

4 Income tax forms

A copy of the supplementary pages to the income tax return that have to be completed by self employed taxpayers are included in appendix to this text. In Unit 18 you will be expected to be aware of how business income is entered in these supplementary pages. However, completion of the full income tax self assessment return will be assessed in Unit 19 only. Please see page (vi) for a note regarding these forms.

You will be able to practice completing tax return forms when you try the activities in BPP's unit 18 Assessment Kit.

5 End of chapter activity

Activity 2.10

The profit and loss account of Mr Brillo for the year ended 31 December 2003 shows the following.

			£		£
Staff wages			2,416	Gross profit from trading	
Wife's wages			624	account	10,326
Rent			630	Profit on sale of plant	240
Light and heat			171	Profit on sale of investment	1,032
Motor car expenses			336	Bank interest received	54
Telephone			79		
Postage, stationery and wrapping			80		
Repairs and renewals			476		
Bad debts written off			100		
Miscellaneous expenses			346		
Advertising			24		
Loan interest			130		
Depreciation:	plant	480			
	motor car	120	600		
Net profit			5,640		
			11,652		11,652

Notes

(a) The Revenue have agreed that one third of the expenditure on rent, light and heat relates to living accommodation at the business premises.

(b) One seventh of the motor expenses relate to private motoring.

(c) Repairs and renewals comprise the following.

	£
Painting shop internally	155
Plant repairs	220
Building extension to stockroom	101
	476

(d) BAD DEBTS ACCOUNT

		£			£
2003			*2003*		
31 Dec	Bad debts written off	102	1 Jan	Balances b/f	
	Balances c/f			General	200
	General	400		Specific	360
	Specific	398			560
			31 Dec	Bad debt recovered	240
				Profit & loss account	100
		900			900

(e) Miscellaneous expenses comprise the following.

	£
Donations to the Spastics Society	10
Subscription to the Chamber of Commerce	8
Entertaining customers	90
Christmas gifts to customers:	
bottles of gin costing £8.75 each, one per customer with 'Mr Brillo' labels	70
Payments to employees in lieu of notice	50
Legal expenses re debt collecting	15
Sundries: all allowable	103
	346

(f) The profit on the sale of an investment relates to the sale of a holding of ordinary shares in a company quoted on the Stock Exchange. The capital gain on these shares was £7,690.

(g) Mrs Brillo assists full time in the business.

(h) Gross profit is 15% of selling price and Brillo estimates that he has withdrawn goods costing £340 for his own use. No entry has been made in the accounts in respect of this.

(i) The staff wages include £260 paid to Brillo.

Task

Compute Mr Brillo's tax adjusted trading profit for the year ended 31 December 2003.

Key learning points

- ☑ The **badges of trade** can be used to decide whether or not a trade exists.
- ☑ If there is a trade, the **accounts profits need to be adjusted** in order to **calculate taxable profits**.
- ☑ **Capital expenditure** is **not allowable** for income tax.
- ☑ Wages or salary **paid to a proprietor** are **not deductible**.
- ☑ Certain types of entertaining (eg **entertaining clients**) are **not deductible**.
- ☑ **General** doubtful debt provisions are **not deductible**.
- ☑ **Basis periods** are used to link **periods of account** to **tax years**.
- ☑ In **opening years**, special rules are applied so that a **new trader can start to be taxed quickly**.
- ☑ In **closing years**, special rules make sure that the **retiring trader need not be taxed long after his retirement**.
- ☑ Certain profits may be **taxed twice** (**'overlap profits'**).
- ☑ **Overlap profits** can be **relieved on cessation**.

Quick quiz

1 List the six traditional badges of trade.

2 Victor has a trading profit of £220,000 after charging entertainment expenses of £3,200, (including £1,000 for a staff dance), legal fees of £4,500 (of which £800 related to the purchase of a property) and depreciation of £32,000. Capital allowances of £47,000 are available to claim.

Victor's Schedule DI trading profits are:

A £205,000
B £205,800
C £208,000
D £221,800

3 Mr Jones provides an analysis of his business legal expenses as follows:

	£
Successful tax appeal to commissioners	1,600
New employment contract for manager	700
Renewal of 18 year lease	950
Raising loan to buy a factory for use in the trade	850
Fine for breach of Factories Act	200

The amount to be added back in arriving at his taxable profits is:

A £Nil
B £200
C £1,600
D £1,800

4 Rachel starts in business on 1 December 2003. She makes up her first set of accounts to 30 November 2004 showing a profit of £6,000. What is her taxable profit for 2003/04?

5 And what are Rachel's overlap profits?

6 Darren has been in business for many years. He had overlap profits of £5,000 on the start of his business. His results to the cessation of his business were:

y/e 30.6.03	£10,000
3 months to 30.9.03	£1,500

What are Darren's taxable profits for the final tax year of trading?

Answers to quick quiz

1 Subject matter
Frequency of transactions
Length of ownership
Supplementary work and marketing
Profit motive
Way the goods were acquired

2 C

		£
Trading profit		220,000
Add:	Entertaining	2,200
	Legal fees	800
Depreciation		32,000
Less: Capital allowances		(47,000)
Schedule D Case I		208,000

3 D

	£
Appeal	1,600
Fine	200
	1,800

The legal fees incurred in renewing the lease are specifically allowable.

4 Basis period 1.12.03 – 5.4.04 = 4 months

Taxable profit 2003/04 is 4/12 x £6,000 = £2,000

5 Taxable profit 2004/05 will be the whole of the y/e 30.11.04

So the profits between 1.12.03 – 5.4.04 will be taxed twice

The overlap profits is therefore 4/12 x £6,000 = £2,000

6 Basis period for 2003/04 is 1.7.02 – 30.9.03

Taxable profits are £(10,000 + 1,500 – 5,000) = £6,500

Overlap profits are relieved on cessation

Activity checklist

This checklist shows which performance criteria or knowledge and understanding point is covered by each activity in this chapter. Tick off each activity as you complete it.

Activity		
2.1	☐	This activity deals with Knowledge and Understanding point 4: basic law and practice.
2.2	☐	This activity deals with Performance Criteria 18.2.A: adjust trading profits and losses for tax purposes.
2.3	☐	This activity deals with Performance Criteria 18.2.A: adjust trading profits and losses for tax purposes.
2.4	☐	This activity deals with Performance Criteria 18.2.A: adjust trading profits and losses for tax purposes.
2.5	☐	This activity deals with Performance Criteria 18.2.A: adjust trading profits and losses for tax purposes.
2.6	☐	This activity deals with Performance Criteria 18.2.A and 18.2.B: adjust trading profits and losses for tax purposes; make adjustments for private use by business owners.
2.7	☐	This activity deals with Performance Criteria 18.2.D: apply the basis of assessment for unincorporated businesses in the opening and closing years.
2.8	☐	This activity deals with Performance Criteria 18.2.D: apply the basis of assessment for unincorporated businesses in the opening and closing years.
2.9	☐	This activity deals with Performance Criteria 18.2.D: apply the basis of assessment for unincorporated businesses in the opening and closing years.
2.10	☐	This activity deals with Performance Criteria 18.1.A, classify expenditure on capital assets in accordance with the distinction between capital and revenue expenditure; 18.2.A and 18.2.B: adjust trading profits and losses for tax purposes; make adjustments for private use by business owners.

chapter 3

Capital allowances

Contents

Performance criteria

18.1 A Classify expenditure on capital assets in accordance with the statutory distinction between capital and revenue expenditure

18.1 B Ensure that entries and calculations relating to the computation of capital allowances for a company are correct

18.1.C Make adjustments for private use by business owners

Range statement

18.1 Business owners: self-employed individuals, partnerships

Knowledge and understanding

5 Availability and types of capital allowances:
- first year allowances
- writing down allowances
- balancing allowance and charge (relevant to industrial buildings and plant and machinery including computers, motor vehicles and short life assets) (Element 18.1)

6 Treatment of capital allowances for unincorporated businesses including private use adjustments (Element 18.1)

1 Capital allowances in general

Capital expenditure is not in itself an allowable Schedule D Case I deduction, but it *may* attract capital allowances. Capital allowances are treated as a trading expense and are deducted in arriving at Schedule D Case I profits. Balancing charges, effectively negative allowances, are added in arriving at those profits.

Capital expenditure on plant and machinery qualifies for capital allowances. Expenditure on industrial buildings may also qualify for allowances.

Both incorporated businesses and companies are entitled to capital allowances. For completeness, in this chapter we will look at the rules for companies alongside those for unincorporated businesses. We will look at companies in more detail later in this text.

For unincorporated businesses, capital allowances are calculated for periods of account. These are simply the periods for which the trader chooses to make up accounts.

For companies, capital allowances are calculated for accounting periods. (See later in this text.)

For capital allowances purposes, expenditure is generally deemed to be incurred when the obligation to pay becomes unconditional. This will often be the date of a contract, but if for example payment is due a month after delivery of a machine, it would be the date of delivery. However, amounts due more than four months after the obligation becomes unconditional are deemed to be incurred when they fall due.

2 The definition of plant

2.1 Introduction

There are two sources of the rules on what qualifies as plant and is therefore eligible for capital allowances. (Machinery is also eligible, but the word 'machinery' may be taken to have its everyday meaning.) **Statute** lists items which do not qualify, but it does not give a comprehensive list of other items which do qualify. There are several **cases** in which certain items have been accepted as plant. A few items such as thermal insulation and computer software are specifically defined as plant by statute.

2.2 The statutory exclusions

2.2.1 Buildings

Expenditure on a building and on any asset which is incorporated in a building or is of a kind normally incorporated into buildings does not qualify as expenditure on plant unless the asset falls within the list of exceptions given below. Even if an asset falls within that list, it does not follow that it is plant although it usually will be.

In addition to complete buildings, **the following assets count as 'buildings', and are therefore not plant**.

- Walls, floors, ceilings, doors, gates, shutters, windows and stairs
- Mains services, and systems, of water, electricity and gas
- Waste disposal, sewerage and drainage systems
- Shafts or other structures for lifts etc.

The following assets which would normally count as 'buildings' **can still be plant**.

- Any machinery not within any other item in this list.
- Electrical (including lighting), cold water, gas and sewerage systems:
  - (i) Provided mainly to meet the particular requirements of the trade, or
  - (ii) Provided mainly to serve particular machinery or plant used for the purposes of the trade.
- Space or water heating systems and powered systems of ventilation.
- Manufacturing and display equipment.
- Cookers, washing machines, refrigeration or cooling equipment, sanitary ware and furniture and furnishings.
- Lifts etc.
- Sound insulation provided mainly to meet the particular requirements of the trade.
- Computer, telecommunication and surveillance systems.
- Sprinkler equipment, fire alarm and burglar alarm systems.
- Strong rooms in bank or building society premises; safes.
- Partition walls, where movable and intended to be moved.
- Decorative assets provided for the enjoyment of the public in the hotel, restaurant or similar trades; advertising hoardings.
- Glasshouses which have, as an integral part of their structure, devices which control the plant growing environment automatically.
- Swimming pools (including diving boards, slides).

In addition, the following items may be 'plant'.

- Caravans provided mainly for holiday lettings
- Movable buildings intended to be moved in the course of the trade

When a building is sold, the vendor and purchaser can make a joint election to determine how the sale proceeds are apportioned between the building and its fixtures. There are anti-avoidance provisions that ensure capital allowances given overall on a fixture do not exceed the original cost of the fixture.

Activity 3.1

One side wall of a building consists of a single sheet of wood, 2cm thick, and advertisements are displayed on the outside. Could this wall qualify as plant?

2.2.2 Structures

Expenditure on structures and on works involving the alteration of land **does not qualify as expenditure on plant** unless the asset falls within the list of exceptions given below. Even if an asset falls within that list, it does not follow that it is plant although it probably will be.

A 'structure' is a fixed structure of any kind, other than a building.

The following items, which would normally count as 'structures' **can still be plant.**

- Expenditure on altering land for the purpose only of installing machinery or plant
- Pipelines, and also underground ducts or tunnels with a primary purpose of carrying utility conduits
- Silos provided for temporary storage and storage tanks
- Fish tanks and fish ponds
- A railway or tramway

In addition, expenditure may qualify as plant despite these rules if the assets bought are items which qualify as plant under the rules discussed below.

2.2.3 Land

Land or an interest in land does not qualify as plant and machinery. For this purpose 'land' excludes buildings, structures and assets which are installed or fixed to land in such a way as to become part of the land for general legal purposes.

2.3 Case law

The original case law **definition of plant** (applied in this case to a horse) **is 'whatever apparatus is used by a businessman for carrying on his business: not his stock in trade which he buys or makes for sale; but all goods and chattels, fixed or movable, live or dead, which he keeps for permanent employment in the business'** (*Yarmouth v France 1887*).

Subsequent cases have refined the original definition and have largely been concerned with the **distinction between plant actively used in the business (qualifying) and the setting in which the business is carried on (non-qualifying). This is the 'functional' test**. Some of the decisions have now been enacted as part of statute law, but they are still relevant as examples of the principles involved.

The whole cost of excavating and installing a swimming pool was allowed to the owners of a caravan park: the pool performed **the function** of giving 'buoyancy and enjoyment' to the persons using the pool (now covered by statute) (*Cooke v Beach Station Caravans Ltd 1974*).

A barrister succeeded in his claim for his law library: 'Plant includes a man's tools of his trade. It extends to what he uses day by day in the course of his profession. It is not confined to physical things like the dentist's chair or the architect's table' (*Munby v Furlong 1977*).

Office partitioning was allowed. Because it was movable it was not regarded as part of the setting in which the business was carried on (now covered by statute) (*Jarrold v John Good and Sons Ltd 1963*).

A ship used as a floating restaurant was regarded as a 'structure in which the business was carried on rather than apparatus employed ... '. No capital allowances could be obtained (*Benson v Yard Arm Club 1978*). The same decision was made in relation to a football club's spectator stand. The stand performed no function in the actual carrying out of the club's trade (*Brown v Burnley Football and Athletic Club 1980*).

At a motorway service station, false ceilings contained conduits, ducts and lighting apparatus. **They did not qualify because they did not perform a function in the business. They were merely part of the setting in which the business was conducted** (*Hampton v Fortes Autogrill Ltd 1979*).

Light fittings, decor and murals can be plant. A company carried on business as hoteliers and operators of licensed premises. The function of the items was the creation of an atmosphere conducive to the comfort and well being of its customers (decorative assets used in hotels etc, now covered by statute) (*CIR v Scottish and Newcastle Breweries Ltd 1982*).

On the other hand, it has been held that when an attractive floor is provided in a restaurant, the fact that the floor performs the function of making the restaurant attractive to customers is not enough to make it plant. It functions as premises, and the cost therefore does not qualify for capital allowances (*Wmpey International Ltd v Warland 1988*).

General lighting in a department store is not plant, as it is merely setting. Special display lighting, however, can be plant (*Cole Brothers Ltd v Phillips 1982*).

Free-standing decorative screens installed in the windows of a branch of a building society qualified as plant. Their function was not to act a part of the setting in which the society's business was carried on; it was to attract local custom, and accordingly the screens formed part of the apparatus with which the society carried on its business (*Leeds Permanent Building Society v Proctor 1982*).

2.4 Expenditure deemed to be on plant and machinery

Plant and machinery capital allowances are also available on:

- Expenditure incurred by a trader in complying with fire regulations for a building which he occupies
- Expenditure by a trader on thermal insulation of an industrial building
- Expenditure by a trader in meeting statutory safety requirements for sports ground
- Expenditure (by an individual or a partnership, not by a company) on *security assets* provided to meet a special threat to an individual's security that arises wholly or mainly due to the particular trade concerned. Cars, ships, aircraft and dwellings are specifically excluded from the definition of a security asset

On disposal, the sale proceeds for the above are deemed to be zero, so no balancing charge (see below) can arise.

2.5 Computer software

Capital expenditure on computer software qualifies as expenditure on **plant and machinery**:

(a) Regardless of whether the software is supplied in a tangible form (such as a disk) or transmitted electronically, and

(b) Regardless of whether the purchaser acquires the software or only a licence to use it.

Disposal proceeds are brought into account in the normal way, except that if the fee for the grant of a licence is taxed as income of the licensor, no disposal proceeds are taken into account in computing the licensee's capital allowances.

Where someone has incurred expenditure qualifying for capital allowances on computer software (or the right to use software), and receives a capital sum in exchange for allowing someone else to use the software, that sum is brought into account as disposal proceeds. However, the cumulative total of disposal proceeds is not allowed to exceed the original cost of the software, and any proceeds above this limit are ignored for capital allowances purposes (although they may lead to chargeable gains).

If software is expected to have a useful economic life of less than two years, its cost may be treated as revenue expenditure.

Activity 3.2

Would lights in a factory qualify as plant if they were:

(a) normal background illumination?
(b) powerful spotlights to assist workers engaged in delicate work?

3 Allowances on plant and machinery

3.1 Pooling expenditure

Most expenditure on plant and machinery is put into a pool of expenditure on which capital allowances may be claimed. An addition increases the pool whilst a disposal decreases it.

Exceptionally the following items are not pooled.

(i) cars costing more than £12,000
(ii) assets with private use by the proprietor
(iii) short life assets where an election has been made.

Each of these items is dealt with in further detail below.

3.2 Writing down allowances

3.2.1 Introduction

A writing down allowance (WDA) is given on pooled expenditure **at the rate of 25% a year** (on a reducing balance basis). The WDA is calculated on the written down value (WDV) of pooled plant, after adding the current period's additions and taking out the current period's disposals.

When plant is sold, proceeds (but **limited to a maximum of the original cost**) are taken out of the pool. Provided that the trade is still being carried on, the pool balance remaining is written down in the future by WDAs, even if there are no assets left.

3.2.2 Example

Elizabeth has a balance of unrelieved expenditure on her general pool of plant and machinery of £16,000 on 1.4.03. In the year to 31.3.04 she bought a car for £8,000 and she disposed of plant which originally cost £4,000 for £6,000.

Calculate the capital allowances available for the year.

	£
Pool value b/f	16,000
Addition	8,000
Less: Disposal (**Limited to cost**)	(4,000)
	20,000
WDA @ 25%	(5,000)
TWDV c/f	15,000

3.2.3 Further points

WDAs are 25% × months/12:

(a) For unincorporated businesses where the period of account is longer or shorter than 12 months

(b) For companies where the accounting period is shorter than 12 months (a company's accounting period for tax purposes is never longer than 12 months), or where the trade concerned started in the accounting period and was therefore carried on for fewer than 12 months. Remember that we will be studying companies in detail later in this text.

Expenditure on plant and machinery by a person about to begin a trade is treated as incurred on the first day of trading. Assets previously owned by a trader and then brought into the trade (at the start of trading or later) are treated as bought for their market values at the times when they are brought in.

Allowances are claimed in the tax return.

Note that from a tax planning point of view any business can claim less than the full allowances. **Adjusting capital allowances may be advantageous, if, for example, a trader wants to avoid making such a large loss claim as to lose the benefit of the personal allowance (see later in this text).** Higher capital allowances will then be available in later years because the WDV carried forward will be higher.

3.3 First year allowances

3.3.1 Spending by small and medium sized enterprises

Expenditure incurred on plant and machinery after 2 July 1998 **by small and medium sized enterprises, in general, qualifies for a first year allowance** (FYA) of 40%.

A **small or medium sized enterprise,** is an individual, partnership or company that either satisfies at least two of the following conditions in the chargeable period/financial year in which the expenditure is incurred.

(a) **Turnover not more than £11.2 million**
(b) **Assets not more than £5.6 million**
(c) **Not more than 250 employees**

or which was small or medium sized in the previous year. A company must not be a member of a large group when the expenditure is incurred.

The definition of small and medium sized companies is to be aligned with the European Union definition which will be published later in 2003. The effect of the change will be to increase the number of businesses eligible for the 40% FYA. At the date of printing this text, this change had not been announced.

3.3.2 Calculation of FYAs

For FYA purposes, the provisions which treat capital expenditure incurred prior to the commencement of trading as incurred on the first day of trading do not apply.

First year allowances are given in the place of writing down allowances. For subsequent years a WDA is given on the balance of expenditure at the normal rate. You should therefore transfer the balance of the expenditure to the pool at the end of the first period.

FYAs are given for incurring expenditure. It is irrelevant whether the basis period of expenditure is twelve months or not. FYAs are not scaled up or down by reference to the length of the period.

Activity 3.3

The tax written down value brought forward on GWC Ltd's general pool of plant and machinery on 1 July 2003 was £48,000. The only addition in the six month accounting period to 31 December 2003 was printing press costing £20,000.

GWC is a small or medium sized enterprise for capital allowance purposes.

What are the maximum capital allowances the GWC will be entitled to claim in the period to 31 December 2003?

3.3.3 100% FYAs

Expenditure by **small enterprises on information and communication technology equipment in the four year period from 1 April 2000 to 31 March 2004 qualifies for a 100% FYA.**

Equipment acquired for leasing does not normally qualify for the 100% FYA. Exceptionally, leased low emission and electric cars, natural gas/hydrogen refuelling equipment and certain energy saving equipment all do qualify for FYAs.

A **small enterprise** is an individual, partnership or company, which satisfies at least two of the following conditions in the chargeable period/financial year in which the expenditure is incurred:

(a) **Turnover not more than £2.8 million**
(b) **Assets not more than £1.4 million**
(c) **Not more than 50 employees**

or which was small in the previous year. If a company is a member of a group, the group must also be small when the expenditure is incurred. Again this definition is due to change.

A 100% FYA is available to all businesses for expenditure incurred on designated energy saving technologies and on plant to refuel vehicles with compressed natural gas or hydrogen (in this case on expenditure between 17 April 2002 and 31 March 2008). Various criteria must be met by qualifying technologies and products before 100% FYAs are available. The equipment must be used in the person's business.

A car registered between 16 April 2002 and 31 March 2008 qualifies for 100% FYAs if it either:

- emits not more than 120 gm/kg CO_2 ; or
- it is electrically propelled

In addition, the special rules for expensive cars (see below), which restrict the availability of capital allowances and the deductibility of lease rental payments, will not apply to low emission cars.

From 1 April 2003 a 100% FYA is available to all businesses in respect of expenditure incurred on plant and equipment meeting strict water saving or efficiency criteria (eg water meters, flow controllers, efficient toilets!).

Activity 3.4

Walton started a trade on 1 March 2000 and prepared his first accounts to 31 July 2001. Thereafter accounts were prepared to 31 July annually. Plant was bought as follows.

Date	*Cost*
	£
1.3.00 (Grinding machine)	13,000
1.6.00 (Grinding machine)	9,603
1.6.02 (Grinding machine)	5,000
31.7.03 (Computer equipment)	2,000

On 1 May 2002, plant which cost £7,000 is sold for £4,000.

Walton's business is a small enterprise for FYA purposes.

Show the capital allowances arising in the first three periods of account.

Note the tax planning opportunities available. It may be important to buy plant just before an accounting date, so that allowances become available as soon as possible. On the other hand, it may be worthwhile to claim less than the maximum allowances so as to even out the annual assessments and avoid higher rate tax.

3.4 The disposal value of assets

The most common disposal value at which assets are entered in a capital allowances computation is the sale proceeds. But there are a number of less common situations.

Where the asset is sold at below market value (or is given away) **the market value is used instead of the actual sale proceeds**. This general rule has two exceptions. The actual proceeds of sale are used:

(a) Where the buyer will be able to claim capital allowances on the expenditure

(b) Where an employee acquires an asset from his employer at undervalue (or as a gift) and so faces a charge under the employment income benefit rules

If the asset is demolished, destroyed or otherwise lost, the disposal value is taken to be the actual sale proceeds from any resulting scrap, plus any insurance or other compensation moneys.

With all these rules, there is an overriding rule that the capital allowances **disposal value cannot exceed the original purchase price**.

Activity 3.5

At the start of its accounting period from 1 January to 31 October 2003, a company had a balance on its plant pool of £123,000. Plant which had cost £27,000 was sold for £32,000 on 1 August. What were the capital allowances for this ten month accounting period?

3.5 Balancing charges and allowances

Balancing charges occur when the disposal value deducted exceeds the balance remaining in the pool. The charge equals the excess and is effectively a negative capital allowance, increasing profits. Most commonly this happens when the trade ceases and the remaining assets are sold. It may also occur, however, whilst the trade is still in progress.

Balancing allowances on the capital allowance pools of expenditure arise only when the trade ceases. The balancing allowance is equal to the remaining unrelieved expenditure after deducting the disposal value of all the assets. Balancing allowances also arise on items which are not pooled (see below) whenever those items are disposed of.

3.6 Assets which are not pooled

A separate record of allowances and WDV must be kept for each asset which is not pooled and when it is sold a balancing allowance or charge emerges.

Motor cars costing more than £12,000 are not pooled. The maximum WDA is £3,000 a year. The limit is £3,000 × months/12:

(a) For short or long periods of account of unincorporated businesses
(b) For short accounting periods of companies

FYAs are not available on cars (except for certain low emission or electric cars – see above).

An asset (for example, a car) which is used partly for private purposes by a sole trader or a partner is not pooled. Make all calculations on the full cost but claim only the business use proportion of the allowances. An asset with some private use by an employee (not a proprietor), however, suffers no such restriction. The employee may be taxed on a benefit so the business gets capital allowances on the full cost of the asset.

Activity 3.6

A trader started to trade on 1 July 2000, making up accounts to 31 December 2000 and each 31 December thereafter. On 1 August 2000 he bought a car for £15,500. The private use proportion is 10%. The car was sold in July 2003 for £4,000. What are the capital allowances?

Short life assets (see below) are not pooled.

3.7 The cessation of a trade

When a business ceases to trade no FYAs or WDAs are given in the final period of account (unincorporated businesses) or accounting period (companies - see later in this text). Each asset is deemed to be disposed of on the date the trade ceased (usually at the then market value). Additions in the relevant period are brought in and then the disposal proceeds (limited to cost) are deducted from the balance of qualifying expenditure. If the proceeds exceed the balance then a balancing charge arises. If the balance of qualifying expenditure exceeds the proceeds then a balancing allowance is given.

4 Short-life assets

A trader can elect that specific items of plant be kept separately from the general pool. The election is irrevocable. For an unincorporated business, the time limit for electing is the 31 January which is 22 months after the end of the tax year in which the period of account of the expenditure ends. (For a company, it is two years after the end of the accounting period of the expenditure.) **Any asset subject to this election is known as a 'short-life asset'**, and the election is known as a **'de-pooling election'**.

Provided that the asset is disposed of within four years of the end of the period of account or accounting period in which it was bought, it is a **short life asset** and a balancing charge or allowance is made on its disposal.

If the asset is not disposed of in the correct time period, its tax written down value is added to the general pool at the end of that time.

The election should be made for assets likely to be sold within four years for less than their tax written down values. It should not be made for assets likely to be sold within four years for more than their tax written down values. (These are, of course, only general guidelines based on the assumption that a trader will want to obtain allowances as quickly as possible. There may be other considerations, such as a desire to even out annual taxable profits.)

Activity 3.7

Caithin bought an asset on 1 May 1999 for £12,000 and elected for de-pooling. His accounting year end is 30 April. Calculate the capital allowances due if:

(a) The asset is scrapped for £300 in August 2003.
(b) The asset is scrapped for £200 in August 2004.

Short-life asset treatment cannot be claimed for:

- Motor cars
- Plant used partly for non-trade purposes
- Plant brought into use for the trade following non-business use
- Plant received by way of gift
- Plant in respect of which a subsidy is received

Where a short-life asset is disposed of within the four year period to a connected person (see below):

(a) The original owner receives a balancing allowance calculated as normal and the new owner receives WDAs on the cost to him, but

(b) **If both parties so elect, the asset is treated as being sold for its tax written down value at the start of the chargeable period in which the transfer takes place, so there is no balancing charge or allowance for the vendor.**

In both situations, the acquiring party will continue to 'de-pool' the asset up to the same date as the original owner would have done.

5 Hire purchase and leasing

5.1 Assets on hire purchase

Any asset (including a car) bought on hire purchase (HP) is treated as if purchased outright for the cash price. Therefore:

(a) The buyer normally obtains **capital allowances on the cash price** when the agreement begins.
(b) He may write off the **finance charge as a trade expense** over the term of the HP contract.

5.2 Leased assets

Under a lease, the lessee merely hires the asset over a period. The hire charge can normally be deducted in computing Schedule D Case I profits.

An expensive car (one costing over £12,000) will attract WDAs limited to £3,000 a year if bought. If it is leased instead, the maximum allowable deduction from trading profits for lease rentals is

$$\frac{£12{,}000 + P}{2P} \times R$$

where P = the purchase price (if bought outright)
R = the annual rental

This restriction does not apply to the finance charges in hire purchase payments (which could be regarded as payment for the hire of the car), provided the amount payable to acquire the car at the end of the hire period is no more than 1% of the car's retail price when new.

5.3 Example: leased cars

A car is used by a business under a lease. The purchase price would have been £20,000. The annual rental is £5,000. The rental allowed for tax purposes is

$$\frac{£12{,}000 + £20{,}000}{2 \times £20{,}000} \times £5{,}000 = £4{,}000$$

Since £5,000 is deducted in the profit and loss account, £5,000 - £4,000 = £1,000 is added back in computing taxable profits.

6 Successions

Balancing adjustments arise on the cessation of a business. No writing down allowances are given, but the final proceeds (limited to cost) on sales of plant are compared with the tax WDV to calculate balancing allowances or charges.

Balancing charges may be avoided where the trade passes from one connected person to another. If a succession occurs both parties must elect if the avoidance of the balancing adjustments is required. **An election will result in the plant being transferred at its tax written down value for capital allowances purposes.** The predecessor can write down the plant for the period prior to cessation and the successor can write it down from the date of commencement. The election must be made within two years of the date of the succession.

If no election is made on a transfer of business to a connected person, assets are deemed to be sold at their market values.

An individual is connected with his spouse and his or his spouse's brothers, sisters, ancestors and lineal descendants, with their spouses, and with a company he controls. Companies under common control are connected.

Where a person succeeds to a business under a will or on intestacy, then even if he was not connected with the deceased he may elect to take over the assets at the lower of their market value and their tax written down value.

For both connected persons transfers and transfers on death, where the elections are made, the limit on proceeds to be brought into account on a later sale of an asset is the original cost of the asset, not the deemed transfer price.

7 Industrial buildings – types

7.1 Introduction

A special type of capital allowance (an **industrial buildings allowance** or IBA) is available in respect of **expenditure on industrial buildings**.

The allowance is available to traders taxable under Schedule D Case I, but not Case II.

7.2 Definition of industrial buildings

Industrial buildings include:

(a) All factories and ancillary premises used in:
   - (i) A manufacturing business
   - (ii) A trade in which goods and materials are subject to any process
   - (iii) A trade in which goods or raw materials are stored

(b) Staff welfare buildings (such as workplace nurseries and canteens, but not directors' restaurants) where the trade is qualifying

(c) Sports pavilions in any trade

(d) Buildings in use for a transport undertaking, agricultural contracting, mining or fishing

(e) Roads operated under highway concessions. The operation of such roads is treated as a trade for capital allowances purposes. The operator is treated as occupying the roads.

The definition in (a) (ii) above is 'the subjection of goods to any process'.

- The unpacking, repacking and relabelling of goods in a wholesale cash and carry supermarket did not amount to a 'process' but was a mere preliminary to sale (*Bestway Holdings Ltd v Luff 1998*).
- The mechanical processing of cheques and other banking documents was a process but pieces of paper carrying information were not 'goods' and thus the building housing the machinery did not qualify (*Girobank v Clarke 1998*).

Estate roads on industrial estates qualify, provided that the estate buildings are used wholly or mainly for a qualifying purpose.

Dwelling houses, retail shops, showrooms and offices are not industrial buildings.

Warehouses used for storage often cause problems in practice. A warehouse used for storage which is merely a transitory and necessary incident of the conduct of the business is not an industrial building. Storage is only a qualifying purpose if it is an end in itself.

Any building is an industrial building if it is constructed for the welfare of employees of a trader whose trade is a qualifying one (that is, the premises in which the trade is carried on are industrial buildings).

Sports pavilions provided for the welfare of employees qualify as industrial buildings. In this case, it does not matter whether the taxpayer is carrying on a trade in a qualifying building or not. Thus a retailer's sports pavilion would qualify for IBAs.

Drawing offices which serve an industrial building are regarded as industrial buildings themselves (*CIR v Lambhill Ironworks Ltd 1950*).

7.3 Buildings in enterprise zones

Any commercial building or hotel **built in an enterprise zone qualifies for industrial buildings allowances**, provided that the construction expenditure is contracted for within ten years of the zone's designation, and actually incurred within 20 years of the zone's designation.

A commercial building is any building that is used for trading purposes or as offices. Dwelling houses are not commercial buildings.

Activity 3.8

A retailer buys a shop, a staff canteen, a staff sports pavilion and a warehouse, none of these buildings being in an enterprise zone. Will any of them qualify as industrial buildings?

7.4 Eligible expenditure

Capital allowances are computed on the amount of eligible expenditure incurred on qualifying buildings. The eligible expenditure is:

- The original cost of a building if built by the trader, or
- The purchase price if the building was acquired from a person trading as a builder.

If the building was acquired other than from a person trading as a builder, the eligible expenditure is the lower of the purchase price and the original cost incurred by the person incurring the construction expenditure.

If a building is sold more than once before being brought into use, the last buyer before the building is brought into use obtains the allowances. If, in such cases, the building was first sold by someone trading as a builder, the eligible expenditure is the lower of the price paid by the first buyer and the price paid by the last buyer.

In all cases where a building is sold before use and artificial arrangements have increased the purchase price, it is reduced to what it would have been without those arrangements.

Where part of a building qualifies as an industrial building and part does not, the whole cost qualifies for IBAs, provided that the cost of the non-qualifying part is not more than 25% of the total expenditure. If the non-qualifying part of the building does cost more than 25% of the total, its cost must be excluded from the capital allowances computation.

Difficulties arise where non-qualifying buildings (particularly offices and administration blocks) are joined to manufacturing areas. For example, a covered walkway linking manufacturing and administrative areas was not regarded as creating a single building. The administrative area was treated as a separate, non-qualifying building (*Abbott Laboratories Ltd v Carmody 1968*).

The cost of land is disallowed but expenditure incurred in preparing land for building does qualify. The cost of items which would not be included in a normal commercial lease (such as rental guarantees) also does not qualify.

Activity 3.9

Sue purchased an industrial building for £2,500,000. This cost was made up of:

	£
Factory	2,100,000
Land	400,000
	2,500,000

The costs attributable to showrooms and offices within the factory were £400,000 and £200,000 respectively.

What is the expenditure qualifying for industrial buildings allowances?

Professional fees, for example architects' fees, incurred in connection with the construction of an industrial building qualify. The cost of repairs to industrial buildings also qualifies, provided that the expenditure is not deductible as a trading expense.

8 Allowances on industrial buildings

8.1 Writing down allowances

A writing down allowance (WDA) is given for a period provided that the industrial building was in use as such on the last day of the period concerned.

If the building was not in use as an industrial building at the end of the relevant period it may have been:

- **Unused** for any purpose, or
- Used for a non-industrial purpose.

The distinction is important in ascertaining whether WDAs are due to the taxpayer. **If any disuse is temporary and previously the building had been in industrial use, WDAs may be claimed in exactly the same way as if the building were in industrial use.** The legislation does not define 'temporary' but in practice, any subsequent qualifying use of the building will usually enable the period of disuse to be regarded as temporary.

Non-industrial use has different consequences, but you will not be expected to deal with these in your assessment.

The WDA is 4% of the eligible expenditure incurred by the taxpayer.

The allowance is calculated on a straight line basis (in contrast to WDAs on plant and machinery which are calculated on the reducing balance), starting when the building is brought into use.

The WDA is 4% × months/12 if the period concerned is not 12 months long.

Buildings in enterprise zones qualify for a 100% allowance when built, without waiting for them to be brought into use (unlike other buildings). However, not all the allowance need be taken, and any expenditure not so allowed is written off straight line, at 25% of the full cost each year, over a period of up to four years starting when the building is brought into use.

Buildings always have a **separate computation for each building**. They are never pooled.

Activity 3.10

Fraser Ltd acquired a factory for £600,000 and started to use it for industrial purposes on 1 July 2003. What industrial buildings allowances are available to Fraser Ltd in its nine month accounting period to 30 September 2003?

8.2 Balancing adjustments on sale

8.2.1 The tax life

The 'tax life' of an industrial building is 25 years (hence the 4% straight line WDA) after it is first used. Balancing adjustments apply *only* if a building is sold within its tax life of 25 years.

On a sale between connected persons, the parties may jointly elect that the transfer price for IBAs purposes should be the lower of the market value and the residue of unallowed expenditure before the sale. This avoids a balancing charge unless there has been non-industrial use.

8.2.2 Sales without non-industrial use

The seller's calculation is quite straightforward. It takes the following form.

	£
Cost	X
Less allowances previously given	(X)
Residue before sale	X
Less proceeds (limited to cost)	(X)
Balancing (charge)/allowance	(X)

The buyer obtains annual straight line WDAs for the remainder of the building's tax life (25 years). This life is calculated to the nearest month. The allowances are granted on the residue after sale which is computed thus.

	£
Residue before sale	X
Plus balancing charge or less balancing allowance	X
Residue after sale	X

This means that **the second owner will write off the lower of his cost or the original cost.**

Activity 3.11

Frankie, who started to trade in 1998 preparing accounts to 31 December, bought an industrial building for £100,000 (excluding land) on 1 October 1999. He brought it into use as a factory immediately. On 1 September 2003 he sells it for £120,000 to Holly, whose accounting date is 30 September and who brought the building into industrial use immediately. Show the IBAs available to Frankie and to Holly.

The Inland Revenue allow IBAs equal to the fall in value of a building over the trader's use of that building. As a general rule if an industrial building is sold for more than its original cost a balancing charge equal to the allowances given to date will arise. This is because there was no fall in value so no allowances are actually due.

If it is sold for less than original cost we could calculate the fall in value of the building and that would equal the allowances available for this building. If we compare this to the allowances already given, the difference would be the balancing adjustment due on the sale.

In the above question if Frankie sold the building Holly for £90,000:

	£
Fall in value (£100,000 – £90,000) = allowances due	10,000
Less: allowances already given to Frankie	16,000
Balancing adjustment = Balancing charge	6,000

Over the use of the building by Frankie £16,000 of IBAs were claimed. On the sale of the building the fall in value is calculated as £10,000. Thus Frankie should only have received £10,000 of allowances not £16,000. So £6,000 is paid back as a balancing charge.

9 End of chapter activities

Now attempt the two activities below. The first is concerned with capital allowances on plant and machinery whilst the second is concerned with industrial buildings allowances.

Activity 3.12

Vivace makes up his accounts to 31 December each year.

After claiming allowances based on the period ended 31 December 2000, the balance of his general pool stood at £8,000.

During the years ended 31 December 2001, 2002 and 2003 Vivace recorded the following capital transactions.

14	September 2001	He sold machinery which originally cost £1,800 for £700.
16	September 2001	He bought a new car for a salesman for £4,000. The employee uses it privately for 25% of all its mileage.
1	December 2001	He bought secondhand machinery for £7,693.
21	March 2002	He sold plant which cost £2,000 in 2000 for £2,500.
22	March 2002	He sold the salesman's car for £3,200.
5	July 2002	He bought a Mercedes car for his own use costing £22,000. Vivace uses the car 60% for business purposes.
4	February 2003	He bought a new machine on hire purchase. A deposit of £1,800 was paid immediately. Four further instalments of £1,000 are payable annually in future years. The cash price would have been £4,000.
5	February 2003	He bought a car for the accountant for £3,000. There is no private use.
15	June 2003	He replaced his car. The Mercedes was sold for £4,000; a Volvo was bought for £18,000. 60% business use continued.
30	June 2003	Plant and equipment which originally cost £10,000 was sold for £2,602.
30	June 2003	He bought new computer equipment for £3,000.

Task

Set out Vivace's capital allowance computations for the periods of account ended 31 December 2001, 2002 and 2003, assuming that maximum claims are made. Assume Vivace's business qualifies as a small enterprise for capital allowances purposes where appropriate.

Activity 3.13

Cuckold Ltd makes up accounts to 31 March each year. It is considering the purchase of an additional, secondhand factory on 1 April 2004. It has decided to spend £150,000 and the following details refer to four possible factories which could each be acquired for that sum. All are equally suitable for Cuckold Ltd's purposes and all have been used for qualifying industrial purposes throughout their lives.

	Original cost to first owner	*Date of first use*
	£	
(i)	100,000	31 March 1980
(ii)	80,000	31 March 1979
(iii)	160,000	31 March 2002
(iv)	120,000	31 March 1996

Task

Advise Cuckold Ltd of the amount of industrial buildings allowances which would be available as a result of purchasing each of the above factories, indicating the periods for which the allowances would be available. Which building would you advise it to purchase?

Key learning points

- ☑ Statutory rules generally exclude specified items from treatment as plant, rather than include them as plant.
- ☑ There is substantial case law dealing with the **function/setting** distinction.
- ☑ The main point about capital allowances is to **get the layout right**. Then the figures should drop into place.
- ☑ Most expenditure on plant and machinery qualifies for a **25% writing down allowance (WDA) on the reducing balance** every 12 months.
- ☑ First year allowances (FYAs) may be available on certain expenditure.
- ☑ **FYAs are never reduced or increased for short or long periods of account**.
- ☑ **Private use assets** by sole traders and partners have **restricted capital allowances**.
- ☑ Short life asset elections can bring forward the allowances due on an asset.
- ☑ Allowances for industrial buildings (IBAs) equal the fall in value of the building whilst in industrial use.
- ☑ **IBAs are 4% a year on straight line basis.**

Quick quiz

1 The tax written down value brought forward on Mr Green's general pool of plant and machinery on 1 July 2003 was £24,000. The only addition in the six month period of account to 31 December 2003 was of a printing press costing £20,000. Mr Green's business is a small or medium sized enterprise for capital allowance purposes.

What are the maximum capital allowances that Mr Green will be entitled to claim in the period to 31 December 2003?

A £14,000
B £11,000
C £7,000
D £5,500

2 JD Ltd prepares accounts for the year to 31 March 2004. During the year the company made the following purchases of capital assets:

1.7.03	Car for managing director (50% private use)	£18,000
1.10.03	New computer	£5,000

The balance on JD Ltd's general pool for capital allowance purposes on 1 April 2003 was £10,000. There were no other balances brought forward. JD qualifies as a small enterprise for capital allowance purposes.

What are the maximum capital allowances that JD Ltd can claim for the year?

A £6,000
B £7,500
C £9,000
D £10,500

3 When may balancing allowances arise?

4 An asset must be disposed of within .... years of the end of the period of account or accounting period to be treated as a short life asset. Fill in the blank.

5 Mr Newell bought a factory on 1 June 2003 for £500,000. The purchase price comprised:

	£
Land	100,000
Drawing office	20,000
General offices	85,000
Factory	295,000
	500,000

On what amount may IBAs be claimed?

A £295,000
B £315,000
C £400,000
D £500,000

6 Louise bought a secondhand factory on 1 July 2003 for £200,000. The factory which had always been used for industrial purposes, originally cost £140,000 on 1 July 1998.

What IBAs will be available to Louise in her year ended 31 December 2003?

A £3,500
B £5,600
C £7,000
D £10,000

Answers to quick quiz

1 B

	£	£	£
WDV b/f		24,000	
WDA @ 25% × $^{6}/_{12}$		(3,000)	3,000
		21,000	
Addition	20,000		
FYA @ 40%	(8,000)		8,000
		12,000	
		54,000	11,000

WDA is pro-rated in a short period of account but the FYA is not.

2 D

	£	Pool £	Car £	£
TWDV b/f		10,000		
WDA @ 25%		(2,500)		2,500
		7,500		
Car addition			18,000	
WDA – restricted			(3,000)	3,000
Computer	5,000			
FYA 100%	(5,000)			5,000
		7,500	15,000	10,500

The private use of an asset has no impact on the capital allowances available to a *company.*

3 Balancing allowances may arise in respect of pooled expenditure only when the trade ceases. They may arise on non-pooled items whenever they are disposed of.

4 An asset must be disposed of within **four** years of the end of the period of account or accounting period to be treated as a short life asset.

5 C IBAs are never allowed on the cost of land.

IBAs are available on drawing offices.

IBAs are available on the general offices as they constitute less than 25% of the qualifying expenditure: 25% × £400,000 = £100,000.

6 C IBAs are available on lower of:

- original cost (£140,000)
- purchase price (£200,000)

Over the remaining tax life: $\frac{140,000}{20}$ = £7,000 pa

IBAs of £7,000 will be available to Louise.

Activity checklist

This checklist shows which performance criteria or knowledge and understanding point is covered by each activity in this chapter. Tick off each activity as you complete it.

Activity		
3.1	☐	This activity deals with Knowledge and Understanding point 5: availability and types of capital allowances
3.2	☐	This activity deals with Performance Criteria 18.1.A: classify expenditure on capital assets in accordance with the distinction between capital and revenue expenditure.
3.3	☐	This activity deals with Performance Criteria 18.1.B: ensure that entries and calculations relating to the computation on capital allowance for a company are correct.
3.4	☐	This activity deals with Knowledge and Understanding point 5: availability and types of capital allowances
3.5	☐	This activity deals with Knowledge and Understanding point 5: availability and types of capital allowances
3.6	☐	This activity deals with Performance Criteria 18.1.C: make adjustments for private use by business owners.
3.7	☐	This activity deals with Knowledge and Understanding point 5: availability and types of capital allowances
3.8	☐	This activity deals with Knowledge and Understanding point 5: availability and types of capital allowances
3.9	☐	This activity deals with Knowledge and Understanding point 5: availability and types of capital allowances
3.10	☐	This activity deals with Performance Criteria 18.1.B: ensure that entries and calculations relating to the computation on capital allowance for a company are correct.
3.11	☐	This activity deals with Knowledge and Understanding point 6: treatment of capital allowances for unincorporated businesses
3.12	☐	This activity deals with Performance Criteria 18.1.C: make adjustments for private use by business owners.
3.13	☐	This activity deals with Performance Criteria 18.1.B: ensure that entries and calculations relating to eh computation on capital allowance for a company are correct.

chapter 4

Trading losses

Contents

Performance criteria

18.2 A Adjust trading profits and losses for tax purposes

Range statement

18.2 Clients: sole traders

Knowledge and understanding

7 Adjustment of trading profits and losses for tax purposes (Element 18.2)

1 Losses

This chapter considers how losses are calculated and how a loss-suffering taxpayer can use a Schedule D Case I trading loss to reduce his tax liability. Losses arising in professions and vocations (Schedule D Case II) are treated in exactly the same way.

The rules covered in this chapter apply only to individuals, trading alone or in partnership. Loss reliefs for companies are completely different and are covered later in this text.

Losses of one spouse cannot be relieved against income of the other spouse.

When computing tax adjusted trading profits, profits may turn out to be negative, that is a loss has been made in the basis period. **A loss is computed in exactly the same way as a profit**, making the same adjustments to the accounts profit or loss.

If there is a loss in a basis period, the taxable income for the tax year based on that basis period is nil.

2 Carry forward of trading losses: s 385 ICTA 1988

2.1 Introduction

A trading loss not relieved in any other way may be **carried forward to set against the first available profits of the same trade**. Losses may be carried forward for any number of years.

2.2 Example: carrying forward losses

B has the following results.

Year ending	£
31 December 2001	(6,000)
31 December 2002	5,000
31 December 2003	11,000

B's taxable profits, assuming that he claims loss relief only under s 385 are:

	2001/02		*2002/03*		*2003/04*
	£		£		£
Schedule D Case I	0		5,000		11,000
Less s 385 relief	(0)	(i)	(5,000)	(ii)	(1,000)
Profits	0		0		10,000

Loss memorandum		£
Trading loss, y/e 31.12.01		6,000
Less: claim in y/e 31.12.02	(i)	(5,000)
claim in y/e 31.12.03 (balance of loss)	(ii)	(1,000)
		0

3 Setting trading losses against total income: s 380 ICTA 1988

3.1 Introduction

Instead of carrying a loss forward against future trading income, it may be relieved against current income of all types.

3.2 The computation of the loss

The loss for a tax year is the loss in the basis period for that tax year. However, if basis periods overlap then a loss in the overlap period is a loss for the earlier tax year only.

3.3 Example

Here is an example of a trader who starts to trade on 1 July 2003 and makes losses in opening years.

Period of account	*Loss*
	£
1.7.03 - 31.12.03	9,000
1.1.04 - 31.12.04	24,000

Tax year	*Basis period*	*Working*	*Loss for the tax year*
			£
2003/04	1.7.03 – 5.4.04	£9,000 + (£24,000 × 3/12)	15,000
2004/05	1.1.04 – 31.12.04	£24,000 – (£24,000 × 3/12)	18,000

3.4 Example

The same rule against using losses twice applies when losses are netted off against profits in the same basis period. Here is an example, again with a commencement on 1 July 2003 but with a different accounting date.

Period of account	(Loss)/profit
	£
1.7.03 – 30.4.04	(10,000)
1.5.04 – 30.4.05	24,000

Tax year	*Basis period*	*Working*	*(Loss)/Profit*
			£
2003/04	1.7.03 – 5.4.04	£(10,000) × 9/10	(9,000)
2004/05	1.7.03 – 30.6.04	£24,000 × 2/12 + £(10,000) × 1/10	3,000

3.5 Relieving the loss

Relief under s 380 **is against the income of the tax year in which the loss arose. In addition or instead,** relief may be claimed **against the income of the preceding year**.

If there are losses in two successive years, and relief is claimed against the first year's income both for the first year's loss and for the second year's loss, relief is given for the first year's loss before the second year's loss.

Claim for a loss must be made by the 31 January which is 22 months after the end of the tax year of the loss: thus by 31 January 2006 for a loss in 2003/04.

The taxpayer cannot choose the amount of loss to relieve: thus the loss may have to be set against income, part of which would have been covered by the personal allowance. However, the taxpayer can choose whether to claim full relief in the current year and then relief in the preceding year for any remaining loss, or the other way round.

Set the loss against non-savings income then against savings (excluding dividend) income and finally against dividend income.

Relief is available by carry forward under s 385 for any loss not relieved under s 380.

Activity 4.1

In 2003/04 Nicola has a loss of £18,000. Her statutory total income in 2003/04 is non-savings investment income totalling £14,000, and her personal allowance for that year is £4,615. She has no other source of income for any year. If she obtains loss relief as soon as possible, what loss is carried forward under s 385 ICTA 1988?

Activity 4.2

Janet started to trade on 1 June 2003 and made a loss of £25,000 in her first period of account to 31 March 2004. Her other income is £18,000 rental income a year, and she wishes to claim loss relief for the year of loss and then for the preceding year. Show her taxable income for each year, and comment on the effectiveness of the loss relief. Assume that tax rates and allowances for 2003/04 have always applied.

3.6 Capital allowances

The trader may adjust the size of the total s 380 claim by not claiming all the capital allowances he is entitled to: a reduced claim will increase the balance carried forward to the next year's capital allowances computation.

3.7 Trading losses relieved against capital gains

Where relief is claimed against total income of a given year, the taxpayer may include **a further claim to set the loss against his chargeable gains for the year** less any allowable capital losses for the same year or for previous years. This amount of net gains is computed ignoring taper relief and the annual exempt amount. We will look at chargeable gains later in this text.

The trading loss is first set against total income of the year of the claim, and only any excess of loss is set against capital gains. The taxpayer cannot specify the amount to be set against capital gains, so the annual exempt amount may be wasted.

3.8 Restrictions on s 380 relief

Relief cannot be claimed under s 380 unless a business is conducted on a commercial basis with a view to the realisation of profits; this condition applies to all types of business.

3.9 The choice between loss reliefs

When a trader has a choice between loss reliefs, he should aim to obtain relief both quickly and at the highest possible tax rate. However, do consider that losses relieved against income which would otherwise be covered by the personal allowance are wasted.

Another consideration is that a trading loss cannot be set against the capital gains of a year unless relief is first claimed under s 380 against income of the same year. It may be worth making the claim against income and wasting the personal allowance in order to avoid a CGT liability.

Before recommending S 380 loss relief consider whether it will result in the waste of the personal allowance. Such waste is to be avoided if at all possible.

4 Trade charges: s 387 ICTA 1988

4.1 Introduction

Annual charges such as patent royalties, although they may be paid out wholly and exclusively for business purposes, are nevertheless not deducted in arriving at the adjusted Schedule D Case I profit or loss. They are deducted in arriving at STI. If these amounts exceed STI there are 'excess charges'.

Excess trade charges can be carried forward against future profits from the same trade in the same way as losses under s 385.

4.2 Example: excess trade charges

A taxpayer has the following results for 2003/04.

	£
Schedule D Case I	4,000
Other income	1,000
	5,000
Less patent royalty	(7,000)
STI	0

The excess trade charge available to carry forward and set against future Schedule D Case I profits is £2,000.

5 Losses in the early years of a trade: s 381 ICTA 1988

S 381 relief is available for **trading losses incurred in the first four tax years of a trade**.

Relief is obtained by **setting the allowable loss against total income in the three years preceding the year of loss**, applying the loss to the earliest year first. Thus a loss arising in 2003/04 may be set off against income in 2000/01, 2001/02 and 2002/03 in that order.

A claim under s 381 applies to all three years automatically, provided that the loss is large enough. The taxpayer cannot choose to relieve the loss against just one or two of the years, or to relieve only part of the loss.

Do not double-count a loss. If basis periods overlap, a loss in the overlap period is treated as a loss for the earlier tax year only. This is the same rule as applies for s 380 purposes.

Claims for the relief must be made by the 31 January which is 22 months after the end of the tax year in which the loss is incurred.

The 'commercial basis' test is stricter for loss relief under s 381 than under s 380. The trade must be carried on in such a way that profits could reasonably have been expected to be realised in the period of the loss or within a reasonable time thereafter.

Activity 4.3

On 1 January 2002 Mr A starts up his own business as a scrap metal merchant, making up his accounts to 30 June each year.

His trading results as a scrap metal merchant are as follows.

	Profit/(Loss)
	£
Six months to 30 June 2002	(3,000)
Year to 30 June 2003	(1,500)
Year to 30 June 2004	(1,200)
Year to 30 June 2005	0

Show the loss available for relief under s 381 ICTA 1998 for each of the years 2001/02 to 2004/05 inclusive. State the years in which these losses may be relieved.

6 Businesses transferred to companies: s 386 ICTA 1988

Although the set-off under s 385 is restricted to future profits of the same business, this is extended to cover income received from a company to which the business is sold.

The amount carried forward is the total unrelieved trading losses of the business. The set-off must be made against the first available income from the company. The order of set-off is:

(a) against **salary** derived from the company by the former proprietor of the business; **then**
(b) against **interest and dividends** from the company.

The consideration for the sale must be wholly or mainly shares, which must be retained by the vendor throughout any tax year in which the loss is relieved; the Revenue treat this condition as being satisfied if 80% or more of the consideration consists of shares.

7 Losses on the cessation of a trade: s 388 ICTA 1988

7.1 Introduction

S 380 relief will often be insufficient on its own to deal with a loss incurred in the last months of trading. For this reason there is a special relief, **terminal loss relief, which allows a loss on cessation to be carried back for relief in previous years.**

7.2 Computing the terminal loss

A terminal loss under s 388 is **the loss of the last 12 months of trading**.

It is built up as follows.

		£
(a)	The actual trading loss for the tax year of cessation (calculated from 6 April to the date of cessation)	X
(b)	The actual trading loss for the period from 12 months before cessation until the end of the penultimate tax year	X
(c)	Any excess trade charges for the tax year of cessation	X
(d)	A proportion of any excess trade charges for the penultimate tax year	X
	Total terminal loss	X

If either (a) or (b) above yields a profit as opposed to a loss, the profit is regarded as zero for this purpose.

The terminal loss cannot include any amounts for which relief has already been given. Make sure that computations exclude any amounts claimed under s 380 and also any losses which have been set off in computing the taxable profits for the final tax year.

The proportion mentioned in (d) above is needed to ensure that only trade charges of the last 12 months are included. The figure included in the terminal loss is limited to the total trade charges multiplied by:

$$\frac{\text{number of months in item (b) in the computation}}{12}$$

Any unrelieved overlap profits may be deducted in the tax year of cessation and should, therefore, be included within (a) above.

7.3 Relieving the terminal loss

The income against which the terminal loss can be set is, broadly, the schedule D Case I income.

Relief is given in the tax year of cessation and the three preceding years, later years first.

Activity 4.4

Set out below are the results of a business up to its cessation on 30 September 2003.

	Profit/(loss)
	£
Year to 31 December 2000	2,000
Year to 31 December 2001	400
Year to 31 December 2002	300
Nine months to 30 September 2003	(1,950)

Overlap profits on commencement were £450. These were all unrelieved on cessation.

Show the available terminal loss relief.

Key learning points

- ☑ **Trading losses** may be **relieved in various ways.**
- ☑ A **trading loss not relieved in any other way** can be **carried forward** to set against the **first available profits** of the **same trade**.
- ☑ Losses can be set against **total income** in the **year the loss arises** or the **preceding year.**
- ☑ Losses arising in the **first four years of trading** may be set against **total income** in the **three years preceding the loss,** taking the **earliest year first.**
- ☑ A loss arising in the **last 12 months of trading** may be set against trading profits of the **tax year of cessation** and the **previous three years**, taking the **last year first**.

Quick quiz

1 Schedule D Case I losses can be carried forward and set off against .... Fill in the blank.

2 Keith makes a loss in his accounts made up to 31 July 2003. In which years can he relieve the loss under s.380 ICTA 1988?

3 Maggie starts in business on 6 April 2003. In her first set of accounts to 5 April 2004, she makes a loss. How can this loss be relived under s.381 ICTA 1988?

4 For what years may terminal loss relief be given?

Answers to quick quiz

1 Schedule D Case I losses can be carried forward and set off against **the first available profits of the same trade.**

2 The year of the loss (2003/04) and the preceding year (2002/03).

3 The year of the loss is 2003/04. Under s.381, Maggie can set the loss against income in 2000/01, 2001/02 and 2002/03 in that order.

4 The year of cessation and then the three preceding years, later years first.

Activity checklist

This checklist shows which performance criteria, range statement or knowledge and understanding point is covered by each activity in this chapter. Tick off each activity as you complete it.

Activity		
4.1	☐	This activity deals with knowledge and understanding point 2: issues of tax liability.
4.2	☐	This activity deals with Performance Criteria 18.2.A: adjust trading profits and losses for tax purposes.
4.3	☐	This activity deals with Performance Criteria 18.2.A: adjust trading profits and losses for tax purposes.
4.4	☐	This activity deals with Performance Criteria 18.2.A: adjust trading profits and losses for tax purposes.

chapter 5

Partnerships

Contents

Performance criteria

18.2 C Divide profits and losses of partnerships amongst partners

Range statement

18.2 Clients: partnerships

Knowledge and understanding

10 Basic allocation of income between partners (Element 18.2)

1 Partnerships

1.1 Introduction

A partnership is treated like a sole trader for the purposes of computing its profits. (As usual, 'trade' in this chapter includes professions and vocations.) Partners' salaries and interest on capital are not deductible expenses and must be added back in computing profits, because they are a form of drawings.

Once the partnership's profits or losses for a period of account have been computed, they are shared between the partners according to the profit sharing arrangements for that period of account.

1.2 The tax positions of individual partners

Each partner is taxed like a sole trader who runs a business which:

- starts when he joins the partnership
- finishes when he leaves the partnership
- has the same periods of account as the partnership (except that a partner who joins or leaves during a period will have a period which starts or ends part way through the partnership's period)
- makes profits or losses equal to the partner's share of the partnership's profits or losses

1.3 Changes in membership

When a trade continues but partners join or leave (including cases when a sole trader takes in partners or a partnership breaks up leaving only one partner as a sole trader), **the special rules for basis periods in opening and closing years do not apply to the people who were carrying on the trade both before and after the change. They carry on using the period of account ending in each tax year as the basis period for the tax year. The commencement rules only affect joiners, and the cessation rules only affect leavers.**

However, when no-one carries on the trade both before and after the change, as when a partnership transfers its trade to a completely new owner or set of owners, the cessation rules apply to the old owners and the commencement rules apply to the new owners.

1.4 Assets owned individually

Where the partners own assets (such as their cars) individually, a capital allowances computation must be prepared for each partner in respect of the assets he owns (not forgetting any adjustment for private use). **The capital allowances must go into the partnership's tax computation.**

1.5 Example: a partnership

Alice and Bertrand start a partnership on 1 July 2000, making up accounts to 31 December each year. On 1 May 2002, Charles joins the partnership. On 1 November 2003, Charles leaves. The profit sharing arrangements are as follows.

	Alice	*Bertrand*	*Charles*
1.7.00 – 30.4.02			
Salaries (per annum)	£3,000	£4,500	
Balance	3/5	2/5	
1.5.02 – 31.10.03			
Salaries (per annum)	£2,400	£3,600	£1,800
Balance	2/5	2/5	1/5
1.11.03 – 31.12.03			
Salaries (per annum)	£1,500	£2,700	
Balance	3/5	2/5	

Profits and losses as adjusted for tax purposes are as follows.

Period	*Profit(loss)*
	£
1.7.00 – 31.12.00	22,000
1.1.01 – 31.12.01	51,000
1.1.02 – 31.12.02	39,000
1.1.03 – 31.12.03	15,000

Show the taxable profits for each partner for 2000/01 to 2003/04.

1.6 Solution

We must first share the profits and losses for the periods of account between the partners, remembering to adjust the salaries for periods of less than a year.

	Total	*Alice*	*Bertrand*	*Charles*
	£	£	£	£
1.7.00 – 31.12.00				
Salaries	3,750	1,500	2,250	
Balance	18,250	10,950	7,300	
Total (P/e 31.12.00)	22,000	12,450	9,550	
1.1.01 – 31.12.01				
Salaries	7,500	3,000	4,500	
Balance	43,500	26,100	17,400	
Total	51,000	29,100	21,900	
1.1.02 - 31.12.02				
January to April				
Salaries	2,500	1,000	1,500	
Balance	10,500	6,300	4,200	
Total	13,000	7,300	5,700	

	Total	*Alice*	*Bertrand*	*Charles*
	£	£	£	£
May to December				
Salaries	5,200	1,600	2,400	1,200
Balance	20,800	8,320	8,320	4,160
Total	26,000	9,920	10,720	5,360
Total for y/e 31.12.02	39,000	17,220	16,420	5,360
1.1.03 - 31.12.03				
January to October				
Salaries	6,500	2,000	3,000	1,500
Balance	6,000	2,400	2,400	1,200
Total	12,500	4,400	5,400	2,700
November and December				
Salaries	700	250	450	
Balance	1,800	1,080	720	
Total	2,500	1,330	1,170	
Total for y/e 31.12.03	15,000	5,730	6,570	2,700

The next stage is to work out the basis periods and hence the taxable profits for the partners. All of them are treated as making up accounts to 31 December, but Alice and Bertrand are treated as starting to trade on 1 July 2000, Charles as trading only from 1 May 2002 to 31 October 2003. Applying the usual rules gives the following basis periods and taxable profits.

Alice

Year	*Basis period*	*Working*	*Taxable profits*
			£
2000/01	1.7.00 – 5.4.01	£12,450 + (£29,100 × 3/12)	19,725
2001/02	1.1.01 – 31.12.01		29,100
2002/03	1.1.02 – 31.12.02		17,220
2003/04	1.1.03 – 31.12.03		5,730

Alice will have overlap profits for the period 1 January to 5 April 2001 (£29,100 × 3/12 = £7,275) to deduct when she ceases to trade.

Bertrand

Year	*Basis period*	*Working*	*Taxable profits*
			£
2000/01	1.7.00 – 5.4.01	£9,550 + (£21,900 × 3/12)	15,025
2001/02	1.1.01 – 31.12.01		21,900
2002/03	1.1.02 – 31.12.02		16,420
2003/04	1.1.03 – 31.12.03		6,570

Bertrand's overlap profits are £21,900 × 3/12 = £5,475.

Charles

Year	*Basis period*	*Working*	*Taxable profits* £
2002/03	1.5.02 – 5.4.03	£5,360 + (£2,700 × 3/10)	6,170
2003/04	6.4.03 – 31.10.03	£2,700 × 7/10	1,890

Because Charles ceased to trade in his second tax year of trading, his basis period for the second year starts on 6 April and he has no overlap profits.

Activity 5.1

A partnership makes profits as follows.

Year ended 31 December	£
2002	34,200
2003	45,600

A partner joins on 1 September 2002, and is entitled to 20% of the profits. What are his taxable profits for 2002/03 and 2003/04?

Remember, partners are effectively taxed in the same way as sole traders with just one difference. Before you tax the partner you need to take each set of accounts (as adjusted for tax purposes) and divide the profit (or loss) between each partner.

Then carry on as normal for a sole trader - each partner is that sole trader in respect of his profits or losses for each accounting period.

2 Inland Revenue forms

A sample of the supplementary pages to the income tax return form that may have to be completed by a member of a partnership is included in the appendix to this text. Each partner must enter their share of the partnership's profits or losses on these pages. For Unit 18 you are expected to be aware of how partnership profits or losses are entered on this form. Completion of the full self assessment income tax return is expected only in Unit 19 *Preparing personal tax computations.* Please see page (vi) for a note regarding the version of the form used.

You will be able to practice completing tax forms when you try the activities in BPP's Assessment Kit for Unit 18.

Activity 5.2

Adam, Bert and Charlie started in partnership as secondhand car dealers on 6 April 2000, sharing profits in the ratio 2:2:1, after charging annual salaries of £1,500, £1,200 and £1,000 respectively.

On 5 July 2001 Adam retires and Bert and Charlie continue, taking the same salaries as before, but dividing the balance of the profits in the ratio 3:2.

On 5 May 2003 Dick is admitted as a partner on the terms that he received a salary of £1,800 a year, that the salaries of Bert and Charlie should be increased to £1,800 a year each and that of the balance of the profits, Dick should take one tenth and Bert and Charlie should divide the remainder in the ratio 3:2.

The profits of the partnership as adjusted for tax purposes are as follows.

		Profits
		£
Year ending 31 March	2001	10,200
	2002	20,800
	2003	12,600
	2004	18,000

Task

Show the taxable profits for each partner for 2000/2001 to 2003/04 inclusive.

Key learning points

- ☑ **A partnership** is a **source of profits and losses** for **trades being carried on** by **individual partners**.
- ☑ The first step is to **divide the profit** (or loss) of each set of accounts **between the partners**.
- ☑ The second step is to **allocate the profit** for each partner for the accounting period to the **correct tax year**.
- ☑ **Commencement** and **cessation** rules apply to partners individually when they join or leave.
- ☑ **Each partner** must enter **his share of partnership profits** in the supplementary pages that accompany **his tax return.**

Quick quiz

1 Rod and Steve have been in partnership for many years. Profits are shared equally. For the year ended 31 December 2002, the partnership made a profit of £40,000 and for the year ended 31 December 2003 the profit was £50,000. Show the profit taxable on Rod and Steve for 2003/04.

2 How would your answer to question 1 be different if Rod took a salary of £10,000?

3 Ethel and Mildred have been in partnership for many years. On 1 December 2003, Maud joins the partnership and profits are shared 40:40:20. For the year to 30 November 2004, the partnership makes a profit of £60,000. Show the profits assessable on Maud in 2003/04 and 2004/05.

Answers to quick quiz

1 The profits of the year to 31 December 2003 are assessable in 2003/04 ie £25,000 each.

2

	£
Profits y/e 31.12.03	50,000
Less: salary for Rod	(10,000)
Profits to allocate	40,000
Rod £(10,000 + 20,000)	30,000
Steve	20,000

3 y/e 30.11.04 20% of the profits are allocated to Maud ie £12,000

2003/04	
1.12.03 – 5.4.04	
4/12 x £12,000	£4,000
2004/05	
1.12.03 – 30.11.04	£12,000

Activity checklist

This checklist shows which performance criteria is covered by each activity in this chapter. Tick off each activity as you complete it.

Activity		
5.1	☐	This activity deals with Performance Criteria 18.2 C: divide profits and losses of partnerships amongst partners.
5.2	☐	This activity deals with Performance Criteria 18.2 C: divide profits and losses of partnerships amongst partners.

PART B

Chargeable gains

chapter 6

Chargeable gains: an outline

Contents

Performance criteria

18.3 A Identify and value correctly any chargeable assets that have been disposed of

18.3 D Apply reliefs, deferrals and exemptions correctly

Range statement

18.3 Chargeable assets that have been: sold, gifted, lost, destroyed

Knowledge and understanding

11 Identification of business assets disposed of including part disposals (Element 18.3)

13 Capital gains exemptions and reliefs on business assets including rollover relief and taper relief but excluding retirement relief (Element 18.3)

14 Rates of tax payable on gains on business assets disposed of by individuals (Element 18.3)

1 The charge to tax

1.1 Individuals

An individual pays CGT on any taxable gains arising in the tax year. **Taxable gains are the net chargeable gains (gains minus losses) of the tax year reduced by unrelieved losses brought forward from previous years, a taper relief and the annual exemption.**

There is an annual exemption for each tax year. For 2003/04 it is £7,900. It is the last deduction to be made in the calculation of taxable gains.

1.2 Calculating CGT

Taxable gains are chargeable to capital gains tax as if the gains were an extra slice of savings (excl dividend) income for the year of assessment concerned. This means that CGT may be due at 10%, 20% or 40%.

The rate bands are used first to cover income and then gains.

Activity 6.1

In 2003/04, Carol, a single woman, has the following income, gains and losses. Find the CGT payable.

	£
Business profits	32,830
Chargeable gains (not eligible for taper relief - see later)	26,100
Allowable capital losses	8,000

Activity 6.2

In 2003/04, Amy had business profits of £23,000 and gains (before the annual exemption) of £22,000. What is her CGT payable for 2003/04?

1.3 Companies

Companies are not liable to CGT as such but any net chargeable gains which arise in an accounting period, minus unrelieved losses brought forward from previous accounting periods, form part of their profits chargeable to corporation tax. Gains and losses are calculated, broadly, in the same way as for individuals (but see below).

The gains of companies are charged at normal corporation tax rates. **Companies do not get the annual exemption or taper relief** (see below). You will study the computation of corporation tax later in this text.

2 Chargeable persons, disposals and assets

2.1 Chargeable persons

The following are chargeable persons.

- Individuals
- Partnerships
- Companies

2.2 Chargeable disposals

The following are chargeable disposals.

- Sales of assets or parts of assets
- Gifts of assets or parts of assets
- Receipts of capital sums following the surrender of rights to assets
- The appropriation of assets as trading stock
- The loss or destruction of assets

A chargeable disposal occurs on the date of the contract (where there is one, whether written or oral), or the date of a conditional contract becoming unconditional. This may differ from the date of transfer of the asset. However, when a capital sum is received on a surrender of rights, the disposal takes place on the day the sum is received.

Where a disposal involves an acquisition by someone else, the date of acquisition is the same as the date of disposal.

The following are exempt disposals.

- Transfers of assets on death (the heirs inherit assets as if they bought them at death for their then market values, but there is no capital gain or allowable loss on death)
- Transfers of assets as security for a loan or mortgage
- Gifts to charities and national heritage bodies

Cashbacks, for example on new mortgages or cars, are also not subject to CGT.

When someone acquires an asset other than as trading stock and then uses it as trading stock, the appropriation to trading stock leads to an immediate chargeable gain or allowable loss, based on the asset's market value at the date of appropriation. The asset's cost for Schedule D Case I purposes is that market value. However, the trader can elect to have no chargeable gain or allowable loss: if he does so, the cost for Schedule D Case I purposes is reduced by the gain or increased by the loss. The time limit for the election, for individuals, is the 31 January which is nearly two years after the end of the tax year which includes the end of the period of account of appropriation. For companies, it is two years after the end of the accounting period of appropriation.

When an asset which is trading stock is appropriated to other purposes, the trader is treated for Schedule D Case I purposes as selling it for its market value, and for those other purposes as having bought it at the time of the appropriation for the same value.

2.3 Chargeable assets

All forms of property, wherever in the world they are situated, are chargeable assets unless they are specifically designated as exempt.

The following are exempt assets (thus gains are not taxable and losses on their disposal are not in general allowable losses.

- Motor vehicles suitable for private use
- Works of art, scientific collections and so on given for national purposes
- Gilt-edged securities (when disposed of by individuals)
- Qualifying corporate bonds (QCBs) (when disposed of by individuals)
- Certain chattels
- Debts (except debts on a security)

Activity 6.3

In 1995, J Ltd bought a vintage motor car as an investment. Nobody in the company ever drove it. The car was sold in 2003, making a gain of £75,000. Is the gain chargeable?

3 Losses

3.1 Set-off of losses

Deduct allowable capital losses from chargeable gains in the tax year in which they arise. Any loss which cannot be set off is carried forward to set against future chargeable gains. Losses must be used as soon as possible (subject to the following paragraph). Losses may not normally be set against income.

Allowable losses brought forward are only set off to reduce current year chargeable gains less current year allowable losses to the annual exempt amount. No set-off is made if net chargeable gains for the current year do not exceed the annual exempt amount. (Companies do not have an annual exempt amount so no such restriction on the set off of losses applies to them.)

3.2 Example: the use of losses

(a) George has chargeable gains for 2003/04 of £10,000 and allowable losses of £6,000. As the losses are *current year losses* they must be fully relieved against the £10,000 of gains to produce net gains of £4,000, despite the fact that net gains are below the annual exemption.

(b) Bob has gains of £12,100 for 2003/04 and allowable losses brought forward of £6,000. Bob restricts his loss relief to £4,200 so as to leave net gains of £(12,100 – 4,200) = £7,900, which will be exactly covered by his annual exemption for 2003/04. The remaining £1,800 of losses will be carried forward to 2004/05.

(c) Tom has chargeable gains of £5,000 for 2003/04 and losses brought forward from 2002/03 of £4,000. He will leapfrog 2003/04 and carry forward all of his losses to 2004/05. His gains of £5,000 are covered by his annual exemption for 2003/04.

4 Taper relief

4.1 Taper relief for business assets

Taper relief may be available to reduce gains realised after 5 April 1998 by individuals. It is not available to reduce gains realised by companies.

Taper relief reduces the percentage of the gain chargeable according to how many complete years the asset had been held since acquisition, or 6 April 1998 if later. Taper relief is more generous for business assets than for non-business assets. In unit 18 you will only be expected to compute gains on the disposal of business assets.

The percentages of gains which remain chargeable after taper relief are set out below.

Business assets *Number of complete years after 5.4.98* *for which asset held*	*% of gain chargeable*
0	100
1	50
2 or more	25

The above percentages will be given in the tax tables that you use in completing your assessment.

4.2 Example: complete years held for taper relief

Peter buys a business asset on 1 January 1998 and sells it on 1 July 2003. For the purposes of the taper Peter is treated as if he had held the asset for five complete years after 5 April 1998.

This means that only 25% of the gain remains chargeable after taper relief.

4.3 Taper relief and losses

Taper relief is applied to net chargeable gains after the deduction of current year and brought forward losses. The annual exemption is then deducted from the tapered gains.

Activity 6.4

William sold a business asset in December 2003 realising a chargeable gain of £40,600 before taper relief. He had purchased the asset in May 1997. In January 2004 William sold another business asset realising a loss of £1,300 but had made no other disposals in 2003/04. What are William's taxable gains (after the annual exemption) for 2003/04?

Losses are dealt with **before** taper relief. However losses brought forward are only deducted from net current gains to the extent that the gains exceed the CGT annual exemption.

Activity 6.5

Sally sold a business asset in July 2003 which she had purchased in January 2002. She realised a chargeable gain (before taper relief) of £17,800. She also sold a business asset in 2003/04 realising a capital loss of £6,000. She has a capital loss brought forward from 2002/2003 of £10,000. What are Sally's taxable gains (after the annual exemption) for 2003/04?

Allocate losses to gains in the way that produces the lowest tax charge. Losses should therefore be deducted from the gains attracting the lowest rate of taper (ie where the highest percentage of the gain remains chargeable).

4.4 Example: allocation of losses to gains

Alan made the following capital losses and gains in 2003/2004:

	£
Loss	10,000
Gains (before taper relief)	
Asset A (business asset)	50,000
Asset B (business asset)	18,000

Asset A was purchased in December 2001 and sold in January 2004. Taper relief reduces the gain to 25% of the original gain (2 years business asset). Asset B was purchased on 5 November 2002 and sold on 17 December 2003. Taper relief reduces the gain to 50% of the original gain (1 year business asset).

The best use of the loss is to offset it against the gain on asset B:

	£	£
Gain – Asset A	50,000	
Gain after taper relief (£50,000 × 25%)		12,500
Gain – Asset B	18,000	
Less loss	(10,000)	
	8,000	
Gain after taper relief (£8,000 × 50%)		4,000
Gains after taper relief		16,500
Less annual exemption		(7,900)
Taxable gains		8,600

4.5 Other points

There are certain special situations which will affect the operation of taper relief:

(a) where there has been a transfer of assets between spouses (a no loss/no gain transfer; see below) the taper on a subsequent disposal will be based on the combined period of holding by the spouses.

(b) where gains have been relieved under a provision which reduces the cost of the asset in the hands of a new owner (such as gift relief, see later in this text) the taper will operate by reference to the holding period of the new owner.

4.6 Shares and securities

Special rules apply to shares and securities. We cover these later in this text.

4.7 Business assets

A business asset is:

(a) an asset **used for the purposes of a trade** carried on by an individual (either alone or in partnership) or by a qualifying company of that individual

(b) an asset **held for the purposes of any office or employment** held by that individual with a person carrying on a trade

(c) **shares in a qualifying company** held by an individual

A **qualifying company** is a trading company (or holding company of a trading group) where:

(a) the company is **not listed** on a recognised stock exchange nor is a 51% subsidiary of a listed company (companies listed on the Alternative Investment Market (AIM) are unlisted for this purpose)

(b) the shareholder is an **officer or employee** of the company (full-time or part-time), or of a company with a **relevant connection**

(c) the shareholder holds at least **5% of the voting rights** in the company

A company is also a qualifying company if it is a **non-trading company** (or holding company of a non-trading group) where:

(a) The individual is an **officer or employee** of the company or a company with a **relevant connection**, and

(b) The individual did not have a **material interest** in the company or in any other company which at that time had control of the company.

A **material interest** is defined as possession or the ability to control more than 10% of the issued shares in the company, or more than 10% of the voting rights in the company, or an entitlement to more than 10% of the income of the company or more than 10% of the assets of the company available for distribution. For this purpose, an individual is treated as having a material interest if he, together with one or more connected persons (see next chapter) has a material interest. For example, if A holds 5% of the voting rights in the company and his brother B (a connected person) has 15% of the voting rights, A will have a material interest in the company as between them A and B hold more than 10% of the voting rights.

A company has a **relevant connection** with another company if:

(a) The companies are both members of a 51% group, or

(b) The companies are under common control and they carry on a complementary business which can reasonably be regarded as one composite undertaking, or

(c) One company (X Ltd) is a joint enterprise company in which 75% or more of the ordinary shares capital is held by five or fewer persons and the other company (Y Ltd) holds 10% or more of the ordinary share capital in X Ltd.

5 Married couples

A husband and wife are taxed as two separate people. Each has an annual exemption, and losses of one spouse cannot be set against gains of the other.

Disposals between spouses who are living together give rise to no gain and no loss, whatever actual price (if any) **was charged by the person transferring the asset** to their spouse. A couple are treated as living together unless they are separated under a court order or separation deed, or are in fact separated in circumstances which make permanent separation likely.

The acquiring spouse normally takes over the taper relief position of the disposing spouse. This means the acquiring spouse is treated as acquiring the asset when the disposing spouse did. For assets other than shares, business use by one spouse is treated as business use by the other spouse.

Where an asset is jointly owned, the beneficial interests of the spouses will determine the treatment of any gain on disposal. If, for example, there is evidence that the wife's share in an asset was 60%, then 60% of any gain or loss on disposal would be attributed to her. If there is no evidence of the relative interests, the Revenue will normally accept that the asset is held in equal shares. Where a declaration of how income from the asset is to be shared for income tax purposes has been made, there is a presumption that the same shares will apply for CGT purposes.

If a spouse whose marginal tax rate is 40% wishes to dispose of an asset at a gain and the other spouse would only be taxed on the gain at a lower rate, the asset should first be transferred to the spouse with the lower tax rate. Similarly, assets or parts of assets should be transferred between spouses to use both CGT annual exemptions.

6 Inland Revenue form

A sample of the supplementary pages to the income tax return form that may need to be completed by individual taxpayers with chargeable gains is included in the appendix to this text. Familiarise yourself with these now. At Unit 18 you will be expected to be aware of how gains are entered on these pages. Full completion of an individual's income tax return will be assessed at Unit 19 only. Please see page (vi) for a note regarding the version of the form we have used.

You will be able to practice completing tax forms when you try the activities in BPP's Unit 18 Assessment Kit.

7 End of chapter activities

Activity 6.6

Eric had business profits of £24,500 and gains of £35,000 in 2003/04.

Task

Calculate Eric's capital gains tax liability for 2003/04.

Activity 6.7

Lorna disposed of assets as follows.

(i) On 1 January 2003 she sold her car at a loss of £10,700.

(ii) On 28 February 2003 she sold some shares at a loss of £6,300.

(iii) On 1 May 2003 she sold some shares (acquired August 2002) and realised a gain of £7,800. The shares were a business asset for taper relief purposes.

(iv) On 1 October 2003 she sold some shares at a loss of £2,000.

(v) On 1 December 2003 she sold a business asset (acquired July 2003) for £50,000, making a gain of £3,000.

(vi) On 1 April 2004 she sold some gilt-edged securities (acquired May 2003), making a gain of £10,000.

Task

What loss, if any, is available to be carried forward at the end of 2003/04?

Key learning points

- ☑ An individual pays **CGT** on his **net chargeable gains** in a tax year.
- ☑ There is an **annual exemption** for an individual for each tax year.
- ☑ Taxable gains are taxed as an extra slice of savings (excluding dividends) income.
- ☑ A company pays **corporation tax** on its **net chargeable gains** in an accounting period.
- ☑ **Capital losses** are deducted against gains in the **same tax year or accounting period.**
- ☑ Excess losses are **carried forward.**
- ☑ There needs to be three things for a capital gain to arise: **chargeable person, chargeable disposal, chargeable asset.**
- ☑ **Taper relief** reduces gains for individuals after 5 April 1998.
- ☑ Disposals between **spouses** are on a **no gain/ no loss** basis.

Quick quiz

1 CGT is payable by individuals at ..... %, ... % and ......%. Fill in the blanks

2 Companies are taxable on net chargeable gains in a tax year. TRUE or FALSE?

3 Tom made a chargeable gain (no taper relief) of £8,000 and an allowable loss of £(5,000) in 2003/04.

His loss carried forward to 2004/05 is:

A Nil
B £(100)
C £(4,900)
D £(5,000)

4 Mark acquired a business asset on 1 July 2001. He sold the asset on 1 May 2003. His gain was £4,000.

What is the gain after taper relief?

A Nil
B £1,000
C £2,000
D £4,000

5 How are disposals between a husband and wife who are living together treated for CGT?

Answers to quick quiz

1 CGT is payable at **10**%, **20**% and **40**%.

2 FALSE. A company is taxed on its net chargeable gains in an **accounting period**.

3 A The loss is set against the gain even though this brings the gain below the annual exemption.

4 C The ownership period runs from 1 July 2001 to 30 April 2003 = 1 complete year, so the taper relief % is 50%.

5 Disposals between spouses who are living together give rise to no gain and no loss.

Activity checklist

This checklist shows which performance criteria, range statement or knowledge and understanding point is covered by each activity in this chapter. Tick off each activity as you complete it.

Activity		
6.1	☐	This activity deals with Knowledge and Understanding point 14: rates of tax payable on gains on business assets disposed of by individuals.
6.2	☐	This activity deals with Knowledge and Understanding point 14: rates of tax payable on gains on business assets disposed of by individuals.
6.3	☐	This activity deals with Performance Criteria 18.3.A: Identify and value correctly any chargeable assets that have been disposed of.
6.4	☐	This activity deals with Performance Criteria 18.3.D: apply reliefs, deferrals and exemptions correctly.
6.5	☐	This activity deals with Performance Criteria 18.3.D: apply reliefs, deferrals and exemptions correctly.
6.6	☐	This activity deals with Knowledge and Understanding point 14: rates of tax payable on gains on business assets disposed of by individuals.
6.7	☐	This activity deals with Performance Criteria 18.3.A and 18.3.D: identify and correctly value any chargeable assets that have been disposed of; apply reliefs, deferrals and exemptions correctly.

chapter 7

The computation of gains and losses

Contents

Performance criteria

18.3 A Identify and value correctly any chargeable assets that have been disposed of

18.3 C Calculate chargeable gains and allowable losses

Range statement

18.3 Chargeable assets that have been: sold, gifted, lost, destroyed

Knowledge and understanding

11 Identification of business assets disposed of including part disposals (Element 18.3)

12 Calculation of gains and losses on disposals of business assets including indexation allowance (Element 18.3)

1 The basic computation

1.1 Proforma

A chargeable gain (or an allowable loss) is generally calculated as follows.

	£
Disposal consideration (or market value)	45,000
Less incidental costs of disposal	(400)
Net proceeds	44,600
Less allowable costs	(21,000)
Unindexed gain	23,600
Less indexation allowance (if available)	(8,500)
Indexed gain	15,100

For individuals, taper relief may then apply.

1.2 Costs

Incidental costs of disposal may include:

- valuation fees (but not the cost of an appeal against the Revenue's valuation)
- estate agency fees
- advertising costs
- legal costs

These costs should be deducted separately from any other allowable costs (because they do not qualify for any indexation allowance if it was available on that disposal).

Allowable costs include:

- the original cost of acquisition
- incidental costs of acquisition
- enhancement expenditure

Incidental costs of acquisition may include the types of cost listed above as incidental costs of disposal, but acquisition costs do qualify for indexation allowance (from the month of acquisition) if it is available on the disposal.

1.3 Enhancement expenditure

Enhancement expenditure is capital expenditure which enhances the value of the asset and is reflected in the state or nature of the asset at the time of disposal, or expenditure incurred in establishing, preserving or defending title to, or a right over, the asset. Excluded from this category are:

- costs of repairs and maintenance
- costs of insurance
- any expenditure deductible for income tax purposes
- any expenditure met by public funds (for example council grants)

Enhancement expenditure may qualify for indexation allowance from the month in which it becomes due and payable.

1.4 Disposal consideration

Usually the disposal consideration is the proceeds of sale of the asset, but a disposal is deemed to take place at market value:

(a) where the disposal is **not a bargain at arm's length**
(b) where the disposal is made for a **consideration which cannot be valued**
(c) where the disposal is by way of a **gift**

Activity 7.1

D Ltd bought a plot of land for £100,000, and spent £6,000 on clearing it. However, by the time D Ltd sold the land (at a large profit) it had become overgrown, and was in the same state as it would have been if the work had not been done. Is the £6,000 deductible as enhancement expenditure?

2 The indexation allowance

2.1 Introduction

Indexation was introduced in March 1982. The purpose of having an indexation allowance was to remove the inflationary element of a gain from taxation. You will not have to deal with assets acquired before March 1982 in your assessment.

Individuals are entitled to an indexation allowance until April 1998, but not thereafter.

The above rule does not apply to companies. Companies are entitled to an indexation allowance until the date of disposal of an asset.

2.2 Example: indexation allowance

John bought a shop for use in his business on 2 January 1987 and sold it on 19 November 2003.

Indexation allowance will be available for the period January 1987 to April 1998 only.

2.3 Calculation of indexation allowance

Indexation is calculated from the month of acquisition of an asset.

The indexation factor is:

$$\frac{\text{RPI for month of disposal (or April 1998)} - \text{RPI for month of acquisition}}{\text{RPI for month of acquisition}}$$

The calculation is expressed as a decimal and is rounded to three decimal places.

The indexation factor is then multiplied by the cost of the asset to calculate the indexation allowance. If the RPI has fallen, the indexation allowance is zero: it is not negative.

Activity 7.2

A business asset is acquired by an individual on 15 February 1983 (RPI = 83.0) at a cost of £5,000. Enhancement expenditure of £2,000 is incurred on 10 April 1984 (RPI = 88.6). The asset is sold for £20,500 on 20 December 2003. Incidental costs of sale are £500. Calculate the indexation allowance. RPI April 1998 = 162.6

Activity 7.3

Z Ltd acquired a freehold factory in July 1999 (RPI = 165.1) for £100,000. It sold the factory for £180,000 in August 2003 (RPI = 180.1). What is the indexed gain on sale?

2.4 Indexation and losses

The indexation allowance cannot create or increase an allowable loss. If there is a gain before the indexation allowance, the allowance can reduce that gain to zero, but no further. If there is a loss before the indexation allowance, there is no indexation allowance.

Activity 7.4

Simon bought a business asset for £97,000 in August 1990 (RPI = 128.1) and sold it for £24,000 in April 2003. What is the allowable loss? RPI April 1998 = 162.6.

3 Valuing assets

3.1 General rule

Where market value is used in a CGT computation (see above), **the value to be used is the price which the assets in question might reasonably be expected to fetch on a sale in the open market.**

3.2 Shares and securities

Quoted shares and securities are valued using prices in The Stock Exchange Daily Official List, taking the lower of:

- lower quoted price + 0.25 × (higher quoted price – lower quoted price);
- the average of the highest and lowest marked bargains (ignoring bargains marked at special prices).

Activity 7.5

Shares in A plc are quoted at 100-110p. The highest and lowest marked bargains were 99p and 110p. What would be the market value for CGT purposes?

Unquoted shares are much harder to value than quoted shares. The Revenue have a special office, the Shares Valuation Division, to deal with the valuation of unquoted shares.

3.3 Negligible value claims

If a chargeable asset's value becomes negligible a claim may be made to treat the asset as though it were sold, and then immediately reacquired at its current market value. This will probably give rise to an allowable loss.

The sale and reacquisition are treated as taking place when the claim is made, or at a specified earlier time. The earlier time can be any time up to two years before the start of the tax year in which the claim is made. The asset must have been of negligible value at the specified earlier time.

On a subsequent actual disposal, any gain is computed using the negligible value as the acquisition cost.

4 Connected persons

A transaction between 'connected persons' is treated as one between parties to a transaction otherwise than by way of a bargain made at arm's length. The effect of this is that the acquisition and disposal are deemed to take place for a consideration equal to the market value of the asset, rather than the actual price paid.

If a loss results, it can be set only against gains arising in the same or future years from disposals to the same connected person and the loss can only be set off if he or she is still connected with the person sustaining the loss.

An individual is connected with:

- his spouse
- his relatives (brothers, sisters, ancestors and lineal descendants)
- the relatives of his spouse
- the spouses of his and his spouse's relatives

A company is connected with:

- a person who (alone or with persons connected with him) controls it
- another company under common control

5 Intraspouse transfers of assets

Disposals between spouses living together do not give rise to chargeable gains or allowable losses.

A special rule applies to indexation on no gain/no loss disposals. To illustrate the rule, we assume a husband (H) buys an asset and later transfers it to his wife (W) who then sells it to an outsider. The rule is exactly the same if the roles of H and W are reversed.

If **H buys the asset** and transfers it to W, W is deemed to have bought the asset when H transferred it to her. Her cost is H's cost plus indexation allowance up to the date of transfer (or 6 April 1998). When W sells the asset, she computes indexation allowance from the time of the transfer. If the transfer was made after 5 April 1998 there is no further indexation allowance.

Activity 7.6

Sylvia bought an asset for £18,000 on 1 January 1991 (RPI = 130.2). On 1 January 2002 she gave it to her husband Michael. On 12 April 2003 he sold it for £50,000. The asset had always been used in Michael's business. What is his chargeable gain after taper relief? RPI April 1998 = 162.6

6 Part disposals

6.1 General rule

The disposal of part of a chargeable asset is a chargeable event. The chargeable gain (or allowable loss) is computed by deducting from the disposal value a fraction of the original cost of the whole asset.

The fraction is:

$$\frac{A}{A+B}=\frac{\text{value of the part disposed of}}{\text{value of the part disposed of}+\text{market value of the remainder}}$$

A is the proceeds (for arm's length disposals) *before* deducting incidental costs of disposal.

The part disposal fraction should not be applied indiscriminately. Any expenditure incurred wholly in respect of a particular part of an asset should be treated as an allowable deduction in full for that part and not apportioned. An example of this is incidental selling expenses, which are wholly attributable to the part disposed of.

Activity 7.7

Mr Smith owns a business asset which originally cost him £27,000 in March 1984 (RPI = 87.5). He sold a quarter interest in the asset in July 2003 for £18,000. The market value of the three-quarter share remaining is estimated to be £36,000. What is the chargeable gain after taper relief? RPI April 1998 = 162.6.

Activity 7.8

Louisa bought a plot of land for use in her business for £150,000 in January 1990. In August 2003, she sold part of the land for £187,000, which was net of legal fees on the sale of £3,000. At that time, the value of the remaining land was £327,000. What expenditure (apart from the indexation allowance) could she deduct in computing her chargeable gain?

7 End of chapter activity

Activity 7.9

Hardup Ltd made the following disposals in the year ended 31 March 2004.

(a) On 12 May 2003 it sold an office block for £120,000. The company had bought the offices for £65,000 on 1 July 1989.

(b) On 18 June 2003 it sold a plot of land for £69,000. It had bought it for £20,000 on 1 April 1982 and had spent £4,000 on defending its title to the land in July 1986.

(c) On 25 June 2003 the company exchanged contracts for the sale of a workshop for £173,000. Completion took place on 24 July 2003. It had bought the workshop for £65,000 on 16 October 1984.

Task

Compute Hardup Ltd's capital gains for the year end 31.3.04.

RPIs	April 1982	81.0
	October 1984	90.7
	July 1986	97.5
	July 1989	115.5
	May 2003	179.5
	June 2003	179.7
	July 2003	179.9

Key learning points

- ☑ A chargeable gain is the **proceeds** less **cost** and **indexation allowance** (if any).
- ☑ **Indexation allowance** runs from the **date of acquisition** to the **date of disposal** (for **companies**) or **April 1998** (for **individuals**).
- ☑ Indexation allowance **cannot create or increase a loss.**
- ☑ In some cases, **market value** is used in a CGT computation.
- ☑ Market value is **the sale price on the open market** that could reasonably be expected.
- ☑ Disposals between **connected persons** are at market value**.**
- ☑ There are **special rules on indexation** for **intraspouse transfers.**
- ☑ On a **part disposal**, the **cost must be apportioned** between the **part disposed of** and the **part retained**.

Quick quiz

1 Lemon Ltd buys a factory. It paints the outside of the factory and builds an extension. The extension is destroyed by fire and is not replaced. It pays legal fees on defending a legal action about the ownership of the land.

Which of the additional expenditure will be allowable on a sale of the factory?

A legal fees only
B legal fees and extension only
C extension and painting only
D all of it

2 How does the calculation of the indexation allowance differ for companies and individuals?

3 Shares in X plc are quoted at 203 – 207, with bargains at 202, 205 and 208. What is the value for CGT?

4 George buys a shop for use in his business in July 2000 for £120,000. He sells it to his wife, Elaine in May 2002 when it is worth £140,000. Elaine uses the shop in her business. She sells it for £180,000 in June 2003. What is her gain on sale after taper relief?

A £15,000
B £30,000
C £40,000
D £60,000

5 10 acres of land are sold for £30,000 out of 25 acres. The original cost was £18,000. The costs of sale were £4,000. The rest of the land is valued at £60,000. What is the allowable expenditure?

Answers to quick quiz

1 A Painting – not allowable because not capital in nature
Extension – not allowable as not reflected in the state of the asset at disposal
Legal fees – allowable as incurred in defending title to asset

2 Indexation runs to the date of disposal for companies. For individuals it stops at April 1998.

3 Lower of:

$203 + \frac{1}{4}(207 - 203) = 204$

$\frac{208 + 202}{2} = 205$

ie 204

4 A

	£
Proceeds	180,000
Less: cost (original cost to George)	(120,000)
Gain before taper relief	60,000

Elaine is treated as owning the asset since July 2000 and George's business use is treated as her business use. So she is entitled to 2 years taper relief.

Gain after taper relief (25%) £15,000

5 $\frac{30{,}000}{30{,}000 + 60{,}000} \times £18{,}000 = £6{,}000 + £4{,}000$ (costs of disposal) = £10,000

Activity checklist

This checklist shows which performance criteria, range statement or knowledge and understanding point is covered by each activity in this chapter. Tick off each activity as you complete it.

Activity		
7.1	☐	This activity deals with Performance Criteria 18.3.C: calculate chargeable gains and allowable losses.
7.2	☐	This activity deals with Knowledge and Understanding point 12: calculation of gains and losses on disposals of business assets including indexation allowance.
7.3	☐	This activity deals with Performance Criteria 18.3.C: calculate chargeable gains and allowable losses.
7.4	☐	This activity deals with Performance Criteria 18.3.C : calculate chargeable gains and allowable losses.
7.5	☐	This activity deals with Performance Criteria 18.3.A : identify and value correctly any chargeable assets that have been disposed of
7.6	☐	This activity deals with Performance Criteria 18.3.C: calculate chargeable gains and allowable losses.
7.7	☐	This activity deals with Performance Criteria 18.3.C: calculate chargeable gains and allowable losses.
7.8	☐	This activity deals with Performance Criteria 18.3.C: calculate chargeable gains and allowable losses.
7.9	☐	This activity deals with Performance Criteria 18.3.C: calculate chargeable gains and allowable losses.

chapter 8

Shares and securities

Contents

Performance criteria

18.3 A Identify and value correctly any chargeable assets that have been disposed of

18.3 B Identify shares disposed of by companies

18.3 C Calculate chargeable gains and allowable losses

Range statement

18.3 Chargeable assets that have been: sold, gifted, lost, destroyed

Knowledge and understanding

11 Identification of business assets disposed of including part disposals (Element 18.3)

12 Calculation of gains and losses on disposals of business assets including indexation allowance (Element 18.3)

1 The matching rules for companies

1.1 The problem

Quoted and unquoted shares and securities and units in a unit trust present special problems when attempting to compute gains or losses on disposal. For instance, suppose that a company buys some quoted shares in X plc as follows.

Date	*Number of shares*	*Cost*
		£
5 May 1993	100	150
17 January 2000	100	375

On 15 June 2003, it sells 120 of its shares for £1,450. To determine its chargeable gain, we need to be able to work out which shares out of the two original holdings were actually sold.

1.2 The solution

We therefore need **matching rules**. These **allow us to decide which shares have been sold and so work out what the allowable cost on disposal should be.**

In what follows, we will use 'shares' to refer to both shares and securities.

The **matching of shares** sold by a company is in the following order.

(a) Shares acquired on the **same day**
(b) Shares acquired in the **previous nine days**, taking earlier acquisitions first
(c) Shares from the **FA 1985 pool** (see below)

If a company owns 2% or more of another company, disposals are matched (after same day acquisitions) with shares acquired within one month before or after the disposal (for Stock Exchange transactions) or six months (in other cases) before being matched with shares from the FA 1985 pool.

Where shares are disposed of within nine days of acquisition, **no indexation allowance is available** even if the acquisition and the disposal fall in different months. Acquisitions matched with disposals under the nine day rule never enter the FA 1985 pool (see below).

2 The FA 1985 pool

2.1 Introduction

For companies we treat shares as a 'pool' which grows as new shares are acquired and shrinks as they are sold. **The FA 1985 pool** (so called because it was introduced by rules in the Finance Act 1985) **comprises the following shares of the same class in the same company.**

- **Shares held by a company on 1 April 1985 and acquired by that company on or after 1 April 1982.**
- **Shares acquired by that company on or after 1 April 1985.**

Note that the FA 1985 pool only contains shares acquired on or after 1 April 1982. You will not be required to deal with shares purchased before this date in your assessment so they are not considered here.

In making computations which use the FA 1985 pool, we must keep track of:

(a) the **number** of shares;
(b) the **cost** of the shares ignoring indexation;
(b) the **indexed cost** of the shares.

Each FA 1985 **pool is started by aggregating the cost and number of shares acquired between 1 April 1982 and 1 April 1985** inclusive. In order to calculate the indexed cost of these shares, an indexation allowance, computed from the relevant date of acquisition of the shares to April 1985, is added to the cost.

2.2 Example: the FA 1985 pool

Oliver Ltd bought 1,000 shares in Judith plc for £2,750 in August 1984 (RPI = 89.9) and another 1,000 for £3,250 in December 1984 (RPI = 90.9). The FA 1985 pool at 1 April 1985 (RPI = 94.8) is as follows.

2.3 Solution

	No of shares	*Cost* £	*Indexed cost* £
August 1984 (a)	1,000	2,750	2,750
December 1984 (b)	1,000	3,250	3,250
	2,000	6,000	6,000
Indexation allowance			
$\frac{94.8 - 89.9}{89.9} = 0.055 \times £2,750$			151
$\frac{94.8 - 90.9}{90.9} = 0.043 \times £3,250$			140
Indexed cost of the pool at 1 April 1985			6,291

2.4 Operative events

Disposals and acquisitions of shares which affect the indexed value of the FA 1985 pool are termed **'operative events'**. **Prior to reflecting each such operative event within the FA 1985 share pool, a further indexation allowance (described as an indexed rise) must be computed up to the date of the operative event concerned from the date of the last such operative event** (or from April 1985 if the operative event in question is the first one).

Indexation calculations within the FA 1985 pool (after its April 1985 value has been calculated) **are not rounded to three decimal places**. This is because rounding errors would accumulate and have a serious effect after several operative events.

If there are several operative events between 1 April 1985 and the date of a disposal, the indexation procedure described above will have to be performed several times over.

Activity 8.1

Following on from the above example, assume that Oliver Ltd acquired 2,000 more shares on 10 July 1986 (RPI = 97.5) at a cost of £4,000. Recalculate the value of the FA 1985 pool on 10 July 1986 following the acquisition.

2.5 Disposals from the FA 1985 pool

In the case of a disposal, following the calculation of the indexed rise to the date of disposal, the cost and the indexed cost attributable to the shares disposed of are deducted from the amounts within the FA 1985 pool. The proportions of the cost and indexed cost to take out of the pool should be computed using the same A/(A + B) fraction that is used for any other part disposal. However, we are not usually given the value of the remaining shares (B in the fraction). We then just use numbers of shares.

The indexation allowance is the indexed cost taken out of the pool minus the cost taken out. As usual, the indexation allowance cannot create or increase a loss.

Activity 8.2

Continuing the above exercise, suppose that Oliver Ltd sold 3,000 shares on 10 July 2003 (RPI = 179.9) for £17,000. Compute the gain, and the value of the FA 1985 pool following the disposal.

3 The matching rules for individuals

3.1 Introduction

For individuals, the pooling of shares ceased for acquisitions on or after 6 April 1998. This means the time of each post April 1998 acquisition can be recorded enabling the length of ownership for each share to be calculated for tapering purposes.

3.2 Matching rules

Share disposals for individuals are matched with acquisitions in the following order.

(a) Same day acquisitions.

(b) Acquisitions within the following 30 days.

(c) Previous acquisitions after 5 April 1998 identifying the most recent acquisition first (a LIFO basis).

(d) Any shares in the FA 1985 pool at 5 April 1998 (the FA 1985 pool runs from 6 April 1982 (instead of 1 April 1982) to 5 April 1998 for individuals).

3.3 Example

Sue acquired the following shares in X plc.

	No of shares
1.4.90	10,000
1.9.98	5,000
10.11.00	7,000
30.12.03	2,000

On 11.12.03 Sue sold 12,000 shares. With which acquisitions is Sue's share disposal matched?

3.4 Solution

Sue will initially match the disposal with the 2,000 shares bought on 30.12.03 (next 30 days). She will then match with the other post April 1998 acquisitions on a LIFO basis, so the 7,000 shares bought on 10.11.00 and 3,000 of the shares bought on 1.9.98 are deemed to be sold. 2,000 of the shares acquired on 1.9.98 and the FA 1985 pool shares remain.

3.5 FA 1985 pool for individuals

For all FA 1985 pools held by an individual at 5 April 1998 indexation allowance to April 1998 is calculated and then effectively the pool is closed.

Activity 8.3

Ron acquired the following shares in First Ltd:

Date of acquisition	*No of shares*	*Cost*
		£
9.11.90 (RPI = 130.0)	10,000	25,000
4.8.02	3,000	11,400
15.7.03	5,000	19,000

He disposed of 18,000 shares on 10 July 2003 for £72,000. The shares are business assets for the purposes of taper relief. Calculate the chargeable gain arising after taper relief but before the deduction of the annual exemption. RPI April 1998 = 162.6.

4 Bonus and rights issues

4.1 Bonus issues (scrip issues)

When a company issues bonus shares all that happens is that the size of the original holding is increased. Since bonus shares are issued at no cost there is no need to adjust the original cost. Instead the numbers purchased at particular times are increased by the bonus. The normal matching rules will then be applied.

4.2 Example: bonus issues

The following transactions by an individual in the ordinary shares of X plc would be matched as shown below

6.4.86	Purchase of 600 shares
6.4.90	Purchase of 600 shares
6.4.02	Purchase of 1,000 shares
6.10.02	Bonus issue of one for four
6.12.03	Sale of 1,500 shares

(a) Post 6.4.98 acquisition

		No of shares
6.4.02	Purchase	1,000
6.10.02	Bonus	250
		1,250
6.12.03	Sold	(1,250)

(b) FA 1985 pool

		No of shares
6.4.86	Purchase	600
6.4.90	Purchase	600
		1,200
6.10.02	Bonus	300
		1,500
6.12.03	Sold	(250)
Number of shares remaining in FA 1985 pool		1,250

4.3 Rights issues

The difference between a bonus issue and a rights issue is that in a rights issue the new shares are paid for and this results in an adjustment to the original cost. As with bonus issues, rights shares derived from shares in the 1985 pool go into that holding and for individuals, those derived from post 5.4.98 holdings attach to those holdings. You should add the number and cost of each of right issue to each holding as appropriate.

The length of the period of ownership for taper relief purposes depends on the date of acquisition of the original holding **not** the date of acquisition of the rights shares.

Let us try an activity with a rights issue made to an individual.

Activity 8.4

Simon had the following transactions in S Ltd.

1.10.95	Bought 10,000 shares (10%) holding for £15,000 (RPI = 149.8)
11.9.00	Bought 2,000 shares for £5,000
1.2.01	Took up rights issue 1 for 2 at £2.75 per share
14.10.03	Sold 5,000 shares for £15,000

Compute the gain arising in October 2003, after taper relief (if applicable). The shares have always been a business asset for taper relief purposes. RPI April 1998 = 162.6.

For companies, you will always need to index the value of the FA1985 pool to the date of the rights issue. Add the number and cost of the rights issue shares after you have added the indexation to the pool. Rights issues made to individuals before 6.4.98 should be dealt with in the FA 1985 pool in a similar way.

Activity 8.5

J Ltd had the following transactions in the shares of T plc.

July 1985	Purchased 1,000 shares for £3,000 (RPI = 95.2)
May 1986	Took up one for four rights issue at £4.20 per share (RPI = 97.8)
October 2003	Sold the shares for £10,000 (RPI = 180.5)

Compute the chargeable gain or allowable loss arising on the sale in October 2003.

5 End of chapter activities

Activity 8.6

Frances sold her ordinary shares in The Hastings Hardening Company Ltd on 17 May 2003 for £24,000. She had bought ordinary shares in the company on the following dates.

	No of shares	*Cost*
		£
19 September 1985 (RPI = 95.4)	2,000	1,700
12 December 2001	2,000	5,500
17 January 2003	2,000	6,000

Task

Calculate, before the annual exemption but after taper relief, the capital gain for 2003/04. The shares are a business asset for taper relief purposes.

Activity 8.7

Lorus Ltd acquired the following shares in Henna plc:

	No of shares	Cost
		£
11 July 1988 (RPI = 106.7)	1,000	5,000
19 September 1999 (RPI = 166.2)	2,000	18,000
28 July 2003 (RPI = 179.9)	1,500	15,000

Lorus Ltd sold 4,000 shares for £44,000 on 3 August 2003 (RPI = 180.1).

Task

Calculate the capital gain arising on the disposal.

Key learning points

- ☑ We need **special rules for matching** shares sold with shares purchased.
- ☑ There are **different rules** for **companies** and for **individuals**.
- ☑ The **FA 1985 pool** for companies contains shares acquired between **1.4.82** and **nine days before the date of the current disposal.**
- ☑ **Indexation allowance for companies** is given to the **date of disposal.**
- ☑ Shares acquired **after 5 April 1998** by an individual are matched on a **last in first out** (LIFO) basis
- ☑ The **FA 1985 pool** for individuals contains shares acquired between **6.4.82** and **5.4.98.**
- ☑ **Bonus and rights issues** are attached to the **holding to which they relate**.

Quick quiz

1 Disposals by companies are generally identified in the following order:

.... acquisitions

Previous........... days acquisitions

Shares in the .... pool

2 What shares are included in the FA 1985 pool for companies?

3 Disposals by individuals are identified in the following order:

.... acquisitions

Next .... days acquisitions

Acquisitions after .... on a .... basis

Shares in the .... pool

4 What shares are included in the FA 1985 pool for individuals?

5 What is the difference between a bonus and a rights issue?

Answers to quick quiz

1 **Same day** acquisitions
Previous **nine** days acquisitions
Shares in the **FA 1985** pool

2 Shares held by a company on 1 April 1985 and acquired by that company on or after 1 April 1982 and shares acquired by that company on or after 1 April 1985.

3 **Same day** acquisitions
Next **30** days acquisitions
Acquisitions after **5.4.98** on a **LIFO** basis
Shares in the **FA 1985** pool

4 Shares acquired by an individual on or after 6 April 1982 held at 5 April 1998.

5 In a rights issue the new shares are paid for. In a bonus issue there is no payment for the issue of the shares.

Activity checklist

This checklist shows which performance criteria, range statement or knowledge and understanding point is covered by each activity in this chapter. Tick off each activity as you complete it.

Activity		
8.1	☐	This activity deals with Performance Criteria 18.3.C: calculate chargeable gains and allowable losses.
8.2	☐	This activity deals with Performance Criteria 18.3.C: calculate chargeable gains and allowable losses.
8.3	☐	This activity deals with Performance Criteria 18.3.A : identify and value correctly any chargeable assets that have been disposed of
8.4	☐	This activity deals with Performance Criteria 18.3.A and 18.3.C : identify and value correctly any chargeable assets that have been disposed of; calculate chargeable gains and allowable losses.
8.5	☐	This activity deals with Performance Criteria 18.3.B: identify shares disposed of by companies.
8.6	☐	This activity deals with Performance Criteria 18.3.A and 18.3.C : identify and value correctly any chargeable assets that have been disposed of; calculate chargeable gains and allowable losses.
8.7	☐	This activity deals with Performance Criteria 18.3.B: identify shares disposed of by companies.

chapter 9

Chattels and wasting assets

Contents

Performance criteria

18.3 A Identify and value correctly any chargeable assets that have been disposed of

18.3 C Calculate chargeable gains and allowable losses

Range statement

18.3 Chargeable assets that have been: sold, gifted, lost, destroyed

Knowledge and understanding

11 Identification of business assets disposed of including part disposals (Element 18.3)

12 Calculation of gains and losses on disposals of business assets including indexation allowance (Element 18.3)

1 Chattels

1.1 Gains on chattels

A **chattel** is tangible movable property.

A **wasting asset** is an asset with an estimated remaining useful life of 50 years or less.

Plant and machinery, whose predictable useful life is always deemed to be less than 50 years, is therefore an example of a wasting chattel (unless it is immovable, in which case it will be wasting but not a chattel). Machinery includes, in addition to its ordinary meaning, motor vehicles (unless exempt as cars), railway engines, engine-powered boats and clocks.

Wasting chattels are exempt from CGT (so that there are no chargeable gains and no allowable losses). There is one exception to this: assets used for the purpose of a trade, profession or vocation in respect of which capital allowances have been or could have been claimed. This means that items of plant and machinery used in a trade are not exempt merely on the ground that they are wasting. (However, cars are always exempt.)

If a chattel is not exempt under the wasting chattels rule, any gain arising on its disposal will still be exempt from CGT if the asset is sold for gross proceeds of £6,000 or less, even if capital allowances were claimed on it.

If sale proceeds exceed £6,000, any gain is limited to a maximum of 5/3 × (gross proceeds – £6,000).

Activity 9.1

A Ltd purchased a Chippendale chair on 1 June 1985 (RPI = 95.4) for £800. On 10 October 2003 (RPI = 180.5) it sold the chair at auction for £6,300 (which was net of the auctioneer's 10% commission). What was the chargeable gain?

1.2 Losses on chattels

Where a chattel, not exempt under the wasting chattels rule is sold for less than £6,000 and a loss arises, the allowable loss is restricted by assuming that the chattel had been sold for £6,000. This rule cannot turn a loss into a gain, only reduce the loss, perhaps to zero.

Activity 9.2

E Ltd purchased a rare first edition on 1 July 1994 for £8,000 which it sold in October 2003 at auction for £2,700 (which was net of 10% commission). Compute the loss.

2 Wasting assets

2.1 Introduction

As we have seen, a wasting asset is one which has an estimated remaining useful life of 50 years or less and whose original value will depreciate over time. **Freehold land is never a wasting asset**. You will not be expected to deal with leases in your assessment.

Wasting chattels are exempt except for those on which capital allowances have been (or could have been) **claimed**. Where capital allowances were available (on any asset, not just a chattel) and a loss would arise, the base cost is reduced by the net capital allowances obtained: the result is no gain and no loss. Gains on such assets may still be exempted or restricted under the chattels rules based on £6,000 as long as the assets are not fixed. Items of fixed plant and machinery are not movable and so are not chattels.

2.2 Example: wasting chattel

X Ltd bought a computer for £17,000 in January 1996. The computer was sold for £8,000 in December 2003. Capital allowances were claimed on the computer which will have equalled £9,000 (£17,000 cost less £8,000 disposal proceeds) in total over the life of the computer.

	£	£
Sale proceeds		8,000
Cost	17,000	
Less net capital allowances claimed	(9,000)	
		(8,000)
Loss on disposal		NIL

2.3 Wasting assets other than chattels

The cost is written down on a straight line basis before calculating the indexation allowance. Thus, if a taxpayer acquires such an asset with a remaining life of 40 years and disposes of it after 15 years (with 25 years remaining) only 25/40 of the cost is deducted from the disposal consideration. Indexation allowance is computed on the written down cost rather than the full original cost.

Examples of such assets are copyrights (with 50 years or less to run) and registered designs, owned by individuals.

Where the asset has an estimated residual value at the end of its predictable life, it is the cost less residual value which is written off on a straight line basis over the asset's life. Where additional expenditure is incurred on a wasting asset the additional cost is written off over the life remaining when it was incurred.

Assets eligible for capital allowances and used throughout the period of ownership in a trade, profession or vocation do not have their allowable expenditure written down.

Activity 9.3

Jeremy bought a copyright on 1 April 1993 (RPI = 140.6), when it had 40 years to run. He paid £7,000 for it, and sold it for £23,000 on 1 July 2003. What was the chargeable gain after taper relief? The copyright was a business asset. RPI April 1998 = 162.6.

3 End of chapter activity

Activity 9.4

Adams Ltd makes the following disposals in its accounting period to 31.3.04.

(a) Painting which hung in the boardroom. Acquired July 1998 (RPI = 163.0) for £3,000. Sold for £7,500 in October 2003 (RPI = 180.5).

(b) Vase which was in the reception area. Acquired May 2000 for £8,000 (RPI = 170.7). Sold for £5,000 in December 2003 (RPI = 180.9).

(c) Lathe used in workshop with a useful life of 10 years. Acquired July 2001 (RPI = 173.3) for £10,000. Sold for £8,000 in December 2003 (RPI = 180.9). Capital allowances of £2,000 were claimed in total.

(d) Racehorse sold for £20,000 in July 2003 (RPI = 179.9). Cost £3,000 in September 2001 (RPI = 174.6).

Task

Calculate the net gains arising to Adams Ltd for the accounting period to 31.3.04.

Key learning points

- ☑ If a **chattel** is sold for **up to £6,000**, there is **no chargeable gain** and any **loss is restricted**.
- ☑ Id sale proceeds on the disposal of a chattel exceed £6,000, any gain is limited to a maximum of $^5/_3$ (gross proceeds - £6,000)
- ☑ **Gains on most wasting chattels** are **exempt** and **losses** are **not allowable.**
- ☑ However, **wasting chattels are not exempt** where **capital allowances** have been or could have been claimed.
- ☑ If a **loss would arise on a wasting chattel with capital allowances**, the interaction between the gains and income tax rules means that there is **no gain or loss for chargeable gains purposes**.
- ☑ **Other wasting assets** have cost **written down** over time.

Quick quiz

1 Marcia sells a painting for £8,000 which she bought last year for £3,000. What is her gain on sale before taper relief?

2 Leslie Ltd sold a vase for £4,500. Cost was £7,000. What is the loss on sale?

3 Trevor bought a copyright on 1 December 2000 for £7,000 when it had 35 years left to run. He sold it on 1 June 2003. What is his base cost for the sale?

Answers to quick quiz

1

	£
Proceeds	8,000
Less: cost	(3,000)
Gain	5,000

Restricted to 5/3 × £(8,000 – 6,000) = £3,333

2

	£
Proceeds (deemed)	6,000
Less: cost	(7,000)
Loss	(1,000)

3 Copyright has 32 ½ years to run at sale. So adjusted cost is:

$$\frac{32\frac{1}{2}}{35} \times £7,000 = £6,500$$

Activity checklist

This checklist shows which performance criteria is covered by each activity in this chapter. Tick off each activity as you complete it.

Activity		
9.1	☐	This activity deals with Performance Criteria 18.3.C: calculate chargeable gains and allowable losses.
9.2	☐	This activity deals with Performance Criteria 18.3.A: identify and value correctly any chargeable assets that have been disposed of.
9.3	☐	This activity deals with Performance Criteria 18.3.C: calculate chargeable gains and allowable losses.
9.4	☐	This activity deals with Performance Criteria 18.3.A and 18.3.C: identify and value correctly any chargeable assets that have been disposed of; calculate chargeable gains and allowable losses.

chapter 10

Deferral reliefs

Contents

Performance criteria

18.3 D Apply reliefs, deferrals and exemptions correctly

Range statement

18.3 Reliefs: rollover relief, relief for gifts

Knowledge and understanding

13 Capital gains exemptions and reliefs on business assets including rollover relief and taper relief but excluding retirement relief (Element 18.3)

1 Gift relief

1.1 Introduction

If an individual gives away a business asset (see below), an election can be made by the 31 January which is nearly six years after the end of the tax year of the transfer, **for the transferor's gain to be reduced to nil.**

If an election is made the transferee is deemed to acquire the asset for market value at the date of transfer less the transferor's deferred gain (no taper relief given). The transferee will qualify for further indexation allowance (if available) on that reduced base cost from the date of the transfer. The transferee will start a new period for taper relief from the date of his acquisition.

Activity 10.1

Tim makes a gain of £50,000 on the gift of an asset to Sue. The market value of the asset on the date of the gift was £120,000 and Sue and Tim elected for Tim's gain to be reduced to £Nil under the gift relief provisions.

At what value is Sue deemed to acquire the gift?

Activity 10.2

On 6 December 2003 Angelo gave to his son Michael a freehold shop valued at £200,000 and claimed gift relief. Angelo had originally purchased the shop from which he had run his business in July 1999 for £30,000. Michael continued to run a business from the shop premises but decided to sell the shop in May 2005 for £195,000. Compute Michael's chargeable gains on sale. Assume the rules of CGT in 2003/04 continue to apply in May 2005.

1.2 Qualifying assets

Transfers of business assets include transfers of :

(a) **Assets used in a trade, profession or vocation carried on**:

  (i) by the donor, or

  (ii) by the donor's personal company or a member of a trading group of which the holding company is his personal company

A **'personal company'** is one in which not less than 5% of the voting rights are controlled by the individual disposing of the shares.

A **'trading company'** is a company whose business is wholly or mainly the carrying on of a trade or trades. A 'trading group' is a group the business of whose members, taken together, consists wholly or mainly of the carrying on of a trade or trades.

(b) **Shares and securities in trading companies**, or holding companies of trading groups, where:

(i) the shares or securities are **not listed on a recognised stock exchange** (but they may be on the AIM); or

(ii) the company concerned is the donor's **personal company**

Activity 10.3

20 years ago, Rupert formed a company with £1,000 in share capital. The company used this money to buy a painting, but has since had no transactions. The painting is now worth £60,000. Rupert wishes to give all of the shares in the company to his daughter, claiming gift relief. Why will gift relief be unavailable?

2 Rollover relief

2.1 Introduction

A gain may be 'rolled over' (deferred) where it arises on the disposal of a business asset which is replaced. This is **rollover relief**. A claim cannot specify that only part of a gain is to be rolled over.

2.2 Conditions

All the following conditions must be met.

- **The old asset sold and the new asset bought are both used only in the trade** or trades carried on **by the person claiming rollover relief.**
- **The old asset and the new asset both fall within one** (but not necessarily the same one) **of the following classes.**

  (i) Land and buildings (including parts of buildings) occupied as well as used only for the purpose of the trade

  (ii) Fixed (that is, immovable) plant and machinery

  (iii) Ships, aircraft and hovercraft

  (iv) Goodwill (until 31.3.02 only for companies)

  (v) Satellites, space stations and spacecraft

- **Reinvestment of the proceeds of the old asset takes place in a period beginning one year before and ending three years after the date of the disposal.**
- **The new asset is brought into use in the trade on its acquisition** (not necessarily immediately, but not after any significant and unnecessary delay).

The new asset can be for use in a different trade from the old asset.

A rollover claim is not allowed when a taxpayer buys premises, sells part of the premises at a profit and then claims to roll over the gain into the part retained. However, a rollover claim is allowed when the proceeds of the old asset are spent on improving a qualifying asset which the taxpayer already owns. The improved asset must already be in use for a trade, or be brought into trade use immediately the improvement work is finished.

2.3 Method of relief

Deferral is obtained by carrying forward the chargeable gain and deducting it from the cost of the new asset. To obtain full relief, the whole of the consideration for the disposal must be reinvested. You will not be expected to deal with partial relief in your assessment.

The new asset will have a CGT 'cost' of its purchase price less the gain rolled over into its acquisition.

If an unincorporated business or a company expects to buy new assets, it can make a provisional rollover claim on the tax return which includes the gain on the old asset. The gain is deferred accordingly. If new assets are not actually acquired, the Revenue collect the tax saved by the provisional claim.

Activity 10.4

A freehold factory was purchased by Zoë for business use in August 1998. It was sold in December 2003 for £70,000, giving rise to a gain of £17,950. A replacement factory was purchased in June 2004 for £80,000. Compute the base cost of the replacement factory, taking into account any possible rollover gain from the disposal in December 2003. Ignore taper relief.

Rollover relief applies to the untapered gain. When the replacement asset is sold taper relief on that sale will only be given by reference to the holding period for that asset (assuming further rollover relief is not claimed on this disposal). **Effectively, taper relief on the rolled over gain, for the period of ownership of the original asset, is lost.**

Activity 10.5

Karen is a sole trader who bought a business asset for £170,625 on 5 November 1991 (RPI = 135.6) and sold it on 31 December 2003 for £491,400. A replacement business asset was acquired on 1 November 2003 at a cost of £546,000. The new asset was sold on 3 September 2005 for £914,550. Karen made a claim for rollover relief on the first asset sale but not on the second asset sale.

Calculate the taxable gains for each asset disposal. RPI April 1998 = 162.6.

3 End of chapter activities

Activity 10.6

Alistair bought 1,000 shares in DEF Ltd, an unquoted trading company, for £10,000 in July 2000. He gave them to his brother Edward in September 2002 when they were worth £25,000. Edward sold the shares for £35,000 in October 2003.

Task

Calculate Edward's gain on sale after taper relief.

Activity 10.7

Louis plc bought a freehold factory for £150,000 in July 1999 (RPI = 165.1). It sold it for £200,000 in October 2002 (RPI = 177.9). It had acquired another factory in June 2002 (RPI = 174.4) at a cost of £250,000. Louis plc sold the second factory for £275,000 in May 2003 (RPI = 179.5).

Task

Calculate the gain on sale of the second factory, assuming all reliefs available were claimed.

Key learning points

- ☑ **Gift relief** is available to **defer gains on the gift of business assets.**
- ☑ The **gain on the gift reduces the base cost** of the asset **for the transferee.**
- ☑ The **transferee** will **start a new period of ownership** for taper relief.
- ☑ When **certain types of assets used in a business** are sold and **other such assets bought**, it is possible to **defer (roll-over) the gains on the assets sold.**
- ☑ The **rolled over gain** will **reduce the base cost of the new asset.**
- ☑ The new asset must be acquired in the period commencing **one year before and ending three years after the disposal.**

Quick quiz

1 What is a personal company for gift relief?

2 Graham buys a shop for use in his business in May 1997 for £100,000. He gives it to his son, Neil, in March 2004 when it is worth £150,000. The indexation factor between May 1997 and April 1998 was 0.036. What is the base cost for Neil?

3 In order to qualify for rollover relief, reinvestment must normally take place within .... year(s) before and .... year(s) after the disposal of the original asset.

4 Rollover relief may be available to defer a gain arising on the disposal of unlisted shares. True/ False?

5 What effect does gift relief or rollover relief have on taper relief?

Answers to quick quiz

1 A personal company is one in which an individual controls not less than 5% of the voting rights.

2

	£
Market value	150,000
Less: cost	(100,000)
	50,000
Less: indexation allowance 0.036 x £100,000	(3,600)
Gain	46,400

Base cost for Neil £(150,000 – 46,400) = £103,600

3 In order to qualify for rollover relief, reinvestment must normally take place within **one year** before and **three years** after the disposal of the original asset.

4 FALSE. Shares are not a qualifying assets for rollover relief purposes.

5 The taper relief period will commence when the 'new' asset is acquired . This means the taper relief period that had been built up on the old asset is lost.

Activity checklist

This checklist shows which performance criteria, range statement or knowledge and understanding point is covered by each activity in this chapter. Tick off each activity as you complete it.

Activity		
10.1	☐	This activity deals with Performance Criteria 18.3.D: apply reliefs, deferrals and exemptions correctly.
10.2	☐	This activity deals with Performance Criteria 18.3.D: apply reliefs, deferrals and exemptions correctly.
10.3	☐	This activity deals with Performance Criteria 18.3.D: apply reliefs, deferrals and exemptions correctly.
10.4	☐	This activity deals with Knowledge and Understanding point 13: capital gains tax exemptions and reliefs on business assets including rollover relief.
10.5	☐	This activity deals with Knowledge and Understanding point 13: capital gains tax exemptions and reliefs on business assets including rollover relief.
10.6	☐	This activity deals with Performance Criteria 18.3.D: apply reliefs, deferrals and exemptions correctly.
10.7	☐	This activity deals with Knowledge and Understanding point 13: capital gains tax exemptions and reliefs on business assets including rollover relief.

PART C

Corporation tax

chapter 11

An outline of corporation tax

Contents

Performance criteria

18.4 A Enter adjusted trading profits and losses, capital allowances, investment income and capital gains in the Corporation Tax computation

18.4 C Calculate Corporation Tax due, taking account of marginal relief

Range statement

There are no additional contextual requirements in this element relevant to this chapter.

Knowledge and understanding

15 The computation of profit for Corporation Tax purposes including income, capital gains and charges (Element 18.4)

16 Calculation of Corporation Tax payable by starting, small, large and marginal companies including those with associated companies (Element 18.4)

1 The scope of corporation tax

1.1 Introduction

Corporation tax is paid by companies. It is charged on the profits (including chargeable gains) arising in each accounting period. Corporation tax is not charged on dividends received from companies resident in the UK.

1.2 Proforma corporation tax computation

The profits chargeable to corporation tax (PCTCT) for an accounting period are derived as follows.

	£
Schedule D Case I	**X**
Schedule D Case III	**X**
Schedule D Case VI	**X**
Schedule A	**X**
Chargeable gains	**X**
Total profits	**X**
Less charges on income	**(X)**
Profits chargeable to corporation tax (PCTCT) for an accounting period	**X**

It would be of great help in the assessment if you could learn the above proforma to calculate PCTCT. Then when answering a corporation tax question you could immediately reproduce the proforma and insert the appropriate numbers into the proforma as you are given the information in the question. We will look at the various items in this proforma as we work through this chapter.

1.3 Accounting periods

Corporation tax is chargeable in respect of **accounting periods** and it is important to understand the difference between an accounting period and a period of account. A period of account is any period for which a company prepares accounts; usually this will be 12 months in length but it may be longer or shorter than this. An accounting period starts when a company commences to trade or otherwise becomes liable to corporation tax, or immediately after the previous accounting period finishes. An accounting period finishes on the earliest of:

- 12 months after its start
- the end of the company's period of account
- the commencement of the company's winding up
- the company's ceasing to be resident in the UK
- the company's ceasing to be liable to corporation tax

If a company has a long period of account, exceeding 12 months, it is split into two accounting periods: the first 12 months and the remainder.

Where the period of account differs from the corporation tax accounting periods (as in the above example), there is the problem of **allocating profits between the relevant periods.** In such cases the following rules apply.

(a) **Trading income** before capital allowances is apportioned on a **time basis**.

(b) **Capital allowances** and balancing charges are **calculated for each accounting period.**

(c) **Other income is allocated to the period to which it relates** (for example interest to the period in which it accrued) (see below). Schedule D Case VI income is apportioned on a time basis.

(d) **Chargeable gains** are taken into account for the accounting **period in which they are realised.**

(e) **Charges on income** are deducted from the profits of the accounting **period in which they are paid**.

Companies' taxable profits are always computed for accounting periods. There are no basis period rules, there is no personal allowance and there is no taper relief or annual exemption for capital gains.

Activity 11.1

Xenon Ltd makes up an 18 month set of accounts to 30 June 2004 with the following results.

	£
Trading profits	180,000
Schedule D Case III	
18 months @ £500 accruing per month	9,000
Capital gain (1 May 2004 disposal)	250,000
Less: Charge on income (paid 31.12.03)	(50,000)
	389,000

What are the profits chargeable to corporation tax for each of the accounting periods based on the above accounts?

2 Profits chargeable to corporation tax

2.1 Schedule D Case I

The Schedule D Case I income of companies is derived from the net profit figure in the accounts, adjusted as follows.

	£	£
Net profit per accounts		X
Add expenditure not allowed for taxation purposes		X
		X
Less: income not taxable under Schedule D Case I	X	
expenditure not charged in the accounts but allowable for the purposes of taxation	X	
capital allowances	X	
		X
Schedule D Case I income		X

The adjustment of profits computation shown above broadly follows that for computing business profits subject to income tax.

Charges are added back in the calculation of Schedule D Case I profit. They are treated instead as a deduction from total profits and the amount allowed is the amount paid. The only charge on income that you will meet in your exam is a gift aid donation (see below).

Investment income including rents is deducted in arriving at trading profit but brought in again further down in the computation.

When adjusting profits as supplied in a profit and loss account confusion can arise as regards whether figures are net or gross. Properly drawn up company accounts should normally include all income gross. However, some questions mention 'net' figures. Read the question carefully.

The calculation of capital allowances follows income tax principles. For companies, there is never any reduction of allowances to take account of any private use of an asset. The director or employee suffers a taxable benefit instead.

2.2 Charges on income

One-off and regular charitable gifts of money qualify for tax relief under the **gift aid scheme** provided the donor gives the charity a gift aid declaration. **Gift aid declarations can be made in writing, electronically through the internet or orally over the phone. A declaration can cover a one off gift or any number of gifts for the future or retrospectively.**

For companies, gift aid donations are a charge on income. They are paid gross and the amount paid is deducted in computing PCTCT. You'll recall from earlier in your studies that this is not the case for income tax. Gift aid donations are not charges on income for income tax purposes. Conversely, **patent royalties paid** by a company are **not** a charge on income. Patent royalties that are paid/ received for trade purposes are included in Schedule D Case I profits on an accruals basis. Royalties paid/ received for non-trade purposes are included in Schedule D Case VI income.

Donations to charities which are incurred wholly and exclusively for the purposes of the trade are Schedule D Case I deductions instead of charges on income.

2.3 Rental income

A company with rental income is treated as running a 'Schedule A business'. All the rents and expenses for all properties are pooled, to give a single profit or loss. Schedule A income is taxed on an **accruals basis**. This means that if you have a long period of account you should allocate the amount accrued to each accounting period. You will not be expected to calculate Schedule A rental income (assessable under Unit 19). However, you may be given a figure for a Schedule A profit or loss and required to deal with it in the corporation tax computation as appropriate.

2.4 Income received net of tax

Income which suffers a deduction of tax at source is included within the corporation tax computation at its gross equivalent. For example £4,875 of patent royalties interest received net of tax would need to be grossed up by multiplying by 100/78 to include £6,250 within either Schedule D Case I or Schedule D Case VI income (see below). The way in which relief is given for the tax credit is covered later in this text. Essentially, if tax suffered on income received net exceeds tax deducted from patent royalties and interest paid net, the difference is subtracted in calculating the mainstream corporation tax due.

Examples of income received net of tax are:

(a) Patent royalties where the payer is not a UK company: tax at 22%

(b) Interest on most gilt edged securities is received gross but in certain limited circumstances it is received net of tax at 20%

Patent royalties and interest which relate to the trade are included in Schedule D Case I profits normally on an accruals basis. Patent royalties which do not relate to the trade are taxed under Schedule D Case VI. Non-trading interest is taxed under Schedule D Case III on an accruals basis.

2.5 Interest received gross

UK companies receive interest gross from banks and building societies. Interest on most gilts is received gross.

Interest received from other UK companies is also received gross. This means debenture interest received from another UK company will be received gross.

2.6 Chargeable gains

2.6.1 Gains for companies

Companies do not pay capital gains tax. Instead their chargeable gains are included in the profits chargeable to corporation tax. A company's capital gains or allowable losses are computed in a similar way to individuals (see earlier in this text) but with a few major differences:

(a) Indexation allowance calculations may include periods of ownership after 6 April 1998. **Indexation is calculated to the month of disposal of an asset.**

(b) **The FA 1985 pool for shares does not close at 5 April 1998: it runs to the month of disposal of the shares**. This means that different matching rules are needed (see Chapter 8)

(c) The **taper relief does not apply**

(d) No **annual exemption is available**

2.6.2 Disposal of substantial shareholdings

A gain arising on the disposal of the whole or a part of a substantial shareholding in another trading company (or in the holding company of a trading group or subgroup) **by a trading company** (or member of a trading group) **is exempt**. Similarly a loss is not allowable.

A **substantial shareholding is one of 10% or more of the share capital**.

2.7 Intellectual property

In general, **the tax relief available to companies for the cost of intangible assets mirrors the amortisation charged in the accounts**. However, there is a long stop **fixed rate of 4% per annum for long life assets**, including assets with an indefinite useful life.

Disposals are taxed on an income basis and royalty payments/receipts are treated for tax purposes as they are in the accounts. Rollover relief applies where proceeds from the sale of intangibles are reinvested in other intangibles.

Goodwill is not a qualifying asset for companies for the purpose of rollover relief.

2.8 Borrowing and lending (loan relationships)

2.8.1 Introduction

If a company borrows or lends money it has a loan relationship. This can be a creditor relationship (where the company lends or invests money) **or a debtor relationship** (where the company borrows money or issues securities).

2.8.2 Treatment of trading loan relationships

If the company is a party to a **loan relationship for trade purposes, any debits – ie interest paid or other debt costs – charged through its accounts are allowed as a trading expense** and are therefore deductible in computing Schedule D Case I profits.

Similarly **if any credits – ie interest income or other debt returns – arise on a trading loan these are treated as a trading receipt and are taxable under Schedule D Case I.** This is not likely to arise unless the trade is one of money lending.

2.8.3 Treatment of non-trading loan relationships

If a loan relationship is not one to which the company is a party for trade purposes any debits or credits must be pooled. A net credit on the pool is chargeable as income under Schedule D Case III. A net deficit on the pool may be:

(a) **set against other income of the same accounting period**

(b) **carried back and set against any surpluses on non-trading loan relationships (taxed under Schedule D Case III) for the previous twelve months**

(c) **carried forward and set against future non-trading profits**

Any deficit remaining after the above claims is automatically carried forward as an opening DIII debit of the next accounting period.

We will look at the reliefs available for non trading deficits later in this text.

Activity 11.2

A company had the following results in the year ended 31 March 2004.

	£
Trading profits	85,000
Bank deposit interest income	6,000
Building society interest income	1,500
Debenture interest income	3,200
Capital gains	2,950
Gift Aid donation paid	15,200

All interest received was on non-trading investments.

What were the company's profits chargeable to corporation tax?

Activity 11.3

The following is a summary of the profit and loss account of A Ltd for the year to 31 March 2004.

	£	£
Gross profit on trading		180,000
3½% War Loan interest (non-trading investment)		700
Dividends from UK companies (net)		3,600
Loan interest from UK company (non-trading investment)		4,000
Building society interest received (non-trading investment)		292
Less: trade expenses (all allowable)	62,000	
gift aid donation paid	1,100	
		(63,100)
		125,492

The capital allowances for the period total £5,500. There was also a capital gain of £13,867.

Compute the profits chargeable to corporation tax.

3 Charge to corporation tax

3.1 Introduction

The rates of corporation tax are fixed for financial years. A financial year runs from 1 April to the following 31 March and is identified by the calendar year in which it begins. For example, the year ended 31 March 2004 is the Financial year 2003 (FY 2003). This should not be confused with a tax year, which runs from 6 April to the following 5 April.

The full rate of corporation tax is 30% for FY 1999 to FY 2003.

Activity 11.4

A company had profits chargeable to corporation tax of £2,000,000 in the year ended 31 March 2004. What was the corporation tax payable?

3.2 The small companies rate (SCR)

The SCR of corporation tax (20% for FY 1999 to FY 2001 and 19% for FY 2002 and FY 2003) applies to the profits chargeable to corporation tax of UK resident companies whose 'profits' are not more than £300,000.

'Profits' means profits chargeable to corporation tax plus the grossed-up amount of dividends received from UK companies. The grossed-up amount of UK dividends is the net dividend plus the tax credit which an individual investor would receive. We gross up by multiplying by 100/90.

Activity 11.5

B Ltd had the following results for the year ended 31 March 2004.

	£
Schedule D Case I	42,000
Dividend received 1 May 2003	9,000

Compute the corporation tax payable.

3.3 The starting rate

A starting rate of corporation tax of 0% applies to companies with 'profits' of up to £10,000 for FY 2002 and FY 2003. The starting rate in FY 2000 and in FY 2001 was 10%.

Activity 11.6

Dexter Limited has the following income for the year ended 31 March 2004.

(a) Schedule D, Case I income of £9,500, and
(b) Dividend received of £270.

Calculate the corporation tax liability for the year.

3.4 Marginal relief

3.4.1 Small companies marginal relief

Small companies marginal relief (sometimes called taper relief) applies where the 'profits' of an accounting period of a UK resident company are over £300,000 but under £1,500,000. We first calculate the corporation tax at the full rate and then deduct:

(M – P) × I/P × marginal relief fraction

where M = upper limit (currently £1,500,000)
P = 'profits' (see above Paragraph)
I = PCTCT

The marginal relief fraction is 1/40 for FY 1997 to FY 2001 and 11/400 for FY 2002 and FY 2003 inclusive.

You will be given the marginal relief formula in your assessment.

Activity 11.7

Lenox Ltd has the following results for the year ended 31 March 2004.

	£
PCTCT	296,000
Dividend received 1 December 2003	12,600

Calculate the corporation tax liability.

In your exam you may need to be aware that there is a **marginal rate of tax of 32.75%** that applies to PCTCT between the small companies' limits.

This is calculated as follows:

	£		£
Upper limit	1,500,000	@ 30%	450,000
Lower limit	(300,000)	@ 19%	(57,000)
Difference	1,200,000		393,000

$$\frac{393,000}{1,200,000} = 32.75\%$$

Effectively the band of profits (here £1,200,000) falling between the upper and lower limits is taxed at a rate of 32.75%

3.4.2 Example

A Ltd has PCTCT of £350,000 for the year ended 31.3.04. Its corporation tax liability is

	£
£350,000 × 30%	105,000
Less: small companies' marginal relief	
11/400 (1,500,000 – 350,000)	(31,625)
	73,375

This is the same as calculating tax at 19% × £300,000 + 32.75% × £50,000 = £57,000 + £16,375 = £73,375.

Consequently tax is charged at an effective rate of 32.75% on PCTCT that exceeds the small companies' lower limit.

Note that although there is an effective corporation tax charge of 32.75%, this rate of tax is never used in actually calculating corporation tax. The rate is just an effective marginal rate that you must be aware of.

3.4.3 Starting rate marginal relief

For companies with 'profits' between £10,001 and £50,000, the small companies rate less a starting rate marginal relief applies. The formula for calculating this marginal relief is the same as that given above except that 'M' is the upper limit for starting rate purposes. (£50,000 – FY 2000 to FY 2003). However the fraction used here is 19/400 for FY2002 and FY 2003 and 1/40 in FY2001. The small companies' rate only applies in full when 'profits' exceed £50,000.

Activity 11.8

Armstrong Ltd has the following income for its year ended 31 March 2004:

		£
(a)	Schedule D Case I	29,500
(b)	Dividend received	2,700

Calculate the corporation tax liability.

The effective marginal rate of tax when PCTCT falls between the starting rate limits is 23.75%. Again, this is an effective marginal rate of tax that you need to be aware of but it is a rate that is never actually used in working out the CT charge. It is calculated as:

£		£
50,000	@ 19%	9,500
(10,000)	@ 0%	Nil
40,000		9,500

$$\frac{9,500}{40,000} = 23.75\ \%$$

PCTCT falling into the band (here £40,000) suffers tax at an effective rate of 23.75%.

3.5 Changes in the rate – Accounting periods straddling 31 March

If there is a change in the corporation tax rate, and a company's accounting period does not fall entirely within one financial year, the profits of the accounting period are apportioned to the two financial years on a time basis. Note that the profits as a whole are apportioned. We do not look at components of the profit individually, unlike apportionment of profits of a long period of account to two accounting periods.

Activity 11.9

Frances Ltd makes up accounts to 31 December each year. For the year ended 31 December 2002 its profit and loss account was as follows.

	£
PCTCT	40,000
Dividends plus tax credits	2,500
'Profits'	42,500

Calculate the corporation tax liability for the year.

The 'profits' falling into each financial year determines the rate of corporation tax that applies to the PCTCT of that year. This could be the full rate, the small companies' rate or the starting rate.

Activity 11.10

Hewson Ltd had the following results for its year ended 30 September 2002.

Schedule D Case I	£9,500
Dividends plus tax credits	£300

Calculate the corporation tax liability for the year.

3.6 Associated companies

The expression **'associated companies'** in tax has no connection with financial accounting. For tax purposes a company is associated with another company if either controls the other or if both are under the control of the same person or persons (individuals, partnerships or companies).

If a company has one or more 'associated companies', then the profit limits for starting rate and small companies rate purposes are divided by the number of associated companies + 1 (for the company itself).

Companies which have only been associated for part of an accounting period are deemed to have been associated for the whole period for the purpose of determining the profit limits.

An associated company is ignored for these purposes if it has not carried on any trade or business at any time in the accounting period (or the part of the period during which it was associated). This means that you should ignore dormant companies.

3.7 Short accounting periods

The profit limits are reduced proportionately if an accounting period lasts for less than 12 months.

Activity 11.11

For the nine months to 31 January 2004 a company with two other associated companies had PCTCT of £78,000 and no dividends received. Compute the corporation tax payable.

4 End of chapter activity

Activity 11.12

Tree Ltd, a company with no associated companies, had the following results for the eighteen months to 31 December 2003:

	£
Trading profits	180,000
Chargeable gain - realised 1.6.03	172,000
Gift aid donation - paid 30.9.03	5,000
Gift aid donation - paid 30.9.02	22,000
Schedule D Case III	36,000
Dividend received 30.3.03	27,000

The Schedule D Case III income accrued evenly over the period

Task

Compute the corporation tax liability in respect of the profits arising in the eighteen months to 31 December 2003.

Key learning points

- ☑ Companies pay **corporation tax** on their profits for each **accounting period**.
- ☑ The **usual length** of an accounting period is **12 months**, but it may be **shorter**.
- ☑ If a company has a **period of account longer than 12 months**, the **first 12 months** will be **one accounting period** and the **remainder** a **second accounting period**.
- ☑ **Profits chargeable to corporation tax** are **income** plus **gains** minus **charges**.
- ☑ All **UK rental activities** are treated as a **single source of income** taxable under **Schedule A** on an accruals basis.
- ☑ If a company **borrows or lends** money it has a **loan relationship**.
- ☑ **Trading loan relationships** are dealt with as part of the **Schedule D Case I profits**.
- ☑ **Non-trading loan relationships** are pooled and a net credit is taxable under **Schedule D Case III**.
- ☑ A **gift aid donation** is a **charge** on income.
- ☑ **Tax rates** are set for **financial years**.
- ☑ Companies pay **corporation tax** at the **starting rate**, **small companies rate** or **full rate**.
- ☑ **Marginal relief** is available for some companies depending on their '**profits**' (chargeable profits plus grossed up dividends received).
- ☑ Adjustments are required for **associated companies** and **short accounting periods**.

Quick quiz

1 Trading profits (before capital allowances) of a long period of account are apportioned .... Fill in the blank.

2 S Ltd, a company with one associated company, had profits chargeable to corporation tax of £8,500 for its six month accounting period to 31 March 2004.

Its corporation tax liability for the period will be:

A £Nil
B £831
C £1,425
D £1,615

3 VAC Ltd, a company with no associated companies, has profits chargeable to corporation tax for the year to 31 March 2004 of £25,000.

What is the marginal rate of corporation tax paid by the company on its profits between £10,000 and £25,000?

A 19%
B 23.75%
C 30%
D 32.75%

4 For the year to 31 March 2004, M Ltd, a company with one associated company, has the following results:

	£
Schedule D Case I profits	110,000
Dividend received from UK company	45,000

What is M Ltd's corporation tax liability for the year?

A £20,900
B £21,388
C £21,845
D £36,845

Answers to quick quiz

1 Trading profits (before capital allowances) of a long period of account are apportioned **on a time basis**.

2 C

Starting rate upper limit = $\frac{50,000}{2} \times \frac{6}{12}$ = £12,500

Starting rate lower limit = $\frac{10,000}{2} \times \frac{6}{12}$ = £2,500

	£
Starting rate marginal relief applies: £8,500 × 19%	1,615
Less 19/400 (£12,500 – £8,500)	(190)
	1,425

3 B

The marginal rate of corporation tax on profits between the starting rate upper and lower limits is 23.75%.

4 C

Small companies' limits

Lower limit = $\frac{£300,000}{2}$ = £150,000

Upper limit = $\frac{£1,500,000}{2}$ = £750,000

'Profits' £110,000 + £45,000 × $^{100}/_{90}$ = £160,000

∴ Small companies' marginal relief applies

	£
£110,000 × 30%	33,000
$^{11}/_{400}(750,000 - 160,000) \times \frac{110,000}{160,000}$	(11,155)
	21,845

Activity checklist

This checklist shows which performance criteria, range statement or knowledge and understanding point is covered by each activity in this chapter. Tick off each activity as you complete it.

Activity		
11.1	☐	This activity deals with Knowledge and Understanding point 15: the computation of profit for Corporation Tax purposes including income, capital gains and charges.
11.2	☐	This activity deals with Performance Criteria 18.4.A: enter adjusted trading profits and losses, capital allowances, investment income and capital gains in the corporation tax computation.
11.3	☐	This activity deals with Performance Criteria 18.4.A: enter adjusted trading profits and losses, capital allowances, investment income and capital gains in the corporation tax computation.
11.4	☐	This activity deals with Performance Criteria 18.4.C: calculate corporation tax payable, taking account of marginal relief.
11.5	☐	This activity deals with Performance Criteria 18.4.C: calculate corporation tax payable, taking account of marginal relief.
11.6	☐	This activity deals with Performance Criteria 18.4.C: calculate corporation tax payable, taking account of marginal relief.
11.7	☐	This activity deals with Performance Criteria 18.4.C: calculate corporation tax payable, taking account of marginal relief.
11.8	☐	This activity deals with Performance Criteria 18.4.C: calculate corporation tax payable, taking account of marginal relief.
11.9	☐	This activity deals with Performance Criteria 18.4.C: calculate corporation tax payable, taking account of marginal relief.
11.10	☐	This activity deals with Performance Criteria 18.4.C: calculate corporation tax payable, taking account of marginal relief.
11.11	☐	This activity deals with Performance Criteria 18.4.C: calculate corporation tax payable, taking account of marginal relief.
11.12	☐	This activity deals with Performance Criteria 18.4.C: calculate corporation tax payable, taking account of marginal relief.

chapter 12

Corporation tax losses

Contents

Performance criteria

18.4 B Set-off and deduct loss reliefs and charges correctly

Range statement

18.4 Loss reliefs relating to: trade losses, non trade losses

Knowledge and understanding

17 Set-off of trading losses incurred by companies (Element 18.4)

1 Reliefs for losses

1.1 Trading losses

The following reliefs are available for trading losses incurred by a company.

(a) **Set-off against current profits**
(b) **Carry back against earlier profits**
(c) **Carry forward against future trading profits**

A claim must be made for reliefs (a) and (b). The reliefs are given in the order shown.

Relief (c) is given automatically for any loss for which the other reliefs are not claimed.

1.2 Non trading deficits

Non-trading deficits on loan relationships can be relieved in the same ways as trading losses, but against different profits. (See below)

1.3 Capital losses

Capital losses can only be set against capital gains in the same or future accounting periods, never against income. Capital losses must be set against the first available gains.

1.4 Schedule D Case VI losses

Where in an accounting period a company makes a loss in a transaction taxable under Schedule D Case VI, the company can set the loss against any income from other transactions taxable under Case VI in the same or later accounting periods. The loss must be set against the earliest income available.

1.5 Schedule A losses

Schedule A losses are first set off against non-Schedule A income and gains of the company for the current period.

Any excess is then carried forward as if a Schedule A loss arising in the later accounting period for offset against future income (of all descriptions).

Activity 12.1

A plc had the following results in the three years to 31.3.04. Show its PCTCT in each year.

		Year ended	
	31.3.02	*31.3.03*	*31.3.04*
	£	£	£
Trading profits/(loss)	20,000	24,000	20,000
Capital gain/(loss)	(8,000)	2,000	7,000

2 Loss relief against future income: s 393(1) ICTA 1988

A company **must set off a trading loss not otherwise relieved against income from the same trade in future accounting periods**. Relief is given against the first available profits. This relief is given automatically, there is no need to make a claim for it.

Activity 12.2

A Ltd has the following results for the three years to 31 March 2004.

		Year ended	
	31.3.02	*31.3.03*	*31.3.04*
	£	£	£
Trading profit/(loss)	(8,550)	3,000	6,000
Schedule A income	0	1,000	1,000

Calculate the profits chargeable to corporation tax for all three years showing any losses available to carry forward at 1 April 2004.

3 Loss relief against total profits: s 393A(1) ICTA 1988

A company may claim to set a trading loss incurred in an accounting period against total profits (before deducting charges) of the same accounting period. Any charges (gift aid donations) that become unrelieved remain unrelieved.

Such a loss may then be carried back and set against total profits (before deducting charges) of an accounting period falling wholly or partly within the 12 months of the start of the period in which the loss was incurred.

If a period falls partly outside the 12 months, loss relief is limited to the proportion of the period's profits (before charges) equal to the proportion of the period which falls within the 12 months.

The 12 month carry back period is extended to 36 months where the trading loss arose in the 12 months immediately before the company ceased to trade.

Any possible s 393A(1) claim for the period of the loss must be made before any excess loss can be carried back to a previous period.

Any carry-back is to more recent periods before earlier periods. Relief for earlier losses is given before relief for later losses.

A claim for relief against current or prior period profits must be made within two years of the end of the accounting period in which the loss arose. Any claim must be for the whole loss (to the extent that profits are available to relieve it). The loss can however be reduced by not claiming full capital allowances, so that higher capital allowances are given (on higher tax written down values) in future years. Any loss remaining unrelieved may be carried forward under s 393(1) to set against future profits of the same trade.

Activity 12.3

Helix Ltd has the following results.

		Year ended	
	30.9.02	*30.9.03*	*30.9.04*
	£	£	£
Trading profit/(loss)	10,500	10,000	(35,000)
Bank interest	500	500	500
Chargeable gains	0	0	4,000
Charges on income:			
Gift Aid donation	250	250	250

Show the PCTCT for all the years affected assuming that s 393A(1) loss relief is claimed. Assume the provisions of FA 2003 continue to apply. Show the amount of loss of remaining to carry forward at 1.10.04.

4 Reliefs for deficits on non-trading loan relationships

A deficit on a non-trading loan relationship may be set, in whole or part, against any profit of the same accounting period. Relief is given after relief for any trading loss brought forward but before relief is given for a trading loss of the same or future period.

Activity 12.4

Witherspoon Ltd has the following results for the two years ended 31 December 2003:

	2002	*2003*
	£	£
Trading profit/(loss)	40,000	(12,000)
Trading losses brought forward	(20,000)	–
Bank interest receivable	2,000	
Interest payable on a loan for non-trading purposes	(11,000)	

Show how relief may be given for the deficit on the non-trading loan relationship in the year ended 31.12.02.

A deficit may be set against non-trading income arising from loan relationships in the previous twelve months provided the income has not been reduced by loss relief in respect of a period prior to the deficit period.

A deficit may be set against the non-trading profits of the company in the following accounting period. Non-trade profits represent PCTCT less Schedule D Case I.

Any deficits unrelieved after claiming the above reliefs are automatically carried forward and treated as a deficit for the next accounting period.

A claim to set the deficit against income of the same or previous accounting period must be made within two years of the deficit period. A claim to use the deficit against income in the following accounting period must be made within two years of the accounting period in which the deficit is used.

A company can choose how much deficit to relieve in the current period, how much to carry back and how much to carry forward: unlike s 393A relief, these are not all or nothing claims, and the company can choose to carry back a deficit even if it does not claim current period relief.

5 Choosing loss reliefs

Several alternative loss reliefs may be available. In making a choice consider:

- **The rate at which relief will be obtained:**

  (i) 30% at the full rate (FY 2003)
  (ii) 19% at the small companies' rate (FY 2003)
  (iii) 0% at the starting rate (FY 2003)
  (iv) 23.75% if the starting rate marginal relief applies (FY 2003)
  (v) 32.75% if the small companies' marginal relief applies (FY 2003)

  We previously outlined how the 23.75% and 32.75% marginal rates are calculated. Remember these are just marginal rates of tax; they are never actually used in computing a company's corporation tax.

  Remember that the rates of corporation tax were different in earlier financial years.

- **How quickly relief will be obtained**: s 393A(1) relief is quicker than s 393(1) relief.
- **The extent to which relief for gift aid donations might be lost.**

When choosing between loss relief claims ALWAYS consider the rate of tax 'saved' by the loss first.

If in the current period the loss 'saves' 19% tax but if carried forward saves 30% tax then a carry forward is the better choice (even though the timing of loss relief is later).

If the tax saved now is 30% and in the future is the same (30%) THEN consider timing (in this example a current claim is better timing wise).

So, first - rate of tax saved, second - timing.

Activity 12.5

M Ltd has had the following results.

	Year ended 31 March		
	2002	*2003*	*2004*
	£	£	£
Schedule D Case I/(loss)	2,000	(1,000,000)	200,000
Chargeable gains	35,000	750,000	0
Gift aid donations paid	30,000	20,000	20,000

Recommend appropriate loss relief claims, and compute the mainstream corporation tax for all years based on your recommendations. Assume that future years' profits will be similar to those of the year ended 31 March 2004.

Assume that tax rates and allowances for FY 2003 apply to all years.

6 End of chapter activity

Activity 12.6

Daley plc has had the following results since it started to trade.

	Year ended 31.12.01	*Six months ended 30.6.02*	*Year ended 30.6.03*
	£	£	£
Schedule D Case I/(loss)	109,000	85,000	(200,000)
Schedule D Case III	11,000	12,000	14,000
Chargeable gains/ (allowable losses)	(5,000)	2,000	(1,000)
Gift aid donation	Nil	3,000	1,000

Reliefs are always claimed as early as possible. There are no associated companies.

Task

Compute the corporation tax liability for all three periods, and show all amounts to be carried forward at 30 June 2003. Assume that tax rates and allowances for FY 2003 apply to all years.

Key learning points

- ☑ **Reliefs for losses** depend on the **type of loss** involved.
- ☑ **Capital losses** can only be set against **capital gains** of the **same or future accounting periods.**
- ☑ **Schedule A losses** are first set-off against **other income and gains** of the **current period** and any **excess is carried forward** as a **Schedule A loss**.
- ☑ **Trading losses** can be **carried forward** against **future Sch D Case I income**.
- ☑ **S393A relief** is given against **total profits before charges**. Gift aid donations remain unrelieved.
- ☑ **S393A relief** may be given against **current period profits** and **against profits of the previous 12 months** (or, **previous 36 months** if the **trade is ceasing**).
- ☑ A claim for **current period S393A relief can be made without a claim for carryback.**
- ☑ However, if a **loss is to be carried back** a claim for **current period relief must have been made first**.
- ☑ A **deficit on a non-trading loan relationship** may be relieved in the **same accounting period**, **previous 12 months or following accounting period**.
- ☑ Any **remaining deficit** is automatically **carried forward**.
- ☑ When **selecting a loss relief**, firstly consider the **rate at which relief is obtained** and, secondly, the **timing of the relief**.

Quick quiz

1 Against what profits may trading losses carried forward be set against?

2 On 1 April 2003 MB Ltd had Schedule D Case I losses of £50,000 brought forward:

MB Ltd's results for the year to 31 March 2004 were:

	£
Schedule D Case I profits	40,000
Schedule A profits	25,000
Capital gain	2,000

What amount, if any, of the Schedule D loss remains to be carried forward at 31 March 2004?

A £10,000
B £5,000
C £3,000
D £Nil

3 CR Ltd has the following results for the two years to 31 March 2004:

	Year ended	
	31.3.03	*31.3.04*
	£	£
Schedule D Case I profit (loss)	170,000	(320,000)
Schedule D Case III	5,000	50,000
Capital gain (loss)	(20,000)	12,000
Gift aid payment	5,000	5,000

What amount of Schedule D Case I losses remain to be carried forward at 1.4.04 assuming that all possible s 393A ICTA 1988 claims are made?

A £83,000
B £95,000
C £100,000
D £105,000

4 Which is the first thing to think about when selecting a loss relief – the rate at which the relief is obtained or the timing of the relief?

Answers to quick quiz

1 Profits from the same trade.

2 A The Schedule D Case I loss can be set only against the Schedule D Case I profits of £40,000. The balance of the loss must be carried forward for relief against future Schedule D Case I profits.

3 B

	Year ended	
	31.3.03	*31.3.04*
	£	£
Schedule D I profits	170,000	–
Schedule D III	5,000	50,000
	175,000	50,000
Less: s 393A loss	(175,000)	(50,000)
	–	–

Loss £320,000 – £50,000 – £175,000 = £95,000

Capital losses are carried forward to set against future capital gains. There are capital losses of £8,000 remaining to be carried forward at 1.4.04.

S393A losses are deducted before gift aid donations in both the year of the loss and in previous years.

4 Rate of relief, then timing.

Activity checklist

This checklist shows which performance criteria is covered by each activity in this chapter. Tick off each activity as you complete it.

Activity		
12.1	☐	This activity deals with Performance Criteria 18.4.B: Set-off and deduct loss reliefs and charges correctly.
12.2	☐	This activity deals with Performance Criteria 18.4.B: Set-off and deduct loss reliefs and charges correctly.
12.3	☐	This activity deals with Performance Criteria 18.4.B: Set-off and deduct loss reliefs and charges correctly.
12.4	☐	This activity deals with Performance Criteria 18.4.B: Set-off and deduct loss reliefs and charges correctly.
12.5	☐	This activity deals with Performance Criteria 18.4.B: Set-off and deduct loss reliefs and charges correctly.
12.6	☐	This activity deals with Performance Criteria 18.4.B: Set-off and deduct loss reliefs and charges correctly.

PART D

National Insurance

chapter 13

National insurance

Contents

Performance criteria

18.4 E Identify the National Insurance Contributions payable by employers

18.2 F Identify the National Insurance Contributions payable by self-employed individuals

Range statement

18.2 Clients: sole traders, partnerships

Knowledge and understanding

18 Calculation of National Insurance Contributions payable by self employed persons and employers of not contracted out employees (Elements 18.2 & 18.4)

1 National insurance for employers

1.1 Introduction

Four classes of national insurance contribution (NIC) exist, as set out below.

(a) **Class 1**. This is divided into:

(i) **Primary**, paid by employees
(ii) **Secondary, Class 1A and Class 1B** paid by employers

(b) **Class 2**. Paid by the self-employed

(c) **Class 3**. Voluntary contributions (paid to maintain rights to certain state benefits)

(d) **Class 4.** Paid by the self-employed

Class 1 Primary, Class 1B and Class 3 contributions are outside the scope of your syllabus.

1.2 Class 1 secondary contributions

The National Insurance Contributions Office (NICO), which is part of the Inland Revenue, examines employers' records and procedures to ensure that the correct amounts of NICs are collected.

Employers pay NICs related to the employee's earnings. Employers' contributions are deductible Schedule D Case I expenses.

'Earnings' broadly comprise gross pay, excluding benefits which cannot be turned into cash by surrender (eg holidays). No deduction is made for employee pension contributions deducted from the employee's pay.

An employer's contribution to an employee's approved personal pension or an approved occupational pension scheme is excluded from the definition of 'earnings'.

There are a number of exclusions from NIC 'earnings' including:

(a) Payment of personal incidental expenses up to £5 (UK)/£10 (non-UK) a night for every night the employee is away from home.

(b) Relocation expenses (although expenses exceeding £8,000 are subject to class 1A NICs as described below).

(c) An expense with a business purpose. For example, if an employee is reimbursed for business travel or for staying in a hotel on the employer's business this is not normally 'earnings'. However, if an employee is reimbursed for his own home telephone charges the reimbursed cost of private calls (and all reimbursed rental) is earnings.

(d) Where an employer reimburses an employee using his own car for business mileage, the earnings element is the excess of the mileage rate paid over the Inland Revenue 'up to 10,000 business miles' 'approved mileage rate'(currently 40p). This applies even where business mileage exceeds 10,000 pa.

(e) In general, non cash vouchers (eg book tokens, high street store vouchers) are subject to NICs. However, the following are exempt.

- Childcare vouchers for children up to 16 years old
- Vouchers for the use of sports and recreational facilities (where tax exempt)
- Vouchers for meals on the employer's premises
- Other meal vouchers to a maximum of 15p per day
- Transport vouchers where the employee earns less than £8,500 a year.

1.3 Rates of contribution

The rates of contribution for 2003/04, and the income bands to which they apply, are set out in the Rates and Allowances Tables in this text.

Employers pay secondary contributions of 12.8% on earnings above the earnings threshold of £4,615 or the equivalent monthly or weekly limit. There is no upper limit.

There is a lower earnings limit of £4,004 (or the equivalent monthly or weekly limit). The significance of the lower earnings limit (LEL) is that 'nil rate contributions' will be credited where the employee's earnings are between the LEL and the earnings threshold. These 'nil rate contributions' frank the employee's record and so create an entitlement to certain state benefits.

There are different rules for employees who are contracted out of the State Second Pension but these are not in your syllabus.

NICs are calculated in relation to an earnings period. This is the period to which earnings paid to an employee are deemed to relate. Where earnings are paid at regular intervals, the earnings period will generally be equated with the payment interval, for example a week or a month. An earnings period cannot usually be less than seven days long.

NIC for employees is calculated on a non-cumulative basis, so only the earnings in the earnings period are considered. The monthly earnings threshold is the annual limit divided by 12. The limit is rounded up to the nearest £1.

Activity 13.1

Sally works for Red plc. She is paid £2,750 per month. Show the secondary class 1 contributions paid by Red plc for 2003/04.

Activity 13.2

Mark works for Black plc. He is paid the following in one week in 2003/04.

	£
Wages	200
Business travel reimbursed	20
Bonus paid in Marks & Spencer plc vouchers	50
Relocation expenses	2,000

Show the secondary contributions payable by Black plc for the week.

1.4 Class 1A contributions

Employers must pay Class 1A NIC in respect of most taxable benefits for example, private medical insurance. However, benefits are exempt if they are:

- Within class 1, or
- Provided for employees earning at a rate of less than £8,500 a year

In addition, all kinds of childcare provision, for example, where the employer contracts for places in commercial nurseries, are exempt from Class 1A NICs. However, if an employer provides cash to meet or reimburse childcare expenses the cash is 'earnings' for employer Class 1 NIC purposes. There is also exemption for certain other minor benefits (eg small private use of employer's assets).

Class 1A contributions are paid at 12.8% of the taxable value of the benefit. There is no earnings threshold.

Class 1A contributions are collected annually in arrears, and are due by 19 July following the tax year.

Activity 13.3

Nitin's employer provides him with a company car throughout 2003/04.

The taxable value of the benefit arising is £10,000.

Calculate the Class 1A national insurance contributions that will be payable by Nitin's employer.

2 National insurance for the self employed

2.1 Class 2 contributions

The self employed (sole traders and partners) **pay NICs in two ways. Class 2 contributions are payable at a flat rate.** It is possible, however, to be excepted from payment of Class 2 contributions (or to get contributions already paid repaid) if annual profits are less than £4,095. **The Class 2 rate for 2003/04 is £2.00 a week.**

Self employed people must register with the Inland Revenue for Class 2 contributions within three months of the end of the month in which they start self employment. People who fail to register may incur a £100 penalty.

2.2 Class 4 contributions

Additionally, **the self employed pay Class 4 NICs, based on the level of the individual's business profits.**

Main rate Class 4 NICs are calculated by applying a fixed percentage (8% for 2003/04) to the individual's profits between the lower limit (£4,615 for 2003/04) and the upper limit (£30,940 for 2003/04). Additional rate contributions are 1% (for 2003/04) on profits above that limit.

Activity 13.4

A sole trader had profits of £13,950 for 2003/04. Show his Class 4 NIC liability.

Activity 13.5

An individual's trade profits were £35,000. Show the Class 4 NICs due.

For Class 4 NIC purposes, profits are the business profits taxable under Schedule D Case I or II, less:

(a) **Trading losses**
(b) **Trade charges on income**

There is no deduction for personal pension premiums.

Class 4 NICs are collected by the Inland Revenue. They are paid **at the same time as the associated income tax liability**. This will be covered later in this text. Interest is charged on overdue contributions.

3 End of chapter activity

Activity 13.6

(a) Arnold is employed by Julius Ltd. In 2003/04, his remuneration package consists of the following.

Monthly salary	£2,500
Company car – taxable benefit	£5,000
Childcare vouchers	£2,250
Private medical insurance – taxable benefit	£750

Task

Show the national insurance contributions payable by Julius Ltd for 2003/04

(b) Marcia is a self-employed florist. In 2003/04, her profits are £38,000.

Task

Show the total national insurance contributions payable by Marcia.

Key learning points

- ☑ **Class 1 secondary national insurance contributions** are paid by employers.
- ☑ Employers pay NICs related to the **employee's earnings**.
- ☑ '**Earnings**' broadly comprise **gross pay** excluding benefits which cannot be turned into cash.
- ☑ There are a number of **exemptions**, for example **relocation expenses, business travel.**
- ☑ Secondary contributions are payable at **12.8%** above the **earnings threshold**.
- ☑ NICs are calculated in relation to **earnings periods**, for example **weekly** or **monthly**.
- ☑ **Class 1A contributions** are payable on **benefits** provided to employees.
- ☑ **Self employed individuals** pay **Class 2** and **Class 4** contributions.
- ☑ **Class 2** contributions are **£2 per week**.
- ☑ **Class 4** contributions are payable at **8%** between **upper and lower limits**.
- ☑ **Additional class 4** contributions are payable at **1%** above the **upper limit**.

Quick quiz

1 Which, if either, of the following types of expenses incurred by a company are allowable for Schedule D Case I purposes?

1 Secondary Class 1 NICs incurred in respect of staff working in the business.

2 The cost of staff entertainment

A 1 only
B 2 only
C Both 1 and 2 are allowable
D Neither 1 nor 2 are allowable

2 On what are Class 1A contributions paid?

3 How are Class 4 NICs calculated?

Answers to quick quiz

1 C Both types of expense are allowable.

2 Class 1A NICs are paid by an employer on taxable benefits.

3 The main rate is a fixed percentage of an individual's profits between an upper and lower limit. The additional rate applies above the upper limit.

Activity checklist

This checklist shows which performance criteria, range statement or knowledge and understanding point is covered by each activity in this chapter. Tick off each activity as you complete it.

Activity		
13.1	☐	This activity deals with Performance Criteria 18.4.E: identify the National Insurance Contributions paid by employers
13.2	☐	This activity deals with Performance Criteria 18.4.E: identify the National Insurance Contributions paid by employers
13.3	☐	This activity deals with Performance Criteria 18.4.E: identify the National Insurance Contributions paid by employers
13.4	☐	This activity deals with Performance Criteria 18.2.F: identify the National Insurance Contributions paid by self-employed individuals
13.5	☐	This activity deals with Performance Criteria 18.2.F: identify the National Insurance Contributions paid by self-employed individuals
13.6	☐	This activity deals with Knowledge and Understanding point 18: calculation of national insurance contributions payable by self-employed persons and employers of not contracted out employees.

PART E

Administration

chapter 14

Administration of income tax and CGT

Contents

Performance criteria

18.2 E Identify the due dates of payment of Income Tax by unincorporated businesses, including payments on account

18.2 G Complete correctly the self employed and partnership supplementary pages for the tax return for individuals, together with relevant claims and elections and submit them within statutory time limits.

18.1 D, 18.3 E

Ensure that computations and submissions are made in accordance with current tax law and take account of current inland Revenue Practice.

18.1 G, 18.2 J, 18.3 H, 18.4 J

Maintain client confidentiality at all times

18.1 F, 18.2 I, 18.3 G

Give timely and constructive advice on the maintenance of accounts and the recording of information relevant to tax returns

Range statement

18.2 Clients: sole traders, partnerships

Knowledge and understanding

19 Self assessment including payment of tax and filing of returns for unincorporated businesses and companies (Elements 18.2 & 18.4)

1 The administration of taxation

The **Treasury** formally imposes and collects taxation. The management of the Treasury is the responsibility of the Chancellor of the Exchequer. The Treasury appoint the **Board of Inland Revenue** (sometimes referred to as the **Commissioners of Inland Revenue (CIR)**), a body of civil servants. The Board administers income tax, capital gains tax and corporation tax.

For income tax purposes, the UK has historically been divided into **tax districts**. These are being merged into larger areas, with separate offices in each **area** being responsible for different aspects of the Revenue's work. Each area is headed by an **area director**.

The Revenue staff were historically described as '**Inspectors**' and '**Collectors**', although these terms are now less commonly used. The legislation now commonly refers to an '**officer of the board**' rather than an 'inspector' when setting out the Revenue's powers. They are responsible for supervising the self-assessment system and agreeing tax liabilities. Collectors may be referred to a **receivables management officers**, and are local officers who are responsible for following up amounts of unpaid tax referred to then by the **Inland Revenue Accounts Office**.

The structure of Revenue offices is also being changed. **Taxpayer service offices** are being set up to do routine checking, computation *and* collection work, while **Taxpayer district offices** investigate selected accounts and enforce the payment of tax. **Taxpayer assistance offices** handle enquiries and arrange specialist help for taxpayers.

The **General Commissioners** (not to be confused with the CIR) are appointed by the Lord Chancellor to hear **appeals** against Revenue decisions. They are part-time and unpaid. They are appointed for a local area (a **division**). They appoint a clerk who is often a lawyer or accountant and who is paid for his services by the Board of Inland Revenue.

The **Special Commissioners** are also appointed by the Lord Chancellor. They are full-time paid professionals. They generally hear the more complex appeals.

Many taxpayers arrange for their accountants to prepare and submit their tax returns. The taxpayer is still the person responsible for submitting the return and for paying whatever tax becomes due: the accountant is only acting as the taxpayer's agent.

2 Notification of chargeability

Individuals who are chargeable to tax for any tax year and who have not received a notice to file a return are, in general, required to give notice of chargeability to an officer of the Board within six months from the end of the year ie by 5 October 2004 for 2003/4.

The maximum mitigable penalty where notice of chargeability is not given is 100% of the tax assessed which is not paid on or before 31 January following the tax year.

3 Tax returns and keeping records

3.1 Tax returns

The tax return comprises a Tax Form, together with supplementary pages for particular sources of income. You will deal with the completion of the tax return if you study Unit 19 *Preparing Personal Tax Computations.*

Partnerships must file a separate return which includes 'a partnership statement' showing the firm's profits, losses, proceeds from the sale of assets, tax suffered, tax credits, charges on income and the division of all these amounts between partners. The partnership return must normally be made by the senior partner (or whoever else may be nominated by the partnership), but the Revenue have power to require any, all, or some of the partners (or their nominated successors) to submit the return.

A partnership return must include a declaration of the name, residence and tax reference of each partner, as well as the usual declaration that the return is correct and complete to the best of the signatory's knowledge.

Each partner must then include his share of partnership profits on his personal tax return. We have included the supplementary pages to the income tax return that must be completed in respect of partnership profits in the appendix to this text. Have a look at them now. You may have to complete these pages in your assessment. You can practice this when you try the activities in BPP's Unit 18 Assessment Kit. Please see page (vi) for a note regarding the version of the form we have used.

3.2 Time limit for submission of tax returns

The **filing due date for filing a tax return is the later of:**

- **31 January following the end of the tax year which the return covers.**
- **three months after the notice to file the return was issued.**

If an individual wishes the Revenue to prepare the self-assessment on their behalf, earlier deadlines apply. The filing date is then the later of:

- **30 September following the tax year; eg for 2003/04, by 30 September 2004.**
- **two months after notice to file the return was issued.**

Since a partnership return does not include a self-assessment these revised deadlines do not apply to partnership returns. This may, of course, create problems if one of the partners wishes the Revenue to complete his personal self-assessment.

3.3 Penalties for late filing

3.3.1 Individual returns

The maximum penalties for delivering a tax return after the filing due date are:

(a)	**Return up to 6 months late:**	**£100**
(b)	**Return more than 6 months but not more than 12 months late:**	**£200**
(c)	**Return more than 12 months late:**	**£200 + 100% of the tax liability**

In addition, the General or Special Commissioners can direct that a maximum penalty of £60 per day be imposed where failure to deliver a tax return continues after notice of the direction has been given to the taxpayer. In this case the additional £100 penalty, imposed under (b) if the return is more than six months late, is not charged.

The fixed penalties of £100/£200 can be set aside by the Commissioners if they are satisfied that the taxpayer had a reasonable excuse for not delivering the return. If the tax liability shown on the return is less than the fixed penalties, the fixed penalty is reduced to the amount of the tax liability. The tax geared penalty is mitigable by the Revenue or the Commissioners.

3.3.2 Partnership returns

The maximum penalties for late delivery of a partnership tax return are as shown above, save that there is no tax-geared penalty if the return is more than 12 months late. The penalties apply separately to each partner.

3.3.3 Reasonable excuse

A taxpayer only has a reasonable excuse for a late filing if a default occurred because of a factor outside his control. This might be non-receipt of the return by the taxpayer, serious illness of the taxpayer or a close relative, or destruction of records through fire and flood. Illness is only accepted as a reasonable excuse if the taxpayer was taking timeous steps to complete the return, and if the return is filed as soon as possible after the illness etc.

3.3.4 Returns rejected as incomplete

If a return, filed before the filing date, is rejected by the Revenue as incomplete later than 14 days before the filing deadline of 31 January, a late filing penalty will not be charged if the return is completed and returned within 14 days of the rejection. This only applies if the omission from the return was a genuine error. It does not apply if a return was deliberately filed as incomplete in the hope of extending the time limit.

3.4 Standard accounting information

'Three line' accounts (ie income less expenses equals profit) only need be included on the tax return of businesses with a turnover (or gross rents from property) of less than £15,000 pa. This is not as helpful as it might appear, as underlying records must still be kept for tax purposes (disallowable items etc) when producing three line accounts.

Large businesses with a turnover of at least £5 million which have used figures rounded to the nearest £1,000 in producing their published accounts can compute their profits to the nearest £1,000 for tax purposes.

The tax return requires trading results to be presented in a standard format. Although there is no requirement to submit accounts with the return, accounts may be filed. If accounts accompany the return, the Revenue's power to raise a discovery assessment (see below) is restricted.

3.5 Keeping of records

All taxpayers must keep and retain all records required to enable them to make and deliver a correct tax return.

Records must be retained until the later of:

(a) (i) **5 years after the 31 January following the tax year where the taxpayer is in business** (as a sole trader or partner or letting property)

(ii) **1 year after the 31 January following the tax year otherwise**

(b) provided notice to deliver a return is given before the date in (a):

(i) **the time after which enquiries by the Inland Revenue into the return can no longer be commenced**

(ii) **the date any such enquiries have been completed**

Where a person receives a notice to deliver a tax return after the normal record keeping period has expired, he must keep all records in his possession at that time until no enquiries can be raised in respect of the return or until such enquiries have been completed.

The maximum (mitigable) penalty for each failure to keep and retain records is £3,000 per tax year/accounting period.

The duty to preserve records can generally be satisfied by retaining copies of original documents except that original documents which show tax deducted or creditable, (eg. dividend certificates) must be kept.

Record keeping failures are taken into account in considering the mitigation of other penalties. Where the record keeping failure is taken into account in this way, a penalty will normally only be sought in serious and exceptional cases where, for example, records have been destroyed deliberately to obstruct an enquiry or there has been a history of serious record keeping failures.

4 Self-assessment and claims

4.1 Self-assessment

Every personal tax return must be accompanied by a self-assessment.

A self assessment is a calculation of the amount of taxable income and gains after deducting reliefs and allowances, and a calculation of the income tax and CGT payable after taking into account tax deducted at source and tax credits.

The self-assessment calculation may either be made by the taxpayer or the Revenue. If a return is filed within certain time limits (normally, 30 September following the tax year to which it relates, see above) an officer of the board must make a self-assessment on the taxpayer's behalf on the basis of the information contained in the return. He must send a copy of the assessment to the taxpayer. These assessments, even though raised by the Revenue, are treated as self-assessments.

If the taxpayer files a return after the above deadline but without completing the self-assessment, the Revenue will not normally reject the return as incomplete. However the Revenue are not then bound to complete the self-assessment in time to notify the taxpayer of the tax falling due on the normal due date (generally the following 31 January), and it is the taxpayer's responsibility to estimate and pay his tax on time.

Within nine months of receiving a tax return, the Revenue can amend a taxpayer's self-assessment to correct any obvious errors or mistakes; whether errors of principle, arithmetical mistakes or otherwise. The taxpayer does have the right to reject any corrections of obvious errors made by the Revenue.

Within 12 months of the due filing date (*not* the actual filing date), the taxpayer can give notice to an officer to amend his tax return and self-assessment. Such amendments by taxpayers are not confined to the correction of obvious errors. They may not be made whilst the Revenue are making enquiries into the return.

The same rules apply to corrections and amendments of partnership statements and stand alone claims (see below).

4.2 Claims

4.2.1 General rules

All claims and elections which can be made in a tax return must be made in this manner if a return has been issued. A claim for any relief, allowance or repayment of tax must normally be quantified at the time it is made.

Certain claims have a time limit that is longer than the time limit for filing or amending a tax return. A claim may therefore be made after the time limit for amending the tax return has expired. Claims not made on the tax return are referred to as **'stand alone' claims**.

Claims made on a tax return are subject to the administrative rules governing returns, for the making of corrections, enquiries etc.

Stand alone claims and elections not made in a tax return are governed by provisions which are similar to the rules governing the treatment of tax returns.

4.2.2 Claims involving more than one year

Self-assessment is intended to avoid the need to reopen earlier years, so relief should be given for the year of the claim. This rule can best be explained by considering a claim to carry back a trading loss to an earlier year of assessment:

(a) the claim for relief is treated as made in relation to the year in which the loss was actually incurred;

(b) the amount of any tax repayment due is calculated in terms of tax of the earlier year to which the loss is being carried back; and

(c) any tax repayment etc is treated as relating to the later year in which the loss was actually incurred.

4.2.3 Error or mistake claims

An error or mistake claim may be made for errors in a return or partnership statement where tax would otherwise be overcharged. The claim may not be made where the tax liability was computed in accordance with practice prevailing at the time the return or statement was made.

An error or mistake claim may not be made in respect of a claim. If a taxpayer makes an error or mistake in a claim, he may make a supplementary claim within the time limits allowed for the original claim.

The taxpayer may appeal to the Special Commissioners against any refusal of an error or mistake claim.

5 Payment of tax, interest and penalties

5.1 Payments of tax

The self-assessment system may result in the taxpayer making three payments of income tax:

Date	**Payment**
31 January in the tax year	**1st payment on account**
31 July after the tax year	**2nd payment on account**
31 January after the tax year	**Final payment to settle the remaining liability**

Payments on account are usually required where the income tax due in the previous year exceeded the amount of income tax deducted at source; this excess is known as **'the relevant amount'**. Income tax deducted at source includes tax suffered, PAYE deductions and tax credits on dividends.

The payments on account are each equal to 50% of the relevant amount for the previous year.

Activity 14.1

Gordon paid tax for 2003/04 as follows:

		£
Total amount of income tax assessed		9,200
This included:	Tax deducted under PAYE	1,700
	Tax deducted on savings income	1,500
He also paid:	Capital gains tax	4,800

How much are the payments on account for 2004/2005?

Payments on account are not required if the relevant amount falls below a de minimis limit of £500. Also, payments on account are not required from taxpayers who paid 80% or more of their tax liability for the previous year through PAYE or other deduction at source arrangements.

If the previous year's liability increases following an amendment to a self-assessment, or the raising of a discovery assessment, an adjustment is made to the payments on account due.

Payments on account are normally fixed by reference to the previous year's tax liability but if a taxpayer expects his liability to be lower than this **he may claim to reduce his payments on account to:**

(a) a **stated amount**, or
(b) **nil.**

The claim must state the reason why he believes his tax liability will be lower, or nil.

If the taxpayer's eventual liability is higher than he estimated he will have reduced the payments on account too far. Although the payments on account will not be adjusted, the taxpayer will suffer an interest charge on late payment.

A penalty of the difference between the reduced payment on account and the correct payment on account may be levied if the reduction was claimed fraudulently or negligently.

The balance of any income tax together with all CGT due for a year, is normally payable on or before the 31 January following the year.

Activity 14.2

Giles made payments on account for 2003/04 of £6,500 each on 31 January 2004 and 31 July 2004, based on his 2002/03 liability. He then calculates his total income tax for 2003/04 at £18,000 of which £2,750 was deducted at source. In addition he calculated that his CGT liability for disposals in 2003/04 is £5,120.

What is the final payment due for 2003/04?

In one case the due date for the final payment is later than 31 January following the end of the year. **If a taxpayer has notified chargeability by 5 October but the notice to file a tax return is not issued before 31 October, then the due date for the payment is three months after the issue of the notice.**

Tax charged in an amended self-assessment is usually payable on the later of:

(a) the normal due date, generally 31 January following the end of the tax year; and
(b) the day following 30 days after the making of the revised self-assessment.

Tax charged on a discovery assessment is due thirty days after the issue of the assessment.

5.2 Surcharges

Surcharges are normally imposed in respect of amounts paid late:

	Paid	*Surcharge*
(a)	within 28 days of due date:	none
(b)	more than 28 days but not more than six months after the due date:	5%
(c)	more than six months after the due date:	10%

Surcharges apply to:

(a) balancing payments of income tax and any CGT under self-assessment or a determination
(b) tax due on the amendment of a self-assessment
(c) tax due on a discovery assessment

The surcharge rules do not apply to late payments on account.

No surcharge will be applied where the late paid tax liability has attracted a tax-geared penalty on the failure to notify chargeability to tax, or the failure to submit a return, or on the making of an incorrect return (including a partnership return).

5.3 Interest

Interest is chargeable on late payment of both payments on account and balancing payments. In both cases interest runs from the due date until the day before the actual date of payment.

Interest is charged from 31 January following the tax year (or the normal due date for the balancing payment, in the rare event that this is later), even if this is before the due date for payment on:

(a) tax payable following an amendment to a self-assessment;
(b) tax payable in a discovery assessment; and
(c) tax postponed under an appeal which becomes payable.

Since a determination (see below) is treated as if it were a self-assessment, interest runs from 31 January following the tax year.

If a taxpayer claims to reduce his payments on account and there is still a final payment to be made, interest is normally charged on the payments on account as if each of those payments had been the lower of:

(a) the reduced amount, plus 50% of the final income tax liability; and
(b) the amount which would have been payable had no claim for reduction been made.

Activity 14.3

Herbert's payments on account for 2003/04 based on his income tax liability for 2002/03 were £4,500 each. However, when he submitted his 2002/03 income tax return in January 2004, he made a claim to reduce the payments on account for 2003/04 to £3,500 each. The first payment on account was made on 29 January 2004, and the second on 12 August 2004.

Herbert filed his 2003/04 tax return in December 2004. The return showed that his tax liabilities for 2003/04 (before deducting payments on account) were income tax: £10,000, capital gains tax: £2,500. Herbert paid the balance of tax due of £5,500 on 19 February 2005.

For what periods and in respect of what amounts will Herbert be charged interest?

Where interest has been charged on late payments on account but the final balancing settlement for the year produces a repayment, all or part of the original interest is remitted.

5.4 Repayment of tax and repayment supplement

Tax is repaid when claimed unless a greater payment of tax is due in the following 30 days, in which case it is set-off against that payment.

Interest is paid on overpayments of:

(a) payments on account
(b) final payments of income tax and CGT, including tax deducted at source or tax credits on dividends
(c) penalties and surcharges

Repayment supplement runs from the original date of payment (even if this was prior to the due date), until the day before the date the repayment is made. Income tax deducted at source and tax credits are treated as if they were paid on the 31 January following the tax year concerned.

6 Enquiries, determinations and discovery assessments

6.1 Enquiries into returns

An officer of the Board has a limited period within which to commence enquiries into a return or amendment. The officer must give written notice of his intention by:

(a) the **first anniversary of the due filing date (not the actual filing date)**; or

(b) **if the return is filed after the due filing date, the quarter day following the first anniversary of the actual filing date. The quarter days are 31 January, 30 April, 31 July and 31 October.**

If the taxpayer amended the return after the due filing date, the enquiry 'window' extends to the quarter day following the first anniversary of the date the amendment was filed. Where the enquiry was not raised within the limit which would have applied had no amendment been filed, the enquiry is restricted to matters contained in the amendment.

Enquiries may be made into partnership returns (or amendments) upon which a partnership statement is based within the same time limits. A notice to enquire into a partnership return is deemed to incorporate a notice, to enquire into each individual partner's return.

Enquiries may also be made into stand alone claims, provided notice is given by the officer of the Board by the later of:

(a) The quarter day following the first anniversary of the making or amending of the claim

(b) 31 January next but one following the tax year, if the claim relates to a tax year

(c) the first anniversary of the end of the period to which a claim relates if it relates to a period other than a tax year

The procedures for enquiries into claims mirror those for enquiries into returns.

The officer does not have to have, or give, any reason for raising an enquiry. In particular the taxpayer will not be advised whether he has been selected at random for an audit. Enquiries may be full enquiries, or may be limited to 'aspect' enquiries.

In the course of his enquiries **the officer may require the taxpayer to produce documents, accounts or any other information required. The taxpayer can appeal to the Commissioners.**

During the course of his enquiries an officer may amend a self-assessment if it appears that insufficient tax has been charged and an immediate amendment is necessary to prevent a loss to the Crown. This might apply if, for example, there is a possibility that the taxpayer will emigrate.

If a return is under enquiry the Revenue may postpone any repayment due as shown in the return until the enquiry is complete. The Revenue have discretion to make a provisional repayment but there is no facility to appeal if the repayment is withheld.

At any time during the course of an enquiry, the taxpayer may apply to the Commissioners to require the officer to notify the taxpayer within a specified period that the enquiries are complete, unless the officer can demonstrate that he has reasonable grounds for continuing the enquiry.

If both sides agree, disputes concerning a point of law can be resolved through litigation without having to wait until the whole enquiry is complete.

An officer must issue a notice that the enquiries are complete, and a statement of the amount of tax that he considers should be included in the tax return, or the amounts which should be contained in the partnership statement, or the amount of the claim. The taxpayer then has thirty days to amend his self-assessment, partnership statement or claim to give effect to the officer's conclusions. He may also make any other amendments that he could have made had the enquiry not been commenced (amendments may not be made whilst enquiries are in progress).

If the officer is not satisfied with the taxpayer's amendment he has thirty days in which to amend the self-assessment, partnership statement or claim. Also if a claim has been disallowed, but does not affect the self-assessment, he must advise the taxpayer of the extent to which it has been disallowed.

If the taxpayer is not satisfied with the officer's amendment he may, within 30 days, appeal to the Commissioners.

Once an enquiry is complete the officer cannot make further enquiries. The Revenue may, in limited circumstances, raise a discovery assessment if they believe that there has been a loss of tax (see below).

The majority of investigation cases are handled by local inspectors, but serious cases are dealt with by the Special Compliance Office.

Where an irregularity is detected, unless it appears to be of a very serious nature, the first overture will often be made by the local inspector writing to the taxpayer or his agent suggesting that he has reason to doubt that full and correct returns have been made and inviting the taxpayer's comments. Correspondence will be followed by interviews at which the inspector will try to collect further evidence, and the taxpayer's accountant may be asked to prepare a detailed report showing the estimated tax unpaid.

The Revenue use various methods to attempt to calculate undisclosed income. Gross profit margins either for previous periods or for similar businesses are standardly used. As a last resort, some indication can be derived from the taxpayer's personal assets. A growth in these, taken together with an assumed level of personal expenditure, can point to an unexplained source, presumably undisclosed income. A sensible taxpayer will co-operate with the Revenue as any resistance on his part at this stage will count heavily against him in the final assessment or penalties.

6.2 The Revenue's powers

The Revenue's powers include the following.

(a) **The power to call for documents of taxpayers and others.** The Revenue may require any person to produce any documents which may contain information relevant to any taxpayer's tax liability. The Revenue may also require the taxpayer to provide written answers about questions of fact. The Inspector must give the person holding the documents reasons for applying for the right to demand documents, unless the commissioner is satisfied that giving reasons would prejudice the assessment or collection of tax.

(b) **The power to call for papers of tax accountants**. The Revenue is not normally empowered to demand documents from the taxpayer's accountant. but if he has either:

   (i) been convicted of an offence in relation to tax
   (ii) been penalised for assisting in making an incorrect return

   the Revenue can, in certain circumstances, demand documents relating to the taxpayer's affairs. A tax accountant is anyone (including a barrister or solicitor) who helps a taxpayer to prepare or deliver documents for tax purposes.

(c) **The power of entry with a warrant to obtain documents**. Where there are reasonable grounds for suspecting that an offence involving fraud in connection with tax has been, is being or is about to be committed and that evidence is to be found on certain premises, a warrant can be obtained authorising an officer of the Board to search the premises and remove anything which he has reasonable cause to suppose may be required as evidence.

(d) **The power to obtain information about interest and dividends**. The Revenue can require details from banks and building societies.

6.3 Determinations

The Revenue may only raise enquiries if a return has been submitted.

If notice has been served on a taxpayer to submit a return but the return is not submitted by the due filing date, an officer of the Board may make a determination of the tax due. Such a determination must be made to the best of the officer's information and belief, and is then treated as if it were a self-assessment. This enables the officer to seek payment of tax, including payments on account for the following year and to charge interest.

6.4 Discovery assessments

If an officer of the Board discovers that profits have been omitted from assessment, that any assessment has become insufficient, or that any relief given is, or has become excessive, an assessment may be raised to recover the tax lost.

If the tax lost results from an error in the taxpayer's return but the return was made in accordance with prevailing practice at the time, no discovery assessment may be made.

A discovery assessment may only be raised where a return has been made if:

(a) there has been fraudulent or negligent conduct by the taxpayer or his agent

(b) at the time that enquiries into the return were completed, or could no longer be made, the officer did not have information to make him aware of the loss of tax

These rules do not prevent the Revenue from raising assessments in cases of genuine discoveries, but prevent assessments from being raised due to the Revenue's failure to make timely use of information or to a change of opinion on information made available.

6.5 Appeals and postponement of payment of tax

A taxpayer may appeal against an amendment to a self-assessment or partnership statement, or an amendment to or disallowance of a claim, following an enquiry, or against an assessment which is not a self-assessment, such as a discovery assessment.

The appeal must normally be made within 30 days of the amendment or self-assessment.

The notice of appeal must state the **grounds** of appeal. These may be stated in general terms. At the hearing the Commissioners may allow the appellant to put forward grounds not stated in his notice if they are satisfied that his omission was not wilful or unreasonable.

In some cases it may be possible to agree the point at issue by negotiation with the Revenue, in which case the appeal may be settled by agreement. If the appeal cannot be agreed, it will be heard by the General or Special Commissioners.

An appeal does not relieve the taxpayer of liability to pay tax on the normal due date unless he obtains a 'determination' of the Commissioners or agreement of the Inspector that payment of all or some of the tax may be postponed pending determination of the appeal. The amount not postponed is due 30 days after the determination or agreement is issued, if that is later than the normal due date.

If any part of the postponed tax becomes due a notice of the amount payable is issued and the amount is payable 30 days after the issue of the notice. Interest, however, is still payable from the normal due date.

7 Client confidentiality

Whenever you prepare accounts or returns on behalf of a client you should remember that you are bound by the ethical guideline of client confidentiality. This means that you should not discuss a client's affairs with third parties without the client's permission. You should also take care not to leave documents relating to a client's affairs in public places such as on trains or in restaurants.

Activity 14.4

Tim is a medical consultant. His total tax liability for 2002/03 was £16,800. Of this £7,200 was paid under the PAYE system, £800 was withheld at source from bank interest and £200 was suffered on dividends received during the year.

Tim's total tax liability for 2003/04 was £22,000. £7,100 of this was paid under PAYE system, £900 was withheld at source from bank interest and there was a £250 tax credit on dividends.

Tim did not make any claim in respect of his payments on account for 2003/04. The Revenue issued a 2003/04 tax return to Tim on 5 May 2004.

Task

State what payments Tim was required to make in respect of his 2003/04 tax liability and the due dates for the payment of these amounts.

Key learning points

- ☑ The **tax return** is due for filing by **31 January following the end of the tax year.**
- ☑ However, if the taxpayer wants the **Revenue to calculate tax**, he must file it by **30 September following the end of the tax year.**
- ☑ **Two payments on account** of income tax are due on **31 January in the tax year** and **31 July following the end of the tax year.**
- ☑ Payments on account are based on the **previous year's tax bill**.
- ☑ On **31 January following the end of the tax year**, the **balance** of any income tax is due.
- ☑ **CGT** is due to be paid on **31 January following the end of the tax year.**
- ☑ There is an extensive regime of **penalties**, **surcharges** and **interest**.
- ☑ The Revenue have extensive, but not unlimited, **powers to enquire into returns**.

Quick quiz

1 Julia is sent her 2003/04 tax return on 6 August 2004.

By what date must she file the tax return if she does not want to calculate her tax liability?

A 30 September 2004
B 5 October 2004
C 5 November 2004
D 31 January 2005

2 What penalty is due if a tax return is delivered 4 months late?

3 Christopher had a tax liability of £6,000 for 2002/03. In 2003/04, his tax liability was £10,000.

How is Christopher's tax liability for 2003/04 paid?

4 Oliver should have made a balancing payment of £10,000 on 31 January 2004. He actually paid it on 31 May 2004.

What surcharge is due?

Answers to quick quiz

1 B later of 30 September 2004 and 2 months after the issue of the tax return.

2 £100

3 Two payments of £3,000 each on 31 January 2004 and 31 July 2004, balance of £4,000 on 31 January 2005.

4 5% x £10,000 = £500

Activity checklist

This checklist shows which performance criteria is covered by each activity in this chapter. Tick off each activity as you complete it.

Activity		
14.1	☐	This activity deals with Performance Criteria 18.2.E: identify the due dates of payment of Income Tax by unincorporated businesses, including payments on account
14.2	☐	This activity deals with Performance Criteria 18.2.E: identify the due dates of payment of Income Tax by unincorporated businesses, including payments on account
14.3	☐	This activity deals with Performance Criteria 18.2.E: identify the due dates of payment of Income Tax by unincorporated businesses, including payments on account
14.4	☐	This activity deals with Performance Criteria 18.2.E: identify the due dates of payment of Income Tax by unincorporated businesses, including payments on account

chapter 15

Payment of tax by companies

Contents

Performance criteria

18.4 D Identify and set off income tax deductions and credits

18.4 F Identify the amount of Corporation Tax payable and the due dates of payment, including payments on account

18.4 G Complete corporation tax returns correctly and submit them, together with relevant claims and elections within statutory time limits

18.4 I Give timely and constructive advice to clients on the maintenance of accounts and the recording of information relevant to tax returns

Range statement

There are no additional contextual requirements in this element relevant to this chapter.

Knowledge and understanding

19 Self assessment including payment of tax and filing of returns for unincorporated businesses and companies (Elements 18.2 & 18.4)

1 Returns under the corporation tax self assessment system

1.1 Returns

A company's tax return (CT600) must include a self assessment of any tax payable.

A copy of the CTSA return form (CT 600) is included in the appendix to this text.

An obligation to file a return arises only when the company receives a notice requiring a return. A return is required for each accounting period ending during or at the end of the period specified in the notice requiring a return.

A company that does not receive a notice requiring a return must, if it is chargeable to tax, **notify the Revenue within twelve months of the end of the accounting period**. Failure to do so results in a maximum penalty equal to the tax unpaid twelve months after the end of the accounting period.

A return for each of the company's accounting periods is due on or before the filing date. This is the later of:

(a) **12 months after the end of the accounting period**

(b) **if the accounting period ends in a period of account which is not more than 18 months long, 12 months from the end of the period of account**

(c) **if the accounting ends in a period of account which is more than 18 months long, 30 months from the start of the period of account; and**

(d) **three months from the date on which the notice requiring the return was made.**

Activity 15.1

A Ltd prepares accounts for the eighteen months to 30 June 2003. A notice requiring a return for the year ended 30 June 2003 was issued to A Ltd on 1 September 2003. State the periods for which A Ltd must file a tax return and the filing dates.

1.2 Penalties

There is a £100 penalty for a failure to submit a return on time, rising to £200 if the delay exceeds three months. These penalties become £500 and £1,000 respectively when a return was late (or never submitted) for each of the preceding two accounting periods.

An additional tax geared penalty is applied if a return is more than six months late. The penalty is 10% of the tax unpaid six months after the return was due if the total delay is up to 12 months, but 20% of that tax if the return is over 12 months late.

There is a tax geared penalty for a fraudulent or negligent return and for failing to correct an innocent error without unreasonable delay. The maximum penalty is equal to the tax that would have been lost had the return been accepted as correct. The Revenue can mitigate (reduce) this penalty. If a company is liable to more than one tax geared penalty, the total penalty is limited to the maximum single penalty that could be charged.

A company may amend a return within twelve months of the filing date. The Revenue may correct obvious errors in a return or amendment within nine months of the day it was filed. The company may amend its return so as to reject the correction. If the time limit for amendments has expired, the company may reject the correction by giving notice within three months.

Wherever possible claims must be made on a tax return or on an amendment to it and must be quantified at the time the return is made.

Activity 15.2

AB Ltd prepares accounts to 30 September each year. Its corporation tax return for the year to 30 September 2001 was filed on time. The return for the year to 30 September 2002 was filed on 1 December 2003 and the return for the year end 30 September 2003 was filed on 1 November 2004. In all cases a notice requiring a return was issued within three months of the end of the period of account concerned.

What fixed penalty is due in respect of the late filing of the return for the period to 30 September 2003?

A £100
B £200
C £500
D £1,000

1.3 Records

Companies must keep records until the latest of:

(a) six years from the end of the accounting period
(b) the date any enquiries are completed
(c) the date after which enquiries may not be commenced

All business records and accounts, including contracts and receipts, must be kept.

If a return is demanded more than six years after the end of the accounting period, any records which the company still has must be kept until the later of the end of any enquiry and the expiry of the right to start an enquiry.

Failure to keep records can lead to a penalty of up to £3,000 for each accounting period affected. However, this penalty does not apply when the only records which have not been kept are ones which could only have been needed for the purposes of claims, elections or notices not included in the return.

The Revenue do not generally insist on original records being kept but original records relating to payments made net of tax must be preserved.

1.4 Enquiries

The Revenue may enquire into a return or an amendment, provided that they give written notice that they are going to enquire by a year after the later of:

(a) the filing date

(b) the 31 January, 30 April, 31 July or 31 October next following the actual date of delivery of the return or amendment

Only one enquiry may be made in respect of any one return or amendment.

If a notice of an enquiry has been given, the Revenue may demand that the company produce documents. Documents relating to an appeal need not be produced and the company may appeal against a notice requiring documents to be produced.

If the Revenue demand documents, but the company does not produce them, there is a penalty of £50. There is also a daily penalty, which applies for each day from the day after the imposition of the £50 penalty until the documents are produced.

The Revenue may amend a self assessment at any time during an enquiry if they believe there might otherwise be a loss of tax. The company may appeal against such an amendment

An enquiry ends when the Revenue give notice that it has been completed and notify what they believe to be the correct amount of tax payable. Before that time, the company may ask the Commissioners to order the Revenue to notify the completion of its enquiry by a specified date. Such a direction will be given unless the Revenue can demonstrate that they have reasonable grounds for continuing the enquiry.

The company has 30 days from the end of an enquiry to amend its self assessment in accordance with the Revenue's conclusions. If the Revenue are not satisfied with the company's amendments, they have a further 30 days to amend the self assessment. The company then has another 30 days in which it may appeal against the Revenues amendments.

Activity 15.3

V Ltd filed its corporation tax return for the year to 30 June 2003 on 30 September 2004. A notice requiring the return was issued on 1 October 2003. What is the latest date by which the Revenue must give notice if they wish to enquire into the return?

A 30 June 2004
B 30 June 2005
C 31 October 2004
D 31 October 2005

1.5 Determinations and discovery assessments

If a return is not delivered by the filing date, the Revenue may issue a determination of the tax payable. There is no appeal against this but it is automatically replaced by any self assessment made by the company by the later of five years from the filing date and 12 months from the determination.

If the Revenue believe that not enough tax has been assessed they can make a discovery assessment. When a tax return has been delivered this power is limited:

(a) No discovery assessment can be made on account of an error as to the basis on which the tax liability ought to be computed, if the basis generally prevailing at the time when the return was made was applied.

(b) A discovery assessment can only be made if either:

  (i) the loss of tax is due to fraudulent or negligent conduct

  (ii) the Revenue could not reasonably be expected to have been aware of the loss, given the information so far supplied to them, when their right to start an enquiry expired or when they notified the company that an enquiry had finished

2 Payment of tax and interest

2.1 Tax payable by small/medium sized companies

Corporation tax is due for payment by small and medium sized companies **nine months after the end of the accounting period**.

2.2 Tax payable by large companies

Large companies must pay their corporation tax in instalments. **Broadly, a large company is any company that pays corporation tax at the full rate** (profits exceed £1,500,000 where there are no associated companies).

Instalments are due on the 14th day of the month, starting in the seventh month. Provided that the accounting period is twelve months long subsequent instalments are due in the tenth month during the accounting period and in the first and fourth months after the end of the accounting period. If an accounting period is less than twelve months long subsequent instalments are due at three monthly intervals but with the final payment being due in the fourth month of the next accounting period.

2.3 Example

X Ltd is a large company with a 31 December accounting year end. Instalments of corporation tax will be due to be paid by X Ltd on:

- 14 July and 14 October in the accounting period;
- 14 January and 14 April after the accounting period ends

Thus for the year ended 31 December 2003 instalment payments are due on 14 July 2003, 14 October 2003, 14 January 2004 and 14 April 2004.

Activity 15.4

S Ltd, a large company, has a corporation tax liability of £700,000 in respect of its accounting year 31 March 2004.

On which date will the company be required to pay the FINAL QUARTERLY instalment of the liability?

A 14 October 2003
B 14 July 2004
C 31 July 2004
D 1 January 2005

2.4 Calculation of instalments

Instalments are based on the estimated corporation tax liability for the current period (not the previous period). This means that it will be extremely important for companies to forecast their tax liabilities accurately. Large companies whose directors are poor at estimating may find their company's incurring significant interest charges. The amount of each instalment is computed by:

(a) working out $3 \times CT/n$ where CT is the amount of the estimated corporation tax liability payable in instalments for the period and n is the number of months in the period;

(b) allocating the smaller of that amount and the total estimated corporation tax liability to the first instalment;

(c) repeating the process for later instalments until the amount allocated is equal to the corporation tax liability. This gives four equal instalments for 12 month accounting periods and also caters for periods which end earlier than expected.

The company is therefore required to estimate its corporation tax liability before the end of the accounting period, and must revise its estimate each quarter.

Activity 15.5

A company has a CT liability of £880,000 for the eight month period to 30 September 2003. Accounts had previously always been prepared to 31 January. Show when the CT liability is due for payment.

A company is not required to pay instalments in the first year that it is 'large', unless its profits exceed £10 million. The £10 million limit is reduced proportionately if there are associated companies. For this purpose only, a company will be regarded as an associated company where it was an associated company at the START of an accounting period. (This differs from the normal approach in CT where being an associated company for any part of the AP affects the thresholds of both companies for the whole of the AP).

There is a de minimis limit in that any company whose liability for its accounting period ending on or after 1 July 2000 does not exceed £10,000 need not pay by instalments.

2.5 Interest

Interest runs from the due date on over/underpaid instalments. The position is looked at cumulatively after the due date for each instalment. The Revenue calculate the interest position after the company submits its corporation tax return.

2.6 Example

X plc prepared accounts to 31.12.03. The company has always prepared accounts to 31 December each year. It paid CT instalments of:

Date	*Amount*
	£m
14.7.03	3.5
14.10.03	8.5
14.01.04	4.5
14.4.04	4.5
	21.0

X plc's CT return showed a CT liability of £22m. The £1m balance was paid on 1.10.04. £22m should have been paid in instalments. The under(over) payments were:

Date	*Paid*	*Correct*	*Under(over) paid*
	£m	£m	£m
14.7.03	3.5	5.5	2
14.10.03	8.5	5.5	
	12.0	11.0	(1)
14.1.04	4.5	5.5	
	16.5	16.5	–
14.4.04	4.5	5.5	
	21.0	22.0	1

Interest would be charged (received) as follows.

14.7.03 – 13.10.03	Interest charged on £2m
14.10.03 – 13.1.04	Interest received on £1m
14.1.04 – 13.4.04	No interest
14.4.04 – 30.9.04	Interest charged on £1m

Interest paid/received on late payments or over payments of corporation tax is dealt with under Schedule D Case III as interest paid/received on a nontrading loan relationship.

2.7 Incorrect instalments

There are penalties if a company deliberately and flagrantly fails to pay instalments of sufficient size. After a company has filed its return or the Revenue has determined its liability, the Revenue may wish to establish the reason for inadequate instalment payments. It can do this by asking the company to produce relevant information or records (presumably to decide if a penalty applies). The failure to supply these will lead to an initial fixed penalty which may also be followed by a daily penalty which may continue until the information/records are produced.

Companies can have instalments repaid if they later conclude they ought not to have been paid.

3 Income tax suffered or withheld

A paying company is not required to withhold income tax on payments of:

(a) annual interest
(b) royalties
(c) annuities
(d) annual payments

if it reasonably believes that the **recipient is chargeable to corporation tax on the payment.**

Thus such payments made by one UK company to another UK company are paid gross.

However such payments made to individuals, partnerships etc (ie non companies) are made under deduction of income tax at 20% (eg debenture interest) or 22% (eg patent royalties).

When the company pays interest or patent royalties it deducts the gross amount in its corporation tax computation. For items paid net (such as debenture interest and patent royalties paid to non corporate recipients), **it acts as an agent for the Revenue and retains income tax at 20% (interest) or 22% (patents) on the gross amount for payment to the Revenue.** The *net* amount is then payable to the payees (for example the individual debenture holders).

Companies may receive some income which has suffered 20% or 22% income tax at source. The cash income plus the income tax suffered, that is the gross figure, forms part of a company's income. The **income tax suffered is deductible from the corporation tax liability**.

Activity 15.6

In its accounting period to 31 March 2004 SB Ltd:

1 Received patent royalties of £7,800 from an individual
2 Paid £5,000 of debenture interest to another UK resident company

The amounts shown are the amounts paid and received by the company. What is the net amount of income tax suffered that SB Ltd may deduct in calculating its corporation tax payable for the period?

A £2,200
B £1,716
C £790
D £616

4 Company return forms

A copy of the corporation tax self assessment return form (CT 600) is included in the appendix at the end of this text. You may be asked to complete this return form as part of your exam and you should start to familiarise yourself with it now. Note that Section 4 of the return is not included here as you will not be required to deal with them in your exam.

You will be able to practice using the above form when you try the questions in BPP's Unit 18 Assessment Kit.

Activity 15.7

(a) Hogg Ltd prepares accounts for the year to 31 December 2003. Its profits chargeable to corporation tax for the year will be £1,750,000. The company has always paid corporation tax at the full rate.

Task

State the amounts and due dates for the payment of corporation tax by Hogg Ltd in respect of the year to 31 December 2003.

(b) In 2005 Hogg Ltd changes its accounting date to 31 October 2005. Assume that the liability for the ten months to 31 October 2005 is expected to be £600,000.

Task

State the due dates for and the amount of instalments of corporation tax that Hogg Ltd will be required to pay in respect of this period.

Key learning points

- ☑ In general, **returns must be filed within 12 months** of the end of an accounting period.
- ☑ The Revenue have **power to enquire into returns**.
- ☑ **Small and medium sized companies** pay corporation tax **nine months after the end of an accounting period**.
- ☑ **Large companies** pay corporation tax in **four quarterly instalments.**
- ☑ **Interest** is payable on **overpaid and underpaid tax**.
- ☑ A paying company is only required to **withhold income tax** on **payments other than to companies**.
- ☑ Any **net income tax suffered** by a company can be **deducted** from the corporation tax liability.

Quick quiz

1 Fairfield Ltd has profits chargeable to corporation tax of £800,000 for its year ended 31 March 2004. It has two wholly owned subsidiaries. If corporation tax is always paid as it falls due, the corporation tax payable on 1 January 2005 will be:

A £Nil
B £60,000
C £240,000
D £800,000

2 Eaton Ltd has profits chargeable to corporation tax of £2,400,000 for its year ended 31 December 2003. The first instalment of the corporation tax liability for this year will be due on:

Due date
A 14 April 2003
B 14 April 2004
C 14 July 2003
D 1 October 2004

3 M Ltd, a large company, has an estimated corporation tax liability of £240,000 in respect of its accounting year 31 March 2004.

What will be the amount of each of the company's quarterly instalments?

A £Nil
B £52,800
C £60,000
D £240,000

4 VW Ltd prepares accounts to 30 June each year. Its corporation tax return for the year to 30 June 2001 was filed on time. The return for the year to 30 June 2002 was filed on 1 November 2003 and the return for the year end 30 June 2003 was filed on 1 December 2004. In all cases a notice requiring a return was issued within three months of the end of the period of account concerned.

What fixed penalty is due in respect of the late filing of the return for the period to 30 June 2003?

Answers to quick quiz

1 A

PCTCT	£800,000
UL = £150,000 ÷ 3 = £500,000	
	£
Gross Corporation Tax (£800,000 × 30%)	240,000
Instalments (100%)	(240,000)
Due 1 January 2005	NIL

A company that pays corporation tax at the full rate of 30% must pay its corporation tax liability in quarterly instalments starting in the seventh month of the accounting period.

2 C Eaton Ltd is a large company paying corporation tax at the full rate of 30%.

The first instalment is paid in the seventh month of the accounting period.

3 C ¼ × £240,000 = £60,000

4 The return is more than three months late but it is only the second late filing of a return so the fixed penalty is £200.

Activity checklist

This checklist shows which performance criteria, range statement or knowledge and understanding point is covered by each activity in this chapter. Tick off each activity as you complete it.

Activity		
15.1	☐	This activity deals with Performance Criteria 18.4 G: complete corporation tax returns correctly and submit them, together with relevant claims and elections within statutory time limits
15.2	☐	This activity deals with Performance Criteria 18.4 I: give timely and constructive advice to clients on the maintenance of accounts and the recording of information relevant to tax returns
15.3	☐	This activity deals with Performance Criteria 18.4 I: give timely and constructive advice to clients on the maintenance of accounts and the recording of information relevant to tax returns
15.4	☐	This activity deals with Performance Criteria 18.2.F: identify the amount of Corporation Tax payable and the due dates of payment, including payments on account
15.5	☐	This activity deals with Performance Criteria 18.2 F: identify the amount of Corporation Tax payable and the due dates of payment, including payments on account
15.6	☐	This activity deals with Performance Criteria 18.4 D: identify and set off income tax deductions and credits
15.7	☐	This activity deals with Performance Criteria 18.2 F: identify the amount of Corporation Tax payable and the due dates of payment, including payments on account

Answers to Activities

Chapter 1: The taxation of business income on individuals

Activity 1.1

The gross amounts are:	Dividends (£2,250 × 100/90)	£2,500
	Building society interest (£2,400 × 100/80)	£3,000

Activity 1.2

	Non-savings income	*Savings (excl dividend) income*	*Dividend income*	*Total*
	£	£	£	£
Schedule D Case I	16,000	0	0	
Building society interest £4,800 × 100/80	0	6,000	0	
Dividends £7,875 × 100/90	0	0	8,750	
STI	16,000	6,000	8,750	30,750
Less: Personal allowance	(4,615)			
Taxable income	11,385	6,000	8,750	26,135

Did you remember to gross up dividends by 100/90 and building society interest by 100/80?

Activity 1.3

	£
£1,960 × 10%	196
£28,540 × 22%	6,279
£19,500 × 40%	7,800
£50,000	14,275

Activity 1.4

	Non-savings income	*Savings (excl dividend) income)*	*Total*
	£	£	£
Schedule D Case I	10,430		
Building society interest (× 100/80)		5,000	
	10,430	5,000	15,430
Less: Personal allowance	(4,615)		
	5,815	5,000	10,815

	£
Tax on non-savings income	
£1,960 × 10%	196
£3,855 × 22%	848
Tax on savings (excl dividend)	
£5,000 × 20%	1,000
Tax Liability	2,044
Less: Tax suffered on building society interest	(1,000)
Tax payable	1,044

The building society interest falls within the basic rate threshold so it is taxed at 20%.

Activity 1.5

	Dividend income
	£
Dividends (× 100/90)	36,000
Less: Personal allowance	(4,615)
Taxable income	31,385

	£
Tax on dividend income	
£30,500 × 10%	3,050
£885 × 32.5%	288
	3,338
Less: Tax credit on dividend (max)	(3,338)
Tax payable	–

The dividend income that falls within the starting and basic rate thresholds is taxed at 10%. Dividend income over the threshold of £30,500 is taxed at 32.5%. The tax credit suffered on the dividend income, £3,600, can be offset against the tax liability to reduce it to £nil. However, the excess tax credit, £262 (£3,600 – £3,338) cannot be repaid. The tax credit is offsettable but not repayable.

Activity 1.6

	Non-savings Income	*Savings (excl dividend) income*	*Dividend income*	
	£	£	£	
Schedule D Case I	8,000			
Building society interest (× 100/80)		17,500		
Dividends (× 100/90)			500	
Charge on income	(8,000)	(4,000)		
	–	13,500	500	14,000
Less personal allowance	–	(4,615)	–	
Taxable income	–	8,885	500	9,385

Chapter 2: Schedule D Cases I and II

Activity 2.1

Supplementary work and marketing (drainage; obtaining planning permission)

A profit motive

The manner of acquisition (extra land was bought)

Activity 2.2

	£
Entertaining Customers	7,300
	7,300

Activity 2.3

They are not worn wholly and exclusively for trade purposes as they are not worn in addition to ordinary clothes.

Activity 2.4

£(230 + 700) = £930

Activity 2.5

	£
Add back loan to customer	1,400
Deduct decrease in general bad debt provision	(3,100)
Net deduction	1,700

Activity 2.6

	£	£
Profit per accounts		12,710
Add: depreciation	1,500	
Provision against a fall in raw material prices	5,000	
Entertainment expenses	750	
Patent royalties (to treat as a charge)	1,200	
Legal expenses	250	
		8,700
		21,410
Less interest received (to tax as savings (excl dividend) income)		(860)
Adjusted trading profit		20,550

Activity 2.7

2003/04	1.7.03 – 5.4.04 9/12 × £10,000	£7,500
2004/05	1.7.03 – 30.6.04	£10,000
2005/06	1.7.04 – 30.6.05	£15,000
2006/07	1.7.05 – 30.6.06	£18,000

Activity 2.8

2002/03	Year ended 30 September 2002	£10,000
2003/04	Year ended 30 September 2003	£7,000
2004/05	1 October 2003 – 31 December 2004 £(6,000 + 2,000)	£8,000

Activity 2.9

Year	Basis period	Working	*Taxable profits* £
1998/99	1.9.98 - 5.4.99	£8,000 × 7/8	7,000
1999/00	1.9.98 - 31.8.99	£8,000 + (£15,000 × 4/12)	13,000
2000/01	1.5.99 - 30.4.00		15,000
2001/02	1.5.00 - 30.4.01		9,000
2002/03	1.5.01 - 30.4.02		10,500
2003/04	1.5.02 - 30.6.03	£(16,000 + 950 - 12,000)	4,950
			59,450

The overlap profits are the profits from 1 September 1998 to 5 April 1999 (taxed in 1998/99 and in 1999/00) and those from 1 May 1999 to 31 August 1999 (taxed in 1999/00 and 2000/01).

	£
1.9.98 - 5.4.99 £8,000 × 7/8	7,000
1.5.99 - 31.8.99 £15,000 × 4/12	5,000
Total overlap profits	12,000

Activity 2.10

		£	£
Profit per accounts			5,640
Add:	salary (a)	260	
	rent (a)	210	
	light and heat (a)	57	
	motor expenses (a)	48	
	stockroom extension (c)	101	
	increase in general provision (a)	200	
	donations (b)	10	
	entertaining (d)	90	
	gifts (e)	70	
	depreciation (c)	600	
	goods withdrawn at selling price (b)	400	
			2,046
			7,686
Less:	profit on sale of plant (c)	240	
	profit on sale of investment (c)	1,032	
	bank interest received (f)	54	
			(1,326)
Adjusted trading profit before capital allowances			6,360

Notes

(a) Appropriation of profit

(b) Not expenditure laid out wholly and exclusively for the purpose of trade

(c) Capital items

(d) Entertaining expenses specifically disallowed

(e) Gifts of drink specifically disallowed

(f) Non-trading income. The bank interest will be taxed as savings (excl. dividend) income

Chapter 3: Capital allowances

Activity 3.1

No: its principal purpose is to provide a permanent wall.

Activity 3.2

(a) No: they would be part of the setting.
(b) Yes: they would perform a specific function.

Activity 3.3

		£	£
TWDV b/f		48,000	
WDA @ 25% × $^6/_{12}$		(6,000)	6,000
		42,000	
	£		
Addition	20,000		
FYA @ 40%	(8,000)		8,000
		12,000	
		54,000	14,000

WDA is pro-rated in a short accounting period but the FYA is not.

Activity 3.4

The capital allowances are as follows.

	FYA	*Pool*	*Allowances*
	£	£	£
1.3.00 – 31.7.01			
Additions (£13,000 + £9,603)	22,603		
FYA 40%	(9,041)		9,041
		13,562	
1.8.01 – 31.7.02			
Disposals		(4,000)	
		9,562	
WDA 25%		(2,391)	2,391
		7,171	
Addition (1.6.02)	5,000		
FYA 40%	(2,000)		2,000
		3,000	4,391
		10,171	
1.8.02 – 31.7.03			
WDA 25%		(2,543)	2,543
		7,628	
Addition (31.7.03)	2,000		
FYA 100%	(2,000)		2,000
		0	
TWDV c/f		7,628	
			4,543

Note: **First year allowances are not pro-rated in a long period of account.**

Activity 3.5

	Pool	*Allowances*
	£	£
Balance brought forward	123,000	
Disposals (limited to cost)	(27,000)	
	96,000	
WDA 25% × 10/12	(20,000)	20,000
Balance carried forward	76,000	

Activity 3.6

	Car	Allowances 90%
	£	£
1.7.00 – 31.12.00		
Purchase price	15,500	
WDA 25% × 6/12 of £15,500 = £1,938,		
Limited to £3,000 × 6/12 = £1,500	(1,500)	1,350
	14,000	
1.1.01 – 31.12.01		
WDA 25% of £14,000 = £3,500,		
Limited to £3,000	(3,000)	2,700
	11,000	
1.1.02 – 31.12.02		
WDA 25% of £11,000	(2,750)	2,475
	8,250	
1.1.03 – 31.12.03		
Proceeds	(4,000)	
Balancing allowance	4,250	3,825

Activity 3.7

(a)

	£
Year to 30.4.00	
Cost	12,000
WDA 25%	(3,000)
	9,000
Year to 30.4.01	
WDA 25%	(2,250)
	6,750
Year to 30.4.02	
WDA 25%	(1,688)
	5,062
Year to 30.4.03	
WDA 25%	(1,266)
	3,796
Year to 30.4.04	
Disposal proceeds	(300)
Balancing allowance	3,496

(b) If the asset is still in use at 30 April 2004, a WDA of 25% × £3,796 = £949 would be claimable in the year to 30 April 2004. The tax written down value of £3,796 - £949 = £2,847 would be added to the general pool at the beginning of the next period of account. The disposal proceeds of £200 would be deducted from the general pool in that period's capital allowances computation.

Activity 3.8

Only the sports pavilion will qualify.

Activity 3.9

The showrooms and offices are non-qualifying parts of the building. As the cost of the non qualifying parts, £600,000, is more than 25% of the total expenditure on the building, industrial buildings allowances are not available on it. The cost of the land is not qualifying expenditure.

Therefore, the qualifying expenditure for industrial buildings allowance purposes is £1,500,000 (£2,100,000 – £600,000)

Activity 3.10

The building was in industrial use at the end of the accounting period so an industrial buildings allowance of 4% of cost per annum is available. The allowance in the nine months to 30.9.03 is, therefore, 9/12 × £600,000 × 4% = £18,000

Activity 3.11

Frankie

	£
Cost 1.10.99	100,000
Y/e 31.12.99 to y/e 31.12.02 WDA 4 × 4%	(16,000)
Residue before sale	84,000
Y/e 31.12.03 Proceeds (limited to cost)	(100,000)
Balancing charge	(16,000)

Holly

	£
Residue before sale	84,000
Balancing charge	16,000
Residue after sale	100,000

The tax life of the building ends on 1.10.99 + 25 years = 30.9.2024

The date of Holly's purchase is 1.9.03

The unexpired life is therefore 21 years 1 month

	£
Y/e 30.9.03 WDA £100,000/21.083333	4,743
Next 20 accounting periods at £4,743 a year	94,860
Y/e 30.9.24 (balance)	397
	100,000

Activity 3.12

Tutorial note. It is important that you become fully competent at spotting when FYAs are available.

(a)

		FYA	*Pool*	*Expensive car (60%)*	*Allowances*
		£	£	£	£
WDV b/f			8,000		
Y/e 31.12.01					
14.9.01	Machinery sold		(700)		
			7,300		
16.9.01	Addition – car		4,000		
			11,300		
	WDA 25%		(2,825)		2,825
1.12.01	Machinery	7,693			
	FYA @ 40%	(3,077)			3,077
			4,616		
	WDV c/f		13,091		
	Total allowances				5,902
Y/e 31.12.02			13,091		
5.7.02	Mercedes			22,000	
21.3.02	Plant sold				
	(restricted to cost)		(2,000)		
22.3.02	Car sold		(3,200)		
			7,891		
	WDA 25%/restricted		(1,973)	(3,000)	3,773
	WDV c/f		5,918	19,000	
	Total allowances				
Y/e 31.12.03					
5.2.03	Car (no FYA)		3,000		
30.6.03	Plant sold		(2,602)		
			6,316		
	WDA 25%		(1,579)		1,579
			4,737		
15.6.03	Mercedes sold			(4,000)	
	Balancing allowance			15,000	9,000
15.6.03	Volvo			18,000	
	WDA restricted			(3,000)	1,800
4.2.03	Machine on HP	4,000			
	FYA @ 40%	(1,600)			1,600
			2,400		
30.6.03	Computer equipment	3,000			
	FYA @ 100%	(3,000)			3,000
	WDV c/f		7,137	15,000	
	Total allowances				16,979

Activity 3.13

Tutorial note. Consider to what extent Cuckold Ltd can claim IBAs. What is the maximum period for IBAs to be claimed?

Cuckold Ltd should acquire factory (i), as shown in the working below.

Factory (ii) is clearly unattractive since, with its tax life expired, industrial buildings allowances cannot be claimed. Factories (iii) and (iv) have greater total allowances available than factory (i) but the annual allowance is much smaller.

Working: industrial buildings allowances on alternative factories

	Factory (i)	*Factory (ii)*	*Factory (iii)*	*Factory (iv)*
Residue after sale*	£100,000	£80,000	£150,000	£120,000
Remaining tax life**	1 yr	0	23 yrs	17 yrs
Allowances available	£100,000 / 1 yr	0	£150,000 / 23 yrs	£120,000 / 17 yrs
in y/e 31.3.2005	= £100,000		= £6,522	= £7,059

* The residue after sale is the lower of the price paid by the new purchaser and the original cost.

** The tax life of an industrial building begins when it is first brought into use and ends 25 years later.

Chapter 4: Trading losses

Activity 4.1

£18,000 – £14,000 (s 380 claim) = £4,000

Activity 4.2

The year of the loss is 2003/04. The loss for 2003/04 is £25,000

	2002/03	*2003/04*
	£	£
Income	18,000	18,000
Less s 380 relief	(7,000)	(18,000)
STI	11,000	0
Less personal allowance	(4,615)	(4,615)
Taxable income	6,385	0

In 2003/04, £4,615 of the loss has been wasted because that amount of income would have been covered by the personal allowance. If Janet claims s 380 relief, there is nothing she can do about this waste of loss relief. However, Janet might have been best advised to claim relief in 2002/03 before making a claim in 2003/04. This would have had the effect of moving the taxable income to 2003/04 and delaying the payment of the associated income tax.

Activity 4.3

The losses available for relief are as follows.

	£	£	*Years against which relief is available*
2001/02 (basis period 1.1.02 - 5.4.02)			
3 months to 5.4.02			
£(3,000) × 3/6		(1,500)	1998/99 to 2000/01
2002/03 (basis period 1.1.02 - 31.12.02)			
3 months to 30.6.02			
(omit 1.1.02 - 5.4.02: overlap)			
£(3,000) × 3/6	(1,500)		
6 months to 31.12.02			
£(1,500) × 6/12	(750)		
		(2,250)	1999/00 to 2001/02
2003/04 (basis period 1.7.02 - 30.6.03)			
6 months to 30.6.03			
(omit 1.7.02 - 31.12.02: overlap)			
£(1,500) × 6/12		(750)	2000/01 to 2002/03
2004/05 (basis period 1.7.03 - 30.6.04)			
12 months to 30.6.04		(1,200)	2001/02 to 2003/04

The Schedule D Case I income for 2001/02 to 2004/05 will all be zero, because there were losses in the basis periods.

Activity 4.4

The terminal loss comes in the last 12 months, the period 1 October 2002 to 30 September 2003. This period is split as follows.

2002/03 Six months to 5 April 2003
2003/04 Six months to 30 September 2003

The terminal loss is made up as follows.

Unrelieved trading losses

		£	£
2002/03			
3 months to 31.12.02	£300 × 3/12	75	
3 months to 5.4.03	£(1,950) × 3/9	(650)	
			(575)
2003/04			
6 months to 30.9.03	£(1,950) × 6/9		(1,300)
Overlap relief	£(450)		(450)
			(2,325)

Schedule D Case I profits will be as follows.

Year	*Basis period*	*Profits*	*Terminal loss relief*	*Final taxable profits*
		£	£	£
2000/01	Y/e 31.12.00	2,000	1,625	375
2001/02	Y/e 31.12.01	400	400	0
2002/03	Y/e 31.12.02	300	300	0
2003/04	1.1.03 – 30.9.03	0	0	0
			2,325	

Chapter 5: Partnerships

Activity 5.1

Year	*Basis period*	*Working*	*Taxable profits* £
2002/03	1.9.02 – 5.4.03	(£34,200 × 20%) × 4/12 + (£45,600 × 20%) × 3/12	4,560
2003/04	1.1.03 – 31.12.03	£45,600 × 20%	9,120

Activity 5.2

Tutorial note. Your first step with a partnership question should be to calculate profits for each period of account. Only after you have done this should you consider allocating the profits to tax years. Remember that the opening year rules apply when a partner joins to that partner. Similarly, when a partner leaves the closing year rules apply to the departing partner. All other partners are assessed on a continuing basis.

	Total £	*A* £	*B* £	*C* £	*D* £
Year ending 31 March 2001					
Salaries	3,700	1,500	1,200	1,000	
Balance	6,500	2,600	2,600	1,300	
Total	10,200	4,100	3,800	2,300	
Year ending 31 March 2002					
April to June					
Salaries	925	375	300	250	
Balance	4,275	1,710	1,710	855	
Total	5,200	2,085	2,010	1,105	
July to March					
Salaries	1,650		900	750	
Balance	13,950		8,370	5,580	
Total	15,600		9,270	6,330	
Totals for the year	20,800	2,085	11,280	7,435	
Year ending 31 March 2003					
Salaries	2,200		1,200	1,000	
Balance	10,400		6,240	4,160	
Total	12,600		7,440	5,160	
Year ending 31 March 2004					
April					
Salaries	183		100	83	
Balance	1,317		790	527	
Total	1,500		890	610	

	Total	*A*	*B*	*C*	*D*
	£	£	£	£	£
May to March					
Salaries	4,950		1,650	1,650	1,650
Balance	11,550		6,237	4,158	1,155
Total	16,500		7,887	5,808	2,805
Totals for the year	18,000		8,777	6,418	2,805

Taxable profits are as follows:

	A	*B*	*C*	*D*
	£	£	£	£
Year 2000/01	4,100	3,800	2,300	
2001/02	2,085	11,280	7,435	
2002/03		7,440	5,160	
2003/04		8,777	6,418	2,805

Chapter 6: Chargeable gains: an outline

Activity 6.1

(a) Carol's taxable income is as follows.

	£
Business profits	32,830
Less personal allowance	(4,615)
Taxable income	28,215

(b) The gains to be taxed are as follows.

	£
Gains	26,100
Less losses	(8,000)
	18,100
Less annual exemption	(7,900)
Taxable gains	10,200

(c) The tax bands are allocated as follows.

	Total	*Income*	*Gains*
	£	£	£
Starting rate	1,960	1,960	0
Basic rate	28,540	26,255	2,285
Higher rate	7,915	0	7,915
		28,215	10,200

(d) The CGT payable is as follows.

	£
£2,285 × 20%	457
£7,915 × 40%	3,166
Total CGT payable	3,623

Activity 6.2

	£
Schedule D Income	23,000
Less personal allowance	(4,615)
Taxable income	18,385
	£
Basic rate band	30,500
Less: used up by income	(18,385)
Available for gains	12,115
	£
Capital gains	22,000
Less: annual exemption	(7,900)
Taxable gains	14,100

CGT:	£
£12,115 × 20%	2,423
1,985 × 40%	794
14,100	3,217

Activity 6.3

No: motor cars are exempt assets.

Activity 6.4

The current year loss must be deducted in full from the gain before taper relief is applied:

	£
Gain	40,600
Loss	(1,300)
Net gain	39,300

The asset was owned for 5 years complete years after 5.4.98 so:

	£
Gain after taper relief (25%)	9,825
Less: Annual exemption	(7,900)
Taxable gain	1,925

Activity 6.5

	£
Gain	17,800
Loss	(6,000)
Current net gains	11,800
Less: brought forward loss	(3,900)
Gains before taper relief	7,900
Gains after taper relief (1 year ownership) £7,900 × 50%	3,950
Less: annual exemption	(7,900)
Taxable gains	Nil

Note that the benefit of the taper relief is effectively wasted since the brought forward loss reduces the gain down to the annual exemption amount but the taper is then applied to that amount reducing it further.

The loss carried forward is £6,100 (£10,000 – £3,900).

Activity 6.6

TAXABLE INCOME AND GAINS

	£
Business Profits	24,500
Less: Personal allowance	(4,615)
Taxable income	19,885

	£
Gains	35,000
Less annual exemption	(7,900)
Taxable gains	27,100

£10,615 (£30,500 – £19,885) of the gains fall within the basic rate band and are taxed at 20%. The remaining gains are taxed at 40%.

The capital gains tax liability is as follows.

	£
£10,615 × 20%	2,123
£16,485 × 40%	6,594
	8,717

Activity 6.7

Motor cars are exempt assets, so the loss brought forward from 2002/03 is £6,300.

The position for 2003/04 is as follows.

	£
Gains	
Shares (no taper relief)	7,800
Business asset (no taper relief)	3,000
	10,800
Less loss on shares	(2,000)
	8,800
Less loss brought forward	(900)
	7,900
Less annual exemption	(7,900)
Chargeable gains	0

Gilt-edged securities are exempt assets. Losses brought forward are (unlike current year losses) only used to bring net gains down to the annual exempt amount.

The loss carried forward at the end of 2003/04 is £(6,300 – 900) = £5,400.

Taper relief was not available on the shares or the business asset as neither had been held for a complete year.

Chapter 7: The computation of gains and losses

Activity 7.1

No: it is not reflected in the state or nature of the asset at the time of disposal.

Activity 7.2

The indexation allowance is available until April 1998 and is computed as follows.

	£
$\frac{162.6 - 83.0}{83.0} = 0.959 \times £5,000$	4,795
$\frac{162.6 - 88.6}{88.6} = 0.835 \times £2,000$	1,670
	6,465

Activity 7.3

	£
Proceeds	180,000
Less: cost	(100,000)
Unindexed gain	80,000
Less: indexation allowance	
$\frac{180.1 - 165.1}{165.1} \times (=0.091)$ £100,000	(9,100)
Indexed gain	70,900

Tutorial note: For companies, indexation runs to the date of disposal of an asset.

Activity 7.4

	£
Proceeds	24,000
Less cost	97,000
Allowable loss	(73,000)

Indexation cannot increase a loss.

Activity 7.5

The value will be the lower of:

(a) $100 + 0.25 \times (110-100) = 102.5$;

(b) $\frac{110 + 99}{2} = 104.5$.

The market value for CGT purposes will therefore be 102.5p per share.

Activity 7.6

	£
No gain/no loss transfer	18,000
Indexation 1.91 – 4.98 $\frac{162.6 - 130.2}{130.2} = 0.249 \times £18,000$	4,482
Cost for Michael	22,482

Sale by Michael

	£
Proceeds	50,000
Less: cost	(22,482)
Gain	27,518

No further indexation allowance.

Michael treated as owning asset from 1.91 for taper relief so taper relief period is 6.4.98 – 5.4.03 = 5 years.

Gain after taper relief £27,518 × 25% = £6,879

Activity 7.7

The amount of the original cost attributable to the part sold is

$$\frac{18,000}{18,000 + 36,000} \times £27,000 = £9,000$$

	£
Proceeds	18,000
Less cost (see above)	(9,000)
Unindexed gain	9,000
Less indexation allowance (March 1984 to April 1998)	
$\frac{162.6 - 87.5}{87.5} = 0.858 \times £9,000$	(7,722)
Indexed gain	1,278

The chargeable gain after taper relief is £319 (£1,278 × 25%)

Activity 7.8

Cost: £150,000 × 190/(190 + 327) = £55,126

Incidental costs of disposal: £3,000

Total: £58,126

Activity 7.9

CAPITAL GAINS COMPUTATION

	£
Office block (W1)	18,990
Plot of land (W2)	17,248
Workshop (W3)	44,235
Taxable gains	80,473

Workings

1 *The office block*

	£
Proceeds	120,000
Less cost	(65,000)
	55,000
Less indexation allowance $\frac{179.5-115.5}{115.5}$ (0.554) × £65,000	(36,010)
Chargeable gain	18,990

2 *The plot of land*

	£
Proceeds	69,000
Less: cost	(20,000)
expenditure in July 1986	(4,000)
	45,000
Less: indexation allowance	
$\frac{179.7-81.0}{81.0}$ (1.219) × £20,000	(24,380)
$\frac{179.7-97.5}{97.5}$ (0.843) × £4,000	(3,372)
	17,248

3 *The workshop*

	£
Proceeds	173,000
Less: cost	(65,000)
	108,000
Less: indexation allowance $\frac{179.7-90.7}{90.7}$ (0.981) × £65,000	(63,765)
	44,235

Tutorial note 1. The date of disposal for chargeable gains purposes is the date that the disposal becomes unconditional. In this case the date of exchange, not the date of completion.

Tutorial note 2. Companies are entitled to the indexation allowance up to the date of the disposal of an asset.

Chapter 8: Shares and securities

Activity 8.1

	No of shares	Cost	Indexed cost
		£	£
Value at 1.4.85	2,000	6,000	6,291
Indexed rise			
$\frac{97.5 - 94.8}{94.8} \times £6,291$			179
	2,000	6,000	6,470
Acquisition	2,000	4,000	4,000
Value at 10.7.86	4,000	10,000	10,470

Activity 8.2

	No of shares	Cost	Indexed cost
		£	£
Value at 10.7.86	4,000	10,000	10,470
Indexed rise			
$\frac{179.9 - 97.5}{97.5} \times £10,470$			8,848
	4,000	10,000	19,318
Disposal	(3,000)		
Cost and indexed cost $\frac{3,000}{4,000} \times £10,000$ and £19,318		(7,500)	(14,489)
Value at 10.7.03	1,000	2,500	4,829

The gain is computed as follows:

	£
Proceeds	17,000
Less cost	(7,500)
	9,500
Less indexation allowance £(14,489 – 7,500)	(6,989)
Chargeable gain	2,511

Note that for companies indexation runs to the date of disposal of an asset.

Activity 8.3

Matching of shares

(a) Acquisition in 30 days after disposal:

	£
Proceeds $\frac{5{,}000}{18{,}000} \times £72{,}000$	20,000
Less cost	(19,000)
Gain	1,000

(b) Post 5.4.98 acquisitions

	£
Proceeds $\frac{3{,}000}{18{,}000} \times £72{,}000$	12,000
Less cost	(11,400)
Gain	600

No taper relief is due since the period of ownership was only 11 months.

(c) FA 1985 pool

	Number of shares	*Cost*	*Indexed cost*
		£	£
11.90 Acquisition	10,000	25,000	25,000
Index to 4.98 $\frac{162.6 - 130.0}{130.0} \times £25{,}000$			6,269
Pool closes at 5.4.98	10,000	25,000	31,269
7.03 sales	10,000	25,000	31,269

Gain

	£
Proceeds $\frac{10{,}000}{18{,}000} \times £72{,}000$	40,000
Less cost	(25,000)
	15,000
Less indexation from FA 1985 pool £(31,269 – 25,000)	(6,269)
Gain	8,731

The gain after taper relief is £2,183 (25% × £8,731)

Total gains after taper relief £(1,000 + 600 + 2,183) £3,783

Activity 8.4

(a) *Post 5.4.98 holding*

	Number	*Cost*
		£
Shares acquired 11.9.00	2,000	5,000
Shares acquired 1.2.01 (rights) 1:2 @ £2.75	1,000	2,750
	3,000	7,750

Gain

	£
Proceeds $\frac{3,000}{5,000} \times £15,000$	9,000
Less: cost	(7,750)
Gain	1,250

Taper relief (based on ownership of original holding 11.9.00 – 10.9.03)

25% (Three years: business asset) × £1,250 £312

(b) *FA 1985 pool*

	Number	*Cost*	*Indexed cost*
		£	£
1.10.95	10,000	15,000	15,000
IA to 4.98 $\frac{162.6 - 149.8}{149.8} \times £15,000$			1,282
Pool at 5.4.98	10,000	15,000	16,282
Rights issues 1.2.01	5,000	13,750	13,750
	15,000	28,750	30,032
14.10.03 Sale	(2,000)	(3,833)	(4,004)
c/f	13,000	24,917	26,028

Gain

		£
Proceeds $\frac{2,000}{5,000} \times$ £15,000		6,000
Less: cost		(3,833)
Unindexed gain		2,167
Less: indexation £(4,004 – 3,833)		(171)
Indexed gain		1,996
Taper relief (based on original holding 6.4.98 – 5.4.03)		
25% (Five years: business asset) × £1,996	£499	

(c) Total gains (after taper relief)

£(312 + 499)	£811

Activity 8.5

The FA 1985 pool

	No of shares	*Cost*	*Indexed cost*
		£	£
July 1985	1,000	3,000	3,000
Indexed rise to May 1986			
$\frac{97.8 - 95.2}{95.2} \times$ £3,000			82
May 1986 one for four rights	250	1,050	1,050
	1,250	4,050	4,132
Indexed rise to October 2003			
$\frac{180.5 - 97.8}{97.8} \times$ £4,132			3,494
	1,250	4,050	7,626
Disposal in October 2003	(1,250)	(4,050)	(7,626)

	£
Proceeds	10,000
Less cost	(4,050)
	5,950
Less indexation allowance £(7,626 – 4,050)	(3,576)
Chargeable gain	2,374

Note that companies do not get taper relief but they get indexation to the date of disposal of an asset.

Activity 8.6

Post 6.4.98 acquisitions: match on a LIFO basis.

17.1.03

	£
Proceeds $\left(\frac{2{,}000}{6{,}000} \times £24{,}000\right)$	8,000
Less: cost	(6,000)
Chargeable gain	2,000

No taper relief as the shares have not been held for a complete year.

12.12.01

	£
Proceeds $\left(\frac{2{,}000}{6{,}000} \times £24{,}000\right)$	8,000
Less: cost	(5,500)
Chargeable gain	2,500

Chargeable gain after taper relief £1,250 (£2,500 × 50%)

The FA 1985 pool

	Shares	*Cost*	*Indexed cost*
		£	£
Acquisition 19.9.85	2,000	1,700	1,700
Indexation to April 1998 (Pool closes)			
$\frac{162.6 - 95.4}{95.4} \times £1{,}700$			1,197
Value when pool closes (5.4.98)	2,000	1,700	2,897
Disposal 17.5.03	(2,000)	(1,700)	(2,897)
	0	0	0

	£
Proceeds $\frac{2{,}000}{6{,}000} \times £24{,}000$	8,000
Less cost	(1,700)
	6,300
Less indexation allowance £(2,897 − 1,700)	(1,197)
Chargeable gain	5,103

The chargeable gain after taper relief is £1,276 (£5,103 × 25%)

The total gains are £(2,000 + 1,250 + 1,276) = £4,526.

Activity 8.7

Previous nine days

	£
Proceeds $\frac{1,500}{4,000} \times £44,000$	16,500
Less: cost	(15,000)
Gain	1,500

No indexation allowance on disposals of shares acquired in previous nine days.

FA 1985 pool

		No of shares	*Cost*	*Indexed cost*
			£	£
11.7.88	Acquisition	1,000	5,000	5,000
19.9.99	Acquisition			
	Indexed rise $\frac{166.2-106.7}{106.7} \times £5,000$			2,788
	Purchase	2,000	18,000	18,000
c/f		3,000	23,000	25,788
3.8.03	Disposal			
	Indexed rise $\frac{180.1-166.2}{166.2} \times £25,788$			2,157
				27,945
	Sale	(2,500)	(19,167)	(23,288)
c/f		500	3,833	4,657

Gain

	£
Proceeds $\frac{2,500}{4,000} \times £44,000$	27,500
Less: cost	(19,167)
	8,333
Less: indexation allowance (23,288 – 19,167)	(4,121)
Indexed gain	4,212
Total gains £(1,500 + 4,212)	£5,712

Chapter 9: Chattels and wasting assets

Activity 9.1

	£
Proceeds	7,000
Less incidental costs of sale	(700)
Net proceeds	6,300
Less cost	(800)
Unindexed gain	5,500
Less indexation allowance (June 1984 to October 2003)	
$\frac{180.5 - 95.4}{95.4} = 0.892 \times £800$	(714)
Indexed gain	4,786

The maximum gain is 5/3 × £(7,000 – 6,000) = £1,667

The chargeable gain is the lower of £4,786 and £1,667, so it is £1,667.

Note: Taper relief is not available to companies. However, indexation is available to the date of disposal of an asset.

Activity 9.2

	£
Proceeds (assumed)	6,000
Less incidental costs of disposal (£2,700 x 10/90)	(300)
	5,700
Less cost	(8,000)
Allowable loss (indexation allowance cannot increase a loss)	(2,300)

Activity 9.3

	£
Proceeds	23,000
Less cost £7,000 × 29.75/40	(5,206)
	17,794
Less indexation allowance to April 1998	
$\frac{162.6 - 140.6}{140.6} = 0.156 \times £5,206$	(812)
Chargeable gain	16,982

Gain chargeable after taper relief £4,226 (£16,904 × 25%)

Activity 9.4

Summary

	£
Painting (W1)	2,500
Lathe (W3)	nil
Racehorse (W4)	nil
	2,500
Less: loss on vase (W2)	(2,000)
Net gains p/e 31.3.04	500

Workings

1 *Painting*

	£
Proceeds	7,500
Less: cost	(3,000)
	4,500
Less: indexation allowance $\frac{180.5 - 163.0}{163.0} = 0.107 \times £3,000$	(321)
	4,179

Restricted to 5/3 × £(7,500 – 6,000) = £2,500

2 *Vase*

	£
Deemed proceeds	6,000
Less: cost	(8,000)
Allowable loss	(2,000)

3 *Lathe*

	£	£
Sale proceeds		8,000
Cost	10,000	
Less: CAs	(2,000)	
		(8,000)
Gain/loss		Nil

4 *Racehorse*

Wasting chattel – exempt.

Chapter 10: Deferral reliefs

Activity 10.1

	£
Market value	120,000
Less: gain	(50,000)
Base cost	70,000

Activity 10.2

(a) *Angelo's CGT position (2003/04)*

	£
Proceeds	200,000
Less cost	(30,000)
Gain	170,000

(b) *Michael's CGT position (2005/06)*

	£
Proceeds	195,000
Less cost £(200,000 – 170,000)	(30,000)
Gain	165,000
Chargeable gain after taper relief (50%)	£82,500

Note. Michael acquired the asset on 6 December 2003 and sold it in May 2005. He therefore owned the asset for one complete year. 50% of the gain is taxable. Michael is not allowed to use any taper relief built up by Angelo.

Activity 10.3

The company is not a trading company

Activity 10.4

	£
Rollover gain	17,950
Cost of new factory	80,000
Less: rolled over gain	(17,950)
Base cost of new factory	62,050

Activity 10.5

31 December 2003 disposal

	£
Sale proceeds	491,400
Cost (5.11.1991)	(170,625)
	320,775
Less: Indexation allowance to April 1998	
$\frac{162.6-135.6}{135.6} = 0.199 \times £170,625$	(33,954)
Chargeable gain before taper relief	286,821

Since a replacement asset was purchased within the required time period, the gain before taper relief of £286,821 is rolled over against the cost of the new asset.

3 September 2005 disposal

	£	£
Sale proceeds		914,550
Cost (1 November 2003)	546,000	
Less: rollover relief	(286,821)	
		(259,179)
Gain		655,371

Ownership period is 1 November 2003 to 3 September 2005
= 1 complete year of ownership

Gain after taper relief	
Taxable gain (50%) for Karen	£327,686

Activity 10.6

Gain on gift

	£
Market value of gift	25,000
Less: cost	(10,000)
Gift relief gain	15,000

Gain on sale

	£
Proceeds	35,000
Less: cost (25,000 – 15,000)	(10,000)
Gift before taper relief	25,000

Taper relief period Sept 2002 – Sept 2003 = 1 year

£25,000 × 50% =	£12,500

Activity 10.7

Gain on first factory

		£
Proceeds		200,000
Less: cost		(150,000)
		50,000
Less: indexation allowance	$\frac{177.9 - 165.1}{165.1} = 0.078 \times £150,000$	(11,700)
Gain		38,300

This was all rolled over into the second factory because the proceeds were 'reinvested' within the required time frame.

Gain on second factory

		£
Proceeds		275,000
Less: cost £(250,000 – 38,300)		(211,700)
		63,300
Less: indexation allowance	$\frac{179.5 - 174.4}{174.4} = 0.029 \times £211,700$	(6,139)
Indexed gain		57,161

Chapter 11: An outline of corporation tax

Activity 11.1

The 18 month period of account is divided into:

Year ending 31 December 2003
6 months to 30 June 2004

Results are allocated:

	Y/e 31.12.03	*6m to 30.6.04*
	£	£
Trading profits 12:6	120,000	60,000
Schedule D Case III		
12 × £500	6,000	
6 × £500		3,000
Capital gain (1.5.04)		250,000
Less: Charge on income	(50,000)	
PCTCT (profits chargeable to corporation tax)	76,000	313,000

Activity 11.2

	£
Schedule D Case I	85,000
Schedule D Case III £(6,000 + 1,500 + 3,200)	10,700
Chargeable gains	2,950
	98,650
Less charges	(15,200)
Profits chargeable to corporation tax	83,450

Note. Debenture interest will be received gross by a UK company.

Activity 11.3

	£	£
Net profit per accounts		125,492
Less: 3½% War Loan interest	700	
dividends received	3,600	
building society interest	292	
loan interest received	4,000	
		(8,592)
		116,900
Add: gift aid donation		1,100
		118,000
Less: capital allowances		(5,500)
Schedule D Case I		112,500
Schedule D Case III £(700 + 292 + 4,000)		4,992
Chargeable gain		13,867
		131,359
Less: charges paid: gift aid donation		(1,100)
Profits chargeable to corporation tax (PCTCT)		130,259

Activity 11.4

£2,000,000 × 30% = £600,000

Activity 11.5

	£
Schedule D Case I	42,000
Dividend plus tax credit £9,000 × 100/90	10,000
'Profits' (below £300,000 limit)	52,000
Corporation tax payable	
£42,000 × 19%	£7,980

Activity 11.6

	£
Schedule D Case I	9,500
Dividend plus tax credit £270 × 100/90	300
'Profits'	9,800
Corporation tax on PCTCT £9,500 × 0%	£ NIL

Activity 11.7

	£
PCTCT	296,000
Dividend plus tax credit £12,600 × 100/90	14,000
'Profits'	310,000

'Profits' are above £300,000 but below £1,500,000, so small companies' marginal relief applies.

	£
Corporation tax on PCTCT £296,000 × 30%	88,800
Less small companies' marginal relief	
£(1,500,000 – 310,000) × 296,000/310,000 × 11/400	(31,247)
	57,553

Activity 11.8

	£
Schedule D Case I	29,500
Dividend plus tax credit £2,700 × 100/90	3,000
Profits	32,500

	£
Corporation tax at small companies rate:	
£29,500 × 19%	5,605
Less: starting rate marginal relief	
19/400 × ((£50,000 – £32,500) × £29,500/£32,500)	(755)
Corporation tax payable	4,850

Activity 11.9

	FY 2001 3 months to 31.3.02	*FY 2002 9 months to 31.12.02*
	£	£
PCTCT (divided 3:9)	10,000	30,000
'Profits' (divided 3:9)	10,625	31,875
Lower limit for Starting rate		
FY 2001 £10,000 × 3/12	2,500	
FY 2002 £10,000 × 9/12		7,500
Upper limit for Starting rate		
FY 2001 £50,000 × 3/12	12,500	
FY 2002 £50,000 × 9/12		37,500
Tax on PCTCT		
FY 2001: £10,000 × 20%		2,000
Less: Starting rate marginal relief		
£(12,500 – 10,625) × 10,000/10,625 × 1/40		(44)
		1,956
FY 2002: £30,000 × 19%	5,700	
Less: starting rate marginal relief		
£(37,500 – 31,875) × 30,000/31,875 × 19/400	(251)	
		5,449
Corporation tax payable		7,405

Activity 11.10

	FY 2001 6 months to 31.3.02	*FY 2002 6 months to 30.9.02*
	£	£
'Profits' (£9,800)	4,900	4,900
Profit chargeable to corporation tax	4,750	4,750
Lower limit for starting rate (– : 6m)	–	5,000
Lower limit for Starting rate (6m : 6m)	5,000	5,000
Corporation tax payable		
£4,750 × 10%		475
£4,750 × 0%		Nil
Total corporation tax payable for 12 months APE 30.9.02		475

Activity 11.11

(a) Division of the lower limit for the starting rate by the number of associated companies + 1

£10,000 × $^1/_3$ = £3,333

(b) Reduction in the lower limit for the starting rate as the accounting period is only nine months long

£3,333 × $^9/_{12}$ = £2,500

(c) Reduction in the upper limit for the starting rate

£50,000 × $^1/_3$ × $^9/_{12}$ = £12,500

(d) Reduction in the lower limit for SCR

£300,000 × $^1/_3$ × $^9/_{12}$ = £75,000

(e) Reduction in the upper limit for SCR

£1,500,000 × $^1/_3$ × $^9/_{12}$ = £375,000

(f) 'Profits' = £78,000

As 'profits' fall between the lower and upper limits for SCR purposes, the full rate less small companies' marginal relief applies:

(g) Corporation tax

	£
£78,000 × 30%	23,400
Less: small companies' marginal relief £(375,000 – 78,000) × 11/400	(8,168)
Corporation tax	15,232

Activity 11.12

Tutorial note. Long periods of account are always split into the first 12 months and the remainder. Schedule D Case I and Schedule D Case III profits are time apportioned. Chargeable gains are allocated to the period they are realised and gift aid donations to the period in which they are paid. When there is a change in the rate of corporation tax it is important that you split the accounting period into financial years in order to calculate the corporation tax.

Tree Ltd

	Year to 30.6.03	*Six months to 31.12.03*
	£	£
Trading profits (12/18: 6/18)	120,000	60,000
Chargeable gain	172,000	
Schedule D Case III (12/18: 6/18)	24,000	12,000
Less: charge on income	(22,000)	(5,000)
Profits chargeable to corporation tax	294,000	67,000
Year to 30.6.03		
Corporation tax (W1)		
FY 02 and FY 03		
£294,000 × 30%	88,200	
Less 11/400 (1,500,000 – 324,000) × $\frac{294,000}{324,000}$	(29,346)	
	58,854	
Six months to 31.12.03 (W2)		
£67,000 × 19%		£12,730

Workings

1 Tax rate: year to 30.6.03

The year to 30.6.03 falls into FY02 and FY03. As the rates of tax and marginal rate bands for both years are the same we do not need to split the profit between the financial years.

As 'profits' are between the small companies' upper and lower limits in both financial years, small companies' marginal relief applies in both financial years. This can be calculated in one step as there has not been a change to the rates.

2 The six month period to 31.12.03 falls in the financial year 2003. As profits of £67,000 are above the starting rate upper limit of £25,000 and below the small companies rate lower limit of £150,000 for this period, the small companies rate applies.

BPP PROFESSIONAL EDUCATION

Chapter 12: Corporation tax losses

Activity 12.1

		Year ended	
	31.3.02	*31.3.03*	*31.3.04*
	£	£	£
Schedule D Case I	20,000	24,000	20,000
Capital gain	–	–	1,000
PCTCT	20,000	24,000	21,000

Tutorial note. The capital loss must be carried forward to set against the gains in future periods. It cannot be set against Schedule D Case I profits.

Activity 12.2

		Year ended	
	31.3.02	*31.3.03*	*31.3.04*
	£	£	£
Schedule D Case I	0	3,000	6,000
Less: s 393(1) loss relief		(3,000)	(5,550)
	0	0	450
Schedule A	0	1,000	1,000
PCTCT	0	1,000	1,450

Note that the trading loss carried forward is set only against the trading profit in future years. It cannot be set against the Schedule A income.

Loss memorandum

	£
Loss for y/e 31.3.02	8,550
Less s 393(1) relief y/e 31.3.03	(3,000)
Loss carried forward at 1.4.03	5,550
Less s 393(1) relief y/e 31.3.04	(5,550)
Loss carried forward at 1.4.04	0

Activity 12.3

The loss of the year to 30.9.04 is relieved under s 393A ICTA 1988 against current year profits and against profits of the previous twelve months.

	Year ended		
	30.9.02	30.9.03	30.9.04
	£	£	£
Schedule D Case I	10,500	10,000	0
Schedule D Case III	500	500	500
Chargeable gains	0	0	4,000
	11,000	10,500	4,500
Less s 393A current period relief	0	0	(4,500)
	11,000	10,500	0
Less s 393A carryback relief	0	(10,500)	0
	11,000	0	0
Less: Non-trade charges	(250)	0	0
PCTCT	10,750	0	0
Unrelieved non-trade charges		250	250

S 393A (1) loss memorandum	£
Loss incurred in y/e 30.9.04	35,000
Less s 393A (1): y/e 30.9.04	(4,500)
y/e 30.9.03	(10,500)
Loss available to carry forward under s 393(1)	20,000

Activity 12.4

	2002
	£
Schedule D Case I	40,000
s 393(1) losses brought forward	(20,000)
	20,000
Less: non-trading deficit £(11,000 – 2,000)	(9,000)
	11,000
Losses carried back s 393A	(11,000)
Chargeable profits	Nil

Activity 12.5

A s 393A(1) claim for the year ended 31 March 2003 will save tax partly in the small companies' marginal relief band, partly at the small companies rate and partly in the starting rate marginal relief band. It will waste the gift aid donation of £20,000.

PCTCT in the previous year is £7,000 (£35,000 + £2,000 – £30,000). This falls into the starting rate band lower limit so no corporation tax would have been due in this year and there is no point in making a loss claim.

If no current period s 393A(1) claim is made, £200,000 of the loss will save tax at the small companies rate and in the starting rate marginal relief band in the year ended 31 March 2004, with £20,000 of gift aid donations being wasted. The remaining £800,000 of the loss, would be carried forward to the year ended 31 March 2005 and later years to save tax at the small companies rate and in the starting rate marginal relief band.

To conclude a s 393A(1) claim should be made for the year of the loss but not in the previous year. £20,000 of gift aid donations would be wasted in the current year, but much of the loss would save tax at the small companies' marginal corporation tax rate and relief would be obtained quickly.

The final computations are as follows.

		Year ended 31 March	
	2002	*2003*	*2004*
	£	£	£
Schedule D Case I	2,000	0	200,000
Less s 393(1) relief	0	0	(200,000)
	2,000	0	0
Chargeable gains	35,000	750,000	0
	37,000	750,000	0
Less: s393A current relief	0	(750,000)	0
	37,000	0	0
Less: gift aid	(30,000)	0	0
Profits chargeable to corporation tax	7,000	0	
MCT at 0%	0	0	0
Unrelieved gift aid donations	0	20,000	20,000

Activity 12.6

Profits chargeable to corporation tax

	Year ended 31.12.01	*6 months ended 30.6.02*	*Year ended 30.6.03*
	£	£	£
Schedule D Case I	109,000	85,000	0
Schedule D Case III	11,000	12,000	14,000
Chargeable gains (losses are carried forward)	0	0	0
	120,000	97,000	14,000
Less s 393A(1) current period relief	-	-	(14,000)
	120,000	97,000	0
Less: s 393A carryback	(60,000)	(97,000)	0
	60,000	0	0
Less: gift aid donation	0	0	0
PCTCT	60,000	0	0
CT @ 19%	11,400	0	0
Unrelieved gift aid donation	0	3,000	1,000

Loss memorandum	£
Loss	200,000
Less s 393A(1) relief	(14,000)
Less s 393A(1) relief (6 months)	(97,000)
Less 6/12 × £120,000 (restricted)	(60,000)
Loss carried forward	29,000

A loss of £29,000 is available at 30 June 2003 to carry forward against future profits of the same trade. The loss carried back under s 393A ICTA 1988 can be carried back only to set against profits of the previous 12 months.

There is also a capital loss of £4,000 to carry forward against future chargeable gains at 30.6.03. Note that capital losses cannot be carried back. The £5,000 capital loss in y/e 31.12.01 is offset to the extent of £2,000 in period ended 30.6.02 and the carried forward balance of £3,000 is added to the carried forward £1,000 capital loss of y/e 30.6.03 to total £4,000.

Chapter 13: National insurance

Activity 13.1

Earnings threshold £4,615 ÷ 12 = £385

Secondary contributions

£(2,750 – 385) = £2,365 × 12.8% × 12 = £3,632.64

Activity 13.2

'Earnings' £(200 + 50)	£250
Business travel reimbursed and relocation expenses are not treated as earnings.	
Earnings threshold - £4,615 ÷ 52 = £89	
£(250 – 89) = £161 × 12.8%	£20.61

Activity 13.3

£10,000 × 12.8% = £1,280

There is no earnings threshold in respect of Class 1A contributions.

Activity 13.4

	£
Profits	13,950
Less lower limit	(4,615)
	9,335

Class 4 NICs = 8% × £9,335 = £746.80 (main only)

Activity 13.5

	£
Profits (upper limit)	30,940
Less lower limit	(4,615)
	26,325

	£
Main rate Class 4 NICs 8% × £26,325	2,106.00
Additional rate class 4 NICs £(35,000 – 30,940) = £4,060 × 1%	40.60
	2,146.60

Activity 13.6

(a) *Class 1*

Earnings £2,500 pa

Monthly earnings threshold £4,615 ÷ 12 = £385

Secondary contributions

£(2,500 – 385) = £2,115 × 12.8% × 12 = £3,248.64

Class 1A

Car and medical insurance

£(5,000 + 750) = £5,750 × 12.8% = £736.00

Total contributions = £3,984.64

Childcare vouchers are not liable to Class 1 NICs, nor Class IA NICs

(b) *Class 2 contributions*

£2 × 52 =	£104
Class 4 contributions	
	£
Profits (upper limit)	30,940
Less: lower limit	(4,615)
	26,325
	£
Main rate Class 4 NICs	
8% × 26,325	2,106.00
Additional rate Class 4 NICs	
1% × (38,000 – 30,940)	70.60
Class 4 contributions	2,176.60
Total contributions (104 + 2,176.60)	£2,281

Chapter 14: Administration of income tax and CGT

Activity 14.1

	£
Total income tax	9,200
Less: tax credits (1,700 + 1,500)	(3,200)
	6,000

Payments on account for 2004/05:

31 January 2005:	Income tax £6,000 × 1/2	£3,000
31 July 2005:	As before, income tax	£3,000

There is no requirement to make payments on account of capital gains tax.

Activity 14.2

Income tax = £18,000 – £2,750 – £6,500 – £6,500 = £2,250

CGT = £5,120

Final payment due on 31 January 2005 for 2003/04 = £2,250 + £5,120 = £7,370

Activity 14.3

Herbert made an excessive claim to reduce his payments on account, and will therefore be charged interest on the reduction. The payments on account should have been £4,500 each based on the 2002/03 liability (not £5,000 each based on the 2003/04 liability). Interest will be charged as follows:

(a) first payment on account

- (i) on £3,500 – nil – paid on time
- (ii) on £1,000 from due date of 31 January 2004 to day before payment, 18 February 2005

(b) second payment on account

- (i) on £3,500 from due date of 31 July 2004 to day before payment, 11 August 2004
- (ii) on £1,000 from due date of 31 July 2004 to day before payment, 18 February 2005

(c) balancing payment

- (i) on £3,500 from due date of 31 January 2005 to day before payment, 18 February 2005

Activity 14.4

Tutorial note. Three payments of income tax may need to be made in respect of a tax year. Two payments of account are normally made on 31 January in the tax year and on the following 31 July. These are based on the prior year tax liability. A final balancing payment of the income tax due for a year is normally made on the 31 January following the year.

Tim's Payments on Account for 2003/04 were based on the excess of his 2002/03 tax liability over amounts deducted under the PAYE system, amounts deducted at source and tax credits on dividends:

		£
2002/03 tax liability		16,800
Less:	PAYE	(7,200)
	Tax deducted at source	(800)
	Tax credit on dividends	(200)
Total payments on account for 2003/04		8,600

Two equal payments on account of £4,300 (£8,600 / 2) were required. The due dates for these payments were 31 January 2004 and 31 July 2004 respectively.

The final payment in respect of Tim's 2003/04 tax liability was due on 31 January 2005 and was calculated as follows:

		£
2003/04 tax liability		22,000
Less:	PAYE	(7,100)
	Tax deducted at source	(900)
	Tax credit on dividends	(250)
		13,750
Less:	Payments on account	(8,600)
Final payment due 31.1.05		5,150

Chapter 15: Payment of tax by companies

Activity 15.1

The company must file a return for the two accounting periods ending in the period specified in the notice requiring a return. The first accounting period is the twelve months to 31 December 2002 and the second is the six months to 30 June 2003. The filing date is twelve months after the end of the relevant period of account, 30 June 2004.

Activity 15.2

A The return is less than three months late and it is only the second late filing of a return so the fixed penalty is £100.

Activity 15.3

D Notice of an enquiry must be given by a year after the later of:

(a) the filing date, 30 June 2005

(b) the 31 January, 30 April, 31 July or 31 October following the actual delivery of the return, 31 October 2005

ie 31 October 2005

Activity 15.4

B The instalments are due on the 14th of the month. For a twelve month accounting period the first instalment is due in the seventh month and thereafter instalments are due at three monthly intervals.

Take care: In this question you were asked for the due date of the **FINAL QUARTERLY INSTALMENT**. This is due in the fourth month after the end of the accounting period.

Activity 15.5

£880,000 must be paid in instalments.

The amount of each instalment is $3 \times \frac{£880,000}{8} = £330,000$

The due dates are:

	£
14 August 2003	330,000
14 November 2003	330,000
14 January 2004 (balance)	220,000

Activity 15.6

A Patent royalties received from individuals are received net of 22% tax:

$$£7{,}800 \times \frac{22}{78} = £2{,}200.$$

As the debenture interest was paid to another UK company, it would have been paid gross

Activity 15.7

Tutorial note. 'Large' companies must pay their CT liabilities in quarterly instalments.

(a) Hogg Ltd's corporation tax liability for the year is £1,750,000 × 30% = £525,000. The due dates for the payment of corporation tax by Hogg Ltd in respect of the year to 31.12.03 are:

	£
14 July 2003 1/4 × £525,000	131,250
14 October 2003 1/4 × £525,000	131,250
14 January 2004 1/4 × £525,000	131,250
14 April 2004 1/4 × £525,000	131,250
Total	525,000

(b) The due dates for the payment of corporation tax instalments by Hogg Ltd in respect of the ten months to 31 October 2005 are:

	£
14 July 2005	180,000
14 October 2005	180,000
14 January 2006	180,000
14 February 2006 (4th month of next accounting period) (balance)	60,000

Tutorial note: The amount of the instalments is $^3/_n$ × CT = $^3/_{10}$ × £600,000 = £180,000.

Appendix

Index to tax forms

Note. We have not included Section 4 of the CT600 return form here as you will not be required to complete it in your assessment

CT600 RETURN FORM

1

Inland Revenue

Company Tax Return

Form CT600 (2002) Version 1

For accounting periods ending on or after 1 July 1999

This form (or an Inland Revenue approved substitute version of it), together with any relevant *Supplementary Pages*, must be used whenever a company is required by form *CT603* (the *Notice*) to deliver a company tax return for any period ended on or after 1 July 1999. This form sets out the information we need and provides a standard format for calculations. Please complete the 'Company information' immediately and then read the notes on pages 2 and 3 and Section 1 on pages 4 and 5 before completing any other sections.

Company information

Company name

Company registration number *(if registered)*

Reference - *as shown on the Notice* / /

Address - Registered office address, or if not registered, Treasurer's address - *complete if different from that shown on the Notice.*

Postcode

Period covered by this return *(cannot exceed 12 months)*

From *(dd/mm/yyyy)* / /

To / /

Now read the notes on pages 2 and 3 and Section 1 on pages 4 and 5 before you complete the rest of the form and any of the Supplementary Pages you might need. Fill in the 'Summary' and 'Declaration' below only when you have completed the relevant sections, and before you send back the return to the issuing Inland Revenue office.

Summary of return information

Is there a repayment? *Put an 'X' in box if 'Yes'*

- for this period?
- for an earlier period?

I have read and completed the appropriate parts of Section 7 on pages 14 and 15

(S102 FA 1989 surrender is a repayment claim for this purpose)

Are you filing more than one return for this company now?

Put an 'X' in box if 'Yes'

Does this return contain estimated figures?

Read note 3 before completing this box

Are you seeking approved investment trust company status under S842(1) ICTA 1988?

Attach a schedule showing how the company has met all the conditions. See note 26

I attach

- accounts and computations for the period to which this return relates
- accounts and computations for a different period
- if no accounts, say why not

I am sending you the following completed ***Supplementary Pages*** **as part of the return form** *Put an 'X' in appropriate box(es)*

Loans to participators by close companies (CT600A)

Controlled foreign companies (CT600B)

Group and consortium (CT600C)

Insurance (CT600D)

Charities and Community Amateur Sports Clubs (CASCs) (CT600E)

Tonnage tax (CT600F)

Corporate Venturing Scheme (CT600G)

Cross-border royalties (CT600H)

Supplementary charge in respect of ring fence trades (CT600I)

Declaration

Warning

Giving false information in the return, or concealing any part of the company's profits or tax payable, can lead to the company and you being prosecuted.

Declaration

The information I have given on this form and the accompanying Supplementary Pages is correct and complete to the best of my knowledge and belief.

Signature

Except where a liquidator has been appointed, any person who is authorised to do so may sign on behalf of the company. A photocopy of a signature is not acceptable

Name *(in capital letters)*

Date *(dd/mm/yyyy)* / /

Status

BS 11/02

CT600 (2002)

2 CT600 (2002) Version 1

General advice on CTSA

Notes here and elsewhere on CT600 forms, including the CT600 Guide (2002) (the *Guide*) do not give a detailed description of corporation tax self assessment (CTSA) for companies.

The notes have been written to help you

- understand your corporation tax obligations
- complete the company tax return form (*CT600*).

Under CTSA, companies have to use the format set out by the Inland Revenue. They will be able to do so by completing the official return form, a photocopy of it, or a software or substitute version approved by the Inland Revenue.

Much basic advice relevant to completing the *CT600*, and any necessary *Supplementary Pages*, is shown on the forms themselves. The *Guide* has additional notes, either relevant to CTSA generally, or specific to box entries you may need to make, where we cannot fit the advice directly onto the relevant return form. We also list at the end of the *Guide* tax rates and limits, and some further information available, and where you can find it.

The notes here and in the *Guide* do not give a detailed account of how to calculate the company's liability. You are advised to seek professional advice about any transactions that seem likely to give rise to the liability, or relief referred to, if you are not a tax expert.

If you make a mistake while completing the *CT600* or any of the *Supplementary Pages*, make a note of the form name and its number and download a copy from the Inland Revenue's website (www.inlandrevenue.gov.uk) or call the **CTSA Orderline** on **0845 300 6555**, or **Fax 0845 300 6777** for a replacement copy. The CTSA Orderline is open 7 days a week between 8am and 10 pm. **Please note that only the Orderline, not local Inland Revenue offices, hold supplies.**

Companies in partnership

If the company carries on a trade, profession or business in partnership, please include with the company tax return a note of the partnership tax reference number. For this purpose a partnership includes a partnership governed by the Partnership Act 1890, a Limited Partnership registered under the Limited Partnership Act 1907, and a Limited Liability Partnership which carries on a business with a view of profit and which is registered under the Limited Liability Partnership Act 2000.

You must also include the profits, gains, losses or income allocated to the company by the partnership statement. The amounts should be included in the appropriate boxes of the form *CT600*. Where the company and the partnership accounting periods are not the same, the company's share of profits should be apportioned (normally on a time basis) to its own accounting periods.

If the company is a member of a foreign partnership, please include with the return a copy of the partnership accounts together with the computation showing its share of partnership taxable profits, gains, losses or income. That share should be included in the appropriate boxes as detailed above.

Companies accounting in foreign currencies

If the company is:

- a UK company which prepares its accounts in a currency other than sterling ("a foreign currency"), or
- a company which prepares its accounts in sterling, but has a branch or other part of its business for which financial records are kept in a foreign currency, or
- a non-resident company which submits a return of accounts in sterling for a UK branch, based on financial records kept in a foreign currency,

special rules apply, but you must still complete each relevant box on the CT600 in sterling.

If the company is a UK company which prepares its accounts in a foreign currency, you should compute all the profits and losses of the company (except capital gains and losses) in that foreign currency. You should then make whatever deductions are appropriate for trading losses, management expenses and non-trade loan relationships deficits which have been brought forward from an earlier accounting period and are expressed in that currency. You then take the sterling equivalent of the resulting figure.

This, when aggregated with chargeable gains, and any reliefs or deductions expressed in sterling (such as group relief), gives the profit chargeable to corporation tax to be entered into box 33. You must, however, translate each item of income comprised within the overall figure of profit, and each deduction claimed, into sterling before entering it on to the CT600.

If the company prepares its accounts partly from financial statements in a foreign currency (the first two bullet points above), you should compute the profits or losses of the branch in the foreign currency, and then translate the result into sterling.

Wherever you need to translate amounts from the foreign currency into sterling, you should do it in a way which accords with generally accepted accounting practice, and you should use the exchange rate employed in the company's accounts (provided it is an arm's length rate).

Important points

- **As soon as you receive the *Notice to deliver a company tax return* (the *Notice*)** make sure you obtain all the *Supplementary Pages* you need. The information on pages 4 and 5 in Section 1 should help you decide which you will need and how to get them. Please contact the Inland Revenue office shown on the *Notice* if you need more help.
- **Members' clubs, societies and voluntary associations** may only need to complete the *Company information, Summary* and *Declaration* sections on page 1, and the short calculation on pages 6 and 7. Community Amateur Sports Clubs (CASCs) need to complete the *Charities and CASC Supplementary Pages (form CT600E)*. Note 1 in the *Company Tax Return Guide (the Guide)* gives advice about what to complete but our leaflet *'Clubs, societies and voluntary associations' (IR46)* gives more detailed information and includes an example of a completed form *CT600*. The leaflet is available to download from the Inland Revenue's website (www.inlandrevenue.gov.uk) or from the CTSA Orderline on 0845 300 6555.
- **'Company' includes** every kind of body, club, society, association or organisation that is chargeable to corporation tax, whether or not it is incorporated.
- **Please** follow the instructions by each box but **do not** make an entry where the company did not have the item specified. Please do **not** enter minus amounts in any box. Enter whole figures only in the boxes unless decimals or pence are shown.
- **Some box numbers** are out of order and there is no box number 113, 161 or 170. Boxes that are out of order have been added to the Version 1 form since 1999 to take account of changes in the law in years 2000 to 2002.
- **References to *notes* throughout the form are to those in the *Guide* which will help you complete this return form.**

Which sections you need to complete

After pages 2 and 3, read Section 1 on pages 4 and 5, then obtain and complete any relevant *Supplementary Pages*.

All trading companies must complete Section 2. All companies must then complete either the Short calculation (Section 3) **or** the Detailed calculation (Section 4). Advice at the beginning of each calculation will help you decide which one is appropriate. If you have no entries, or only zero entries (where there are losses), to make you need not complete Section 3 or 4, but you should complete Sections 5 or 6 as appropriate.

Complete Section 5 if you are claiming capital allowances or enhanced expenditure on Research and Development or land remediation expenditure.

Complete Section 6 if, in this period, the company has any of the losses or excess amounts listed there. Group companies must also show the maximum amounts they intend to surrender by way of group or consortium relief.

Complete Section 7 if you wish to give us general or specific instructions about repayments, including any surrenders.

Completion of Section 8 is optional but we would like you to complete it if the company charges directors' remuneration in its accounts.

What to do when you have completed the return form

When you have completed the appropriate sections make sure you give us all the information requested in the Summary on page 1. Once you have done this, sign and date the *Declaration* and send the **whole** form to us. Attach any supporting calculations, claims or surrender documentation. Send them along with the relevant completed *Supplementary Pages*, company accounts, computations and, where prepared, directors' and auditors' reports. *Note 3* tells you the date by which you must do this (the filing date).

It is a good idea to keep a copy of the completed return for your own records.

You must pay any tax outstanding that you calculate is due. A payslip was attached to the *Notice, which also includes advice on how to pay. Note 20* tells you about payment dates.

Do not send back the *Guide* but please keep it for reference purposes.

When we receive the return

When we receive your completed return we will process it, based on your figures, and record the amount you have shown on form CT600 as the tax due for this period. At this stage we will acknowledge receipt of the return.

The *note* on page 12 of the *Guide* tells you the time limits within which you can amend the return, and within which we can correct or enquire into it.

Remember

- **Interest is charged on tax paid late.**
- **The company may be liable to penalties if its return is late or incorrect.**

4 CT600 (2002) Version 1

Section 1: Which *Supplementary Pages* must be completed?

This Section will help you decide if you need any *Supplementary Pages*. Most company agents have supplies but if you do not have an agent, or your agent does not hold stocks, please call the CTSA Orderline on 0845 300 6555, or fax on 0845 300 6777. Make a note of the name and form number of the *Supplementary Page(s)* you want before calling. The CTSA Orderline is open 7 days a week from 8am to 10pm. Also you can download them from the Inland Revenue's website **www.inlandrevenue.gov.uk**

If you need further advice please contact the Inland Revenue office shown on the *Notice*. ***Please note that local offices do not hold stocks of forms.***

Members' clubs, societies and voluntary associations are unlikely to need any *Supplementary Pages* unless registered with the Inland Revenue as a Community Amateur Sports Club.

Close companies *(see note 2)*

If the company is close and made a loan, or loans, to an individual participator, or associate of a participator, in the return period which has not been repaid within the return period, **you must complete** the *Loans to participators by close companies Supplementary Pages (form CT600A)* and the Detailed calculation on pages 8 to 11.

Controlled foreign companies (CFCs) *(See 'Other publications of interest' on page 12 of the Guide)*

If, in this period, the company had an interest of 25% or more in a foreign company which was controlled from the UK, **you must complete** the *Controlled foreign companies Supplementary Pages (form CT600B)* and, if there is a charge under S747 ICTA 1988, the Detailed calculation on pages 8 to 11.

Group and/or consortium companies

If the company is claiming or surrendering any amounts under the group relief or consortium relief provisions or is claiming or surrendering any eligible unrelieved foreign tax (EUFT) for this period **you must complete**

- the *Group and consortium Supplementary Pages (form CT600C)*
- the Detailed calculation on pages 8 to 11, if you are claiming group or consortium relief or EUFT, and
- Section 6 on page 13 if you are surrendering any group or consortium relief.

Insurance companies and friendly societies

If the company or society

- made claims in this period under Schedule 19AB ICTA 1988 to provisional payments (including notional repayments in respect of tax on gilt interest) or
- has entered into business in the accounting period which it treats as overseas life assurance business (OLAB)

you must complete the *Insurance Supplementary Pages (form CT600D)* and the Detailed calculation on pages 8 to 11.

Charities and Community Amateur Sports Clubs (CASCs)

If, in this period, the charity/CASC is claiming exemption or partial exemption from tax **you must complete** the *Charities and Community Amateur Sports Clubs Supplementary Pages (form CT600E)* and any relevant section of the *CT600* for taxable income.

Tonnage tax

If, for a period beginning on or after 1 January 2000, the company or group operates ships and has elected for the tonnage tax regime, **you must complete** the *Tonnage tax Supplementary Pages (form CT600F)* and the Detailed calculation on pages 8 to 11.

Corporate Venturing Scheme (CVS)

If, for shares issued on or after 1 April 2000 but before 1 April 2010, the company is claiming under CVS:

- investment relief on the amount subscribed for shares, or
- relief against income for losses on disposals of shares, whether the claim is to be given effect to in this or an earlier period, or
- postponement of certain chargeable gains where the gains are reinvested

you must complete the *Corporate Venturing Scheme Supplementary Pages (form CT600G)* and the Detailed calculation on pages 8 to 11.

Cross-border royalties

If the company makes royalty payments overseas after 1 October 2002, and reasonably believes that the recipient of the royalties would be entitled to treaty relief on any tax deducted, the company is entitled to make such payments without deduction of tax or at the rate specified by reference to the double taxation treaty appropriate to the country of residence of the payee.

All UK companies that make such payments **must complete** the *Cross-border royalties Supplementary Pages (form CT600H)*, as well as any relevant section of *form CT600*. All companies that make any cross-border royalty payment, whether or not under such reasonable belief, should also complete box 165 at the end of either Section 3 or 4.

Oil extraction activities subject to the supplementary charge in respect of ring fence trades

If, for any period beginning (or deemed to have begun) on or after 17 April 2002 the company carried on a ring fence trade **you must complete** the *Supplementary charge in respect of ring fence trades Supplementary Pages (form CT600I)* and the Detailed calculation on pages 8 to 11.

Section 2: Turnover of the company *(see note 4)*

You must complete this Section if the company has trading or professional income.

Members' clubs, societies and voluntary associations that do not trade outside their membership need not complete this Section.

Investment companies and Unit Trusts need not complete this Section.

Turnover

1 **Total turnover from trade or profession**
Enter the total for this return period. Enter whole figures only — 1 £

2 **Banks, building societies, insurance companies and other financial concerns**
Put an 'X' in this box if you do not have a recognised turnover and have not made an entry in box 1. See note 4 — 2

This is the end of Section 2. Unless you have no entries to make, please now complete either Section 3 on pages 6 and 7, OR Section 4 on pages 8 to 11.

6 CT600 (2002) Version 1

Section 3: Short calculation

You may complete this section if it covers all the entries you need to make and each entry is less than £10 million.

In all other cases, or if you prefer, complete Section 4 instead. You should enclose explanations and calculations of any figures you have estimated or which are not immediately recognisable from the company's accounts and complete the box in the Summary on page 1. If you include a valuation you should state from where you obtained it. The figures to be entered are those adjusted for tax purposes, after deducting capital allowances and adding balancing charges, where appropriate.

If the company is close and has made loans to an individual participator, or associate of a participator, in this period that were not repaid within the period, you need to complete Section 4 instead.

Please note that certain numbered boxes are missing from the Short calculation.

Income

Enter whole figures only, unless decimals or pence are shown.

3 **Trading and professional profits**
Complete Section 6 if there is a loss. See note 5 — 3 £

4 **Trading losses brought forward claimed against profits**
Only include losses made in the same trade. Include charges treated as losses. ***Do not enter an amount larger than is needed to cover the profits in box 3.*** *See notes 5 and 6* — 4 £

5 **Net trading and professional profits**
If box 4 equals box 3, enter '0'. Leave this box blank if there are no trading profits in box 3 — box 3 minus box 4 — 5 £

7 **Profits and gains from non-trading loan relationships and derivative contracts (financial instruments)**
Include bank, building society or other interest, taking into account gains and losses from exchange fluctuations, and any other profits and gains even if tax has been deducted. Also include intra-group income under S247(4) ICTA 1988 which represents interest on loan relationships. You will need to complete the 'Detailed calculation', at Section 4 and Section 6 if you have deficits on non-trading loan relationships from this, earlier or later accounting periods to include. See note 8 — 7 £

8 **Annuities, annual payments and discounts not arising from loan relationships and from which income tax has not been deducted**
Exclude any amount included in box 7 — 8 £

10 **Income from which income tax has been deducted**
Enter the gross amount before tax and exclude any amount included in box 7. See note 9 — 10 £

12 **Income from UK land and buildings**
Enter the amount net of allowable expenses. Complete Section 6 if there is a loss. See note 10 — 12 £

159 **Non-trading gains on intangible fixed assets**
From assets created or acquired on or after 1 April 2002. See note 35 — 159 £

146 **Annual profits and gains not falling under any other heading**
Enter amount net of losses. Complete Section 6 if there is a loss. See note 7 — 146 £

Chargeable gains

14 **Gross chargeable gains**
Complete Section 6 if there is a loss. See note 11 — 14 £

15 **Allowable losses including losses brought forward**
Do not enter an amount larger than the amount of gross gains shown in box 14. *See note 11* — 15 £

16 **Net chargeable gains**
If box 15 equals box 14, enter '0' — box 14 minus box 15 — 16 £

19 **Profits before other deductions and reliefs** — total of boxes 5, 7, 8, 10, 12, 159, 146 and 16 — 19 £

Deductions and reliefs

26 & 27 **Trading losses of this or a later accounting period under S393A ICTA 1988**
Put an 'X' in box 26 if amounts carried back from later accounting periods are included in box 27. See note 12 — 26 [ ] 27 £

30 **Profits before charges** — box 19 minus box 27 — 30 £

31 **Charges paid**
Include qualifying charity giving. This figure must not exceed profits shown in box 30. See note 13 — 31 £

Corporation tax profits

33 Profits chargeable to corporation tax — box 30 minus box 31 — 33 £

Copy this figure in box 33 to the box at the top of page 7

BPP PROFESSIONAL EDUCATION

Section 3: Short calculation continued

33 Profits chargeable to corporation tax *Enter the figure from box 33 on page 6* £

Tax calculation If you claim tax is chargeable at the starting or small companies' rate, or if you are claiming marginal starting rate or small companies' relief, complete boxes 34 - 38. If there are no associated companies, or franked investment income, please enter the financial year(s) in boxes 35 and 37, and '0' in boxes 34, 36 and, if necessary, 38. *See notes 15 and 20*

34 Franked investment income and foreign income dividends arising in the period covered by the return. *See note 15* — **34** £

35 - 38 Number of companies associated with this company in the/each financial year covered by this return
Exclude this company. See note 15

Financial year *(yyyy)*	Number of associated companies
35	**36**
37	**38**

39 - 59 Corporation tax chargeable *See note 16 and page 12 of the Guide*

Financial year *(yyyy)*	Amount of profit	Rate of tax	Tax
39	**40** £	**41** • %	**42** £ p
49	**50** £	**51** • %	**52** £ p

59 Corporation tax chargeable — box 42 plus box 52 — **59** £ p

Reliefs and deductions in terms of tax

60 Marginal starting rate or small companies' relief
Attach your computation. See notes 15 and 16 — **60** £ p

62 Advance corporation tax (restricted if necessary)
See note 17 — **62** £ p

63 Total reliefs and deductions in terms of tax
Cannot exceed corporation tax chargeable amount in box 59 — box 60 plus box 62 — **63** £ p

68 Tax chargeable — box 59 minus box 63 — **68** £ p

69 Income tax deducted from gross income included in profits
Do not include deductions used to cover income tax for which the company was liable to account to the Inland Revenue on payments it has made. See note 18 — **69** £ p

70 Income tax repayable to the company
Complete if box 69 is greater than box 68. Also complete Section 7 — **70** £ p

72 Tax payable - this is your self-assessment of tax payable
Follow the instructions over the box. Enter 0.00 if you calculate that no tax is payable. See notes 20 and 34 — box 68 minus box 69 — **72** £ p

Tax reconciliation

73 Deductions (before 6 April 2002 only) under the Construction Industry Scheme
Enclose forms CIS25 for amount entered. See note 19 — **73** £ p

74 Construction industry deductions repayable - before 6 April 2002 only
Complete if box 73 is greater than box 72. Also complete Section 7 — box 73 minus box 72 — **74** £ p

75 Tax already paid (and not already repaid)
Exclude amounts entered in boxes 69 and 73. See note 21 — **75** £ p

76 Tax outstanding
This amount is payable to the Accounts Office. See note 23 — box 72 minus boxes 73 and 75 — **76** £ p

77 Tax overpaid
Complete Section 7 — box 75 plus box 73 minus box 72 — **77** £ p

Indicators

Put an 'X' in the relevant box(es) if, in the period, the company

79 should have made (whether it has or not) quarterly instalment payments under the Corporation Tax (Instalment Payments) Regulations 1998 *See notes 20 and 34* — **79**

80 is within a group payment arrangement for this period *See note 34* — **80**

164 has written down or sold intangible assets *See note 35* — **164**

165 has made cross-border royalty payments *whether or not form CT600H completed. See Section 1 note on page 5* — **165**

This is the end of the Short calculation.

12 CT600 (2002) Version 1

Section 5: Capital allowances and enhanced expenditure

Complete this section if you are claiming capital allowances or enhanced expenditure. You should also show balancing charges taken into account in Section 3 or 4 calculations. Show details of qualifying expenditure on which writing-down allowances may be claimed, even if you are not claiming any allowances for this period. *See notes 25, 31 and 33. Enter whole figures only.*

Research and Development (R&D) enhanced expenditure *See note 31 for information on R&D, including vaccine research*

166 & Put an 'X' in box 166 if the claim is made by a small or medium-sized enterprise (SME), including a SME subcontractor to a large company — 166

167 Put an 'X' in box 167 if the claim is made by a large company — 167

151 **R&D enhanced expenditure**
SMEs or large companies. Enter enhanced expenditure figure on which claim is based — 151 £

169 **R&D enhanced expenditure of an SME on work sub-contracted to it by a large company**
Enter enhanced expenditure on which claim is based. — 169 £

168 **Vaccines research expenditure**
Enter additional deduction under Paragraph 14(2)(a) or 21(2) of Schedule 13 FA 2002 — 168 £

Land remediation enhanced expenditure

156 *Enter amount equal to 150% of actual expenditure. See note 33* — 156 £

Capital allowances and balancing charges *See note 25*

81 & 171 **Expenditure on machinery and plant on which first year allowance is claimed**
Put an 'X' in box 171 if claim includes enhanced capital allowances for energy-saving investments. See note 25 — 171 — 81 £

82 **Qualifying expenditure on machinery and plant on long-life assets** — 82 £

83 **Qualifying expenditure on machinery and plant on other assets** — 83 £

Exclude any amounts included in box 81

Charges and allowances included in calculation of trading profits or losses

	Balancing charges	Capital allowances
84 - 85 Cars *Any cars not included in the general pool*	84 £	85 £
86 - 87 Machinery and plant - long-life assets	86 £	87 £
88 - 89 Machinery and plant - other assets	88 £	89 £
90 - 91 Industrial buildings and structures *Including qualifying hotels, and commercial buildings and hotels in enterprise zones*	90 £	91 £
92 - 93 Other charges and allowances *For example agricultural buildings, mineral extraction, research and development, patents*	92 £	93 £

Charges and allowances not included in calculation of trading profits or losses

	Balancing charges	Capital allowances
94 - 95	94 £	95 £

157 **Flat conversion** *Put an 'X' in box 157 if box 95 includes flat conversion allowances* — 157

This is the end of Section 5.

Section 6: Losses, deficits and excess amounts

Complete this section if the company has incurred, in this period, any of the losses or deficits shown below, or if it has, for this period, any of the excess amounts shown below. Companies that are proposing to surrender any amount as group or consortium relief should also complete the second column. *See note 27.*

Enter whole figures only, unless decimals or pence are shown.

Box	Item	Arising	Maximum available for surrender as group relief
96 - 97	**Trading losses Case I** *See note 5*	calculated under S393 ICTA 1988 **96** £	calculated under S393A ICTA 1988 **97** £
98	**Trading losses Case V**	calculated under S393 ICTA 1988 **98** £	
99 - 100	**Non-trade deficits on loan relationships and derivative contracts** *See note 8*	calculated under S82 FA 1996 **99** £	calculated under S83 FA 1996 **100** £
101 - 102	**Schedule A losses** *UK land and buildings. See note 10*	calculated under S392A ICTA 1988 **101** £	calculated under S403 ICTA 1988 **102** £
103	**Overseas property business losses Case V**	calculated under S392B ICTA 1988 **103** £	
104	**Losses Case VI**	calculated under S396 ICTA 1988 **104** £	
105	**Capital losses**	calculated under S16 TCGA 1992 **105** £	
172 - 173	**Non-trading losses on intangible fixed assets** *See note 35*	calculated under Schedule 29 FA 2002 **172** £	calculated under S403 ICTA 1988 **173** £
		Excess	
106	**Excess non-trade capital allowances** *Excess over income in period*		calculated under S403 ICTA 1988 **106** £
107	**Excess charges** *See note 13*		calculated under S403 ICTA 1988 **107** £
108 - 109	**Excess management expenses** *See note 32*	calculated under S75(3) ICTA 1988 **108** £	calculated under S403 ICTA 1988 **109** £
110	**Excess interest distributions**	calculated under S468L(7) ICTA 1988 **110** £	

This is the end of Section 6.

14 CT600 (2002) Version 1

Section 7: Overpayments and repayments (including S102 FA 1989 surrenders)

Complete this section if you believe there is

- a repayment due for the period covered by this return
- a repayment due for an earlier period as a result of events in the period covered by this return.

Small repayments

If you do not want us to make small repayments please either put an 'X' in box 174 or complete box 175 below. 'Repayments' here include tax, payable credits, interest, and late-filing penalties or any combination of them.

You must renew or change any authority you give each time you complete a return. This authority overrides any previous authority given, so if you leave boxes 174 and 175 blank we will make any repayment arising subsequently, however small, and even if it is for an accounting period previously covered by a limit for repayment. If you want to change your instructions before you next complete a return you must tell us in writing, signed by an authorised person (as for the return).

If you complete either of these boxes we will not make any repayment to the company or any authorised nominee unless it is more than the limit you have chosen. Any amounts below the limit will be allocated to any other CT liabilities, if there are any, or to a later accounting period.

Once a small repayment has been reallocated to another accounting period it is treated as if it had been paid for that period and any subsequent reallocations or repayments are treated as coming from that period, not its original period.

Any overpayment automatically reallocated cannot be surrendered under S102 FA 1989 to other group companies for the period in which the overpayment arose. If you think you will or might want to make such a surrender, do not complete this authority but consider completing box 124 below.

Do not repay £20 or less. 174 [ ] **Do not repay sums of** 175 £ [ ] **or less.** *Enter whole figure only*

Repayments for the period covered by this return

We will pay the company, or its nominee, the repayable amounts entered in the Tax Reconciliation (boxes 150, 155, 74 and 77). We can also repay to the company Income Tax (box 70) and it can claim for a repayment of ACT (for payments up to 6 April 1999).

If you have completed boxes 70, 74, 150, 155 or 77, attach your calculations. Make sure you have put an 'X' in the appropriate box(es) on page 1 (under 'Is there a repayment?'). If there is a surrender under S102 FA 1989 enclose the notice of surrender.

111	**Repayment of corporation tax** *Include CIS deductions before 6 April 2002 repayable and enclose forms CIS25.* *Enter amount from box 74, or CT overpaid from box 77*	111 £	p
112	**Repayment of income tax** *Enter amount from box 70*	112 £	p
114	**Repayment of advance corporation tax** *See note 22*	114 £	p
152	**Payable Research and Development tax credit** *Enter amount from box 150. See note 31*	152 £	p
158	**Payable land remediation or life assurance company tax credit** *Enter amount from box 155. See note 33*	158 £	p

Surrender under S102 FA 1989 (including surrenders under Regulation 9 Quarterly Instalments Regulations)
Repayments of advance corporation tax cannot be surrendered.

124 **The following amount is to be surrendered under S102 FA 1989,** 124 £ [ ] p

and

either

125 **the joint Notice is attached** 125 [ ]

or *(put an 'X' in either box 125 or box 126)*

126 **will follow** 126 [ ]

127 **Please stop repayment of the following amount until I send you the Notice** 127 £ [ ] p

Make sure you have put an 'X' in the appropriate box(es) on page 1 (under 'Is there a repayment?'). If there is a surrender under S102 FA 1989 enclose the letter of surrender. For a surrender under Regulation 9 (Quarterly Instalments Regulations) supply a schedule of the amount(s) and date(s) of each instalment surrendered.

Repayments for an earlier period

Events in the period covered by this return may allow claims for repayment(s) for earlier periods, for example a claim to carry back trading losses.

If the company claims when it is still able to amend its return for the previous period we wil treat the claim as an amendment. (The company can amend its return within 12 months from the statutory filing date for that period.) If it is too late to amend the return we will deal with the claim without amending the return.

Please make the claim on a separate sheet of paper sent with the return, or in the body of the covering letter. If the company is still in time it can send us an amended return for the earlier accounting period.

Put an 'X' in the appropriate box on page 1 (under 'Is there a repayment?') if you are making a repayment claim, or S102 FA 1989 surrender.

Section 7: Overpayments and repayment claims continued

Repayment claim

121 The following amount is to be repaid — **121** £ ___ p

either

122 • to the company — **122** ☐

or

123 • to the nominee in the authority given below — **123** ☐

put an 'X' in either box 122 or box 123, ***but not in both***

Bank details (for person to whom the repayment is to be made)

Repayments of corporation tax (but not currently income tax, advance corporation tax, construction industry deductions, or payable tax credits) can be made quickly and safely by direct credit (BACS) to a bank or building society account.

You should provide details of the account which is to be credited. If the details are those of the nominee you want to receive the repayment, remember to complete the authority below.

Name of bank or building society

115

Branch sort code

116

Account number

117

Name of account

118

Building society reference

119

Signature

120

Except where a liquidator has been appointed, any person who is authorised to do so may sign the BACS details on behalf of the company. A photocopy of a signature is not acceptable

Name *(in capital letters)*

120A

Payments to a person other than the company (Nominee)

Complete the authority below if you want the repayment to be made to a person **other than the company**. The Inland Revenue reserves the right not to repay to a nominee.

Please note that this authority overrides any previous authority given. Repayments will be made to the person entered here, until you tell us in this section of a later return that there is a different nominee or you give no nominee details (showing that there is now **no nominee** to receive repayments). If you want to change the nominee before you send in the next return please tell us in writing.

I, as *(enter status - company secretary, treasurer, liquidator or authorised agent, etc.)*

128

of *(enter name of company)*

129

authorise *(enter name)*

130

(enter address)

131

Postcode

Nominee reference

132

to receive on the company's behalf the amount due.

Signature

133

Except where a liquidator has been appointed, any person who is authorised to do so may sign the BACS details or an authority on behalf of the company. A photocopy of a signature is not acceptable

Name *(in capital letters)*

133A

This is the end of Section 7.

16 CT600 (2002) Version 1

Section 8: Directors' remuneration - optional section

Please complete this section if directors' remuneration is charged in the accounts supporting this form *CT600*.

Attach a continuation sheet if you need more space. *Enter whole figures only.*

Company name

134

PAYE District

135

PAYE reference

136

Accounts for the period
From *(dd/mm/yyyy)* **to**

137 **138**

Remuneration claimed as a deduction in the accounts
Show total figure for all directors

139 £

Date when accounts laid before the company in general meeting or, if resolved not to lay accounts, the date on which the accounts were approved by the directors

140

Analysis

Net remuneration voted after adjustments

Enter the net figure of remuneration after deducting employers' National Insurance contributions, employers' and employees' superannuation contributions and any benefits which have been included in the accounts' figure

141 Name of director	National Insurance number	Salary £	Bonus, fees or commission £

Put an 'X' in here if a continuation sheet is used **142**

143 **Adjustments to reconcile the analysis above with total accounts' deductions claimed - please give details** **£**

Date of commencement or cessation of directorship during the period of account

144 Name of director	National Insurance number	Date commenced	Date ceased

SELF EMPLOYMENT PAGES

Inland Revenue

Income for the year ended 5 April 2004

SELF-EMPLOYMENT

Fill in these boxes first

Name

Tax reference

If you want help, look up the box numbers in the Notes

Business details

Name of business **3.1**

Description of business **3.2**

Address of business **3.3**

Postcode

Accounting period - *read the Notes, page SEN2 before filling in these boxes*

Start **3.4** / /

End **3.5** / /

- Tick box 3.6 if details in boxes 3.1 or 3.3 have changed since your last Tax Return **3.6**
- Date of commencement if after 5 April 2000 **3.7** / /
- Date of cessation if before 6 April 2004 **3.8** / /
- Tick box 3.9 if the special arrangements for certain trades apply - *read the Notes, pages SEN11 and SEN12* **3.9**
- Tick box 3.10 if you entered details for all relevant accounting periods on last year's Tax Return and boxes 3.14 to 3.73 and 3.99 to 3.115 will be blank *(read Step 3 on page SEN2)* **3.10**
- Tick box 3.11 if your accounts do not cover the period from the last accounting date (explain why in the 'Additional information' box, box 3.116) **3.11**
- Tick box 3.12 if your accounting date has changed (only if this is a permanent change and you want it to count for tax) **3.12**
- Tick box 3.13 if this is the second or further change (explain in box 3.116 on Page SE4 why you have not used the same date as last year) **3.13**

Capital allowances - summary

	Capital allowances	Balancing charges
• Cars costing more than £12,000 (A separate calculation must be made for each car.)	**3.14** £	**3.15** £
• Other business plant and machinery	**3.16** £	**3.17** £
• Agricultural or Industrial Buildings Allowance (A separate calculation must be made for each block of expenditure.)	**3.18** £	**3.19** £
• Other capital allowances claimed (Separate calculations must be made.)	**3.20** £	**3.21** £
Total capital allowances/balancing charges	total of column above **3.22** £	total of column above **3.23** £
• Tick box 3.22A if box 3.22 includes enhanced capital allowances for environmentally friendly expenditure	**3.22A**	

Income and expenses - annual turnover below £15,000

If your annual turnover is £15,000 or more, ***ignore*** *boxes 3.24 to 3.26. Instead fill in Page SE2*

If your annual turnover is below £15,000, ***fill in boxes 3.24 to 3.26 instead of Page SE2****. Read the Notes, page SEN2.*

- Turnover including other business receipts and goods etc. taken for personal use (and balancing charges from box 3.23) **3.24** £
- Expenses allowable for tax (including capital allowances from box 3.22) **3.25** £

Net profit (put figure in brackets if a loss) box 3.24 *minus* box 3.25 **3.26** £

You must now fill in Page SE3

SA103

BS 12/2002net

TAX RETURN ■ SELF-EMPLOYMENT: PAGE SE1

Income and expenses - annual turnover £15,000 or more

You must fill in this Page if your annual turnover is £15,000 or more - read the Notes, page SEN2

If you were registered for VAT, do the figures in boxes 3.29 to 3.64, include VAT? **3.27** [ ] or exclude VAT? **3.28** [ ]

Sales/business income (turnover) **3.29** £

	Disallowable expenses included in boxes 3.46 to 3.63	Total expenses	
• Cost of sales	3.30 £	3.46 £	
• Construction industry subcontractor costs	3.31 £	3.47 £	
• Other direct costs	3.32 £	3.48 £	
		Gross profit/(loss)	box 3.29 *minus* (boxes 3.46 + 3.47 + 3.48) 3.49 £
		Other income/profits	3.50 £
• Employee costs	3.33 £	3.51 £	
• Premises costs	3.34 £	3.52 £	
• Repairs	3.35 £	3.53 £	
• General administrative expenses	3.36 £	3.54 £	
• Motor expenses	3.37 £	3.55 £	
• Travel and subsistence	3.38 £	3.56 £	
• Advertising, promotion and entertainment	3.39 £	3.57 £	
• Legal and professional costs	3.40 £	3.58 £	
• Bad debts	3.41 £	3.59 £	
• Interest	3.42 £	3.60 £	
• Other finance charges	3.43 £	3.61 £	
• Depreciation and loss/(profit) on sale	3.44 £	3.62 £	
• Other expenses	3.45 £	3.63 £	
	Put the total of boxes 3.30 to 3.45 in box 3.66 below	Total expenses	total of boxes 3.51 to 3.63 3.64 £
		Net profit/(loss)	boxes 3.49 + 3.50 *minus* 3.64 3.65 £

Tax adjustments to net profit or loss

• Disallowable expenses	boxes 3.30 to 3.45 3.66 £	
• Adjustments (apart from disallowable expenses) that increase profits. Examples are goods taken for personal use and amounts brought forward from an earlier year because of a claim under ESC B11 about compulsory slaughter of farm animals	3.67 £	
• Balancing charges (from box 3.23)	3.68 £	
Total additions to net profit (deduct from net loss)		boxes 3.66 + 3.67 + 3.68 3.69 £
• Capital allowances (from box 3.22)	3.70 £	
• Deductions from net profit (add to net loss)	3.71 £	boxes 3.70 + 3.71 3.72 £
Net business profit for tax purposes (put figure in brackets if a loss)		boxes 3.65 + 3.69 *minus* 3.72 3.73 £

BS 12/2002net TAX RETURN ■ SELF-EMPLOYMENT: PAGE SE2 *Now fill in Page SE3*

*You **must** fill in boxes 3.74 and 3.75 and **all other boxes** that apply to you, on this Page*

Adjustments to arrive at taxable profit or loss

Basis period begins	3.74 / /	and ends	3.75 / /
Profit or loss of this account for tax purposes (box 3.26 or 3.73)			3.76 £
Adjustment to arrive at profit or loss for this basis period			3.77 £
• Overlap profit brought forward	3.78 £	• Deduct overlap relief used this year	3.79 £
• Overlap profit carried forward	3.80 £		
Averaging for farmers and creators of literary or artistic works *(see Notes, page SEN9, if you made a loss for 2003-04)*			3.81 £
Adjustment on change of basis			3.82 £
Net profit for 2003-04 (if you made a loss, enter '0')			3.83 £
Allowable loss for 2003-04 (if you made a profit, enter '0')	3.84 £		
• Loss offset against other income for 2003-04	3.85 £		
• Loss to carry back	3.86 £		
• Loss to carry forward (that is allowable loss not claimed in any other way)	3.87 £		
• Losses brought forward from earlier years	3.88 £		
• Losses brought forward from earlier years used this year			3.89 £
Taxable profit after losses brought forward			box 3.83 *minus* box 3.89 3.90 £
• Any other business income (for example, Business Start-up Allowance received in 2003-04)			3.91 £
Total taxable profits from this business			box 3.90 + box 3.91 3.92 £
• Tick box 3.93 if the figure in box 3.92 is provisional			3.93

Class 4 National Insurance contributions

• Tick box 3.94 if exception or deferment applies	3.94
• Adjustments to profit chargeable to Class 4 National Insurance contributions	3.95 £
Class 4 National Insurance contributions due	3.96 £

Subcontractors in the construction industry

• Deductions made by contractors on account of tax (please send your CIS25s to us)	3.97 £

Tax deducted from trading income

• Any tax deducted (excluding deductions made by contractors on account of tax) from trading income	3.98 £

BS 12/2002net TAX RETURN ■ SELF-EMPLOYMENT: PAGE SE3 *Please turn over*

Summary of balance sheet

Leave these boxes blank if you do not have a balance sheet

		Box	£
Assets	• Plant, machinery and motor vehicles	3.99	£
	• Other fixed assets (premises, goodwill, investments etc.)	3.100	£
	• Stock and work-in-progress	3.101	£
	• Debtors/prepayments/other current assets	3.102	£
	• Bank/building society balances	3.103	£
	• Cash in hand	3.104	£
	total of boxes 3.99 to 3.104	3.105	£
Liabilities	• Trade creditors/accruals	3.106	£
	• Loans and overdrawn bank accounts	3.107	£
	• Other liabilities	3.108	£
	total of boxes 3.106 to 3.108	3.109	£
Net business assets (put the figure in brackets if you had net business liabilities)	box 3.105 *minus* 3.109	3.110	£
Represented by	**Capital Account**		
	• Balance at start of period*	3.111	£
	• Net profit/(loss)*	3.112	£
	• Capital introduced	3.113	£
	• Drawings	3.114	£
	• Balance at end of period* (total of boxes 3.111 to 3.113 *minus* box 3.114)	3.115	£

*If the Capital Account is overdrawn, or the business made a net loss, enter the figure in brackets.

3.116 ***Additional information***

Now fill in any other supplementary Pages that apply to you.
Otherwise, go back to Page 2 of your Tax Return and finish filling it in.

BS 12/2002net

TAX RETURN ■ SELF-EMPLOYMENT: PAGE SE4

PARTNERSHIP (SHORT) PAGES

Inland Revenue

Income for the year ended 5 April 2004

PARTNERSHIP (SHORT)

Fill in these boxes first

Name

Tax reference

If you want help, look up the box numbers in the Notes

Partnership details

Partnership reference number	4.1	Description of partnership trade or profession	4.2
• Date you started being a partner (if during 2003-04)	4.3 / /	• Date you stopped being a partner (if during 2003-04)	4.4 / /

Your share of the partnership's trading or professional income

Basis period begins	4.5 / /	**and ends**	4.6 / /

• Your share of the profit or loss of this year's account for tax purposes (enter a loss in brackets)			4.7 £
• Adjustment to arrive at profit or loss for this basis period			4.8 £
• Overlap profit brought forward	4.9 £	Deduct overlap relief used this year	4.10 £
• Overlap profit carried forward	4.11 £		
• Averaging for farmers and creators of literary or artistic works (see Notes, page PN3 if the partnership made a loss in 2003-04) or foreign tax deducted, if tax credit relief not claimed			4.12 £
• Adjustment on change of basis			4.12A £
Net profit for 2003-04 (if loss, enter '0' in box 4.13 and enter the loss in box 4.14)			4.13 £
Allowable loss for 2003-04		4.14 £	
• Loss offset against other income for 2003-04		4.15 £	
• Loss to carry back		4.16 £	
• Loss to carry forward (that is, allowable loss not claimed in any other way)		4.17 £	
• Losses brought forward from last year		4.18 £	
• Losses brought forward from last year used this year			4.19 £
Taxable profit after losses brought forward			box 4.13 *minus* box 4.19 4.20 £
• Add amounts **not** included in the partnership accounts that are needed to calculate your taxable profit (for example, Enterprise Allowance (Business Start-up Allowance) received in 2003-04)			4.21 £
Total taxable profits from this business			box 4.20 + box 4.21 4.22 £

Class 4 National Insurance contributions

• Tick this box if exception or deferment applies	4.23
• Adjustments to profit chargeable to Class 4 National Insurance contributions	4.24 £
Class 4 National Insurance contributions due	4.25 £

SA104

BS 12/2002net — TAX RETURN ■ PARTNERSHIP: PAGE P1 — *Please turn over*

Your share of the partnership taxed income

- Share of taxed income (liable at 20%) — **4.70** £

Your share of the partnership trading and professional profits

- Share of partnership profits (other than that liable at 20%) — from box 4.22 — **4.73** £

Your share of the partnership tax paid

- Share of Income Tax deducted from partnership income — **4.74** £
- Share of CIS25 deductions — **4.75** £
- Share of tax deducted from trading income (not CIS25 deductions) — **4.75A** £

boxes 4.74 + 4.75 + 4.75A — **4.77** £

4.79 ***Additional information***

Now fill in any other supplementary Pages that apply to you.
Otherwise, go back to page 2 in your Tax Return and finish filling it in

BS 12/2002net

TAX RETURN ■ PARTNERSHIP: PAGE P2

CAPITAL GAINS PAGES

Inland Revenue

For the year ended 5 April 2004

CAPITAL GAINS

Fill in these boxes first

Name

Tax reference

Only use this Page if all your transactions were in quoted shares or other securities unless taper relief is due on any of them, or any were held at 31 March 1982, or you are claiming a relief, for example, Enterprise Investment Scheme deferral relief. Otherwise you cannot use this page and must use Pages CG2 to CG6 to work out all of your capital gains or allowable losses.

A Enter details of quoted shares or other securities disposed of	B Tick box if estimate or valuation used	C Enter the date of disposal	D Disposal proceeds	E Gain or loss after indexation allowance, if due (enter loss in brackets)	F Further information, including any elections made
1		/ /	£	£	
2		/ /	£	£	
3		/ /	£	£	
4		/ /	£	£	
5		/ /	£	£	
6		/ /	£	£	
7		/ /	£	£	
8		/ /	£	£	

Total gains	F1	£	*Total your gains in column E and enter the amount in box F1*
Total losses	F2	£	*Total your losses in column E and enter the amount in box F2*
Net gain/(loss)	F3 (box F1 *minus* box F2)	£	*If your net gains are below £7,900 **or** you have a net loss, there is no liability. If you have a net loss, please fill in the losses summary on Page CG8 otherwise carry on to box F4*
minus income losses set against gains	F4	£	
	F5 (box F3 *minus* box F4)	£	*If your gains are now below £7,900, there is no liability; copy box F5 to box F7 and complete Page CG8. Otherwise, carry on to box F6*
minus losses brought forward	F6	£	*Enter losses brought forward up to the **smaller** of either the total losses brought forward or the figure in box F5 **minus** £7,900*
Total taxable gains	F7 (box F5 *minus* box F6)	£	*Copy this figure to box 8.7 on Page CG8 (if F7 is blank because there is no liability, leave 8.7 blank).*

Note:
This Page is only for transactions in quoted shares or other securities. See the definition on page CGN3 of the Notes on Capital Gains.

SA108

BS 12/2002net

TAX RETURN ■ CAPITAL GAINS: PAGE CG1

Go to Page CG8

Your 2003-04 Capital Gains Tax liability

A Brief description of asset	AA* Type of disposal. Enter Q, U, L, T or O	B Tick box if estimate or valuation used	C Tick box if asset held at 31March 1982	D Enter the later of date of acquisition and 16 March 1998	E Enter the date of disposal	F Disposal proceeds	G Enter details of any elections made, reliefs claimed or due and state amount (£)
Gains on assets which are either wholly business or wholly non-business							
1				/ /	/ /	£	
2				/ /	/ /	£	
3				/ /	/ /	£	
4				/ /	/ /	£	
5				/ /	/ /	£	
6				/ /	/ /	£	
7				/ /	/ /	£	
8				/ /	/ /	£	
Gains on assets which are partly business and partly non-business (see the notes on page CGN4)							
9				/ /	/ /	£	
10				/ /	/ /	£	

* Column AA: for
- quoted shares or other securities, (see the definition on page CGN3 of the Notes) enter **Q**
- other shares or securities, enter **U**
- land and property, enter **L**
- amounts attributable to settlor (see page CGN4) enter **T**
- other assets (for example, goodwill), enter **O**

Complete Pages CG4 to CG6 for all U, L and O transactions

Losses

Description of asset	Type of * disposal. Enter Q, U, L or O	Tick box if estimate or valuation used	Tick box if asset held at 31March 1982	Enter the later of date of acquisition and 16 March 1998	Enter the date of disposal	Disposal proceeds	Enter details of any elections made, reliefs claimed or due and state amount (£)
13				/ /	/ /	£	
14				/ /	/ /	£	
15				/ /	/ /	£	
16				/ /	/ /	£	

Total losses of

BS 12/2002net   TAX RETURN ■ CAPITAL GAINS: PAGE CG2

	H Chargeable Gains after reliefs but before losses and taper	I Enter 'Bus' if business asset	J Taper rate	K Losses deducted K1 Allowable losses of the year	K2 Income losses of 2003-04 set against gains	K3 Unused losses b/f from earlier years	L Gains after losses	M Tapered gains (gains from column L x % in column J)
	£		%	£	£	£	£	£
	£		%	£	£	£	£	£
	£		%	£	£	£	£	£
	£		%	£	£	£	£	£
	£		%	£	£	£	£	£
	£		%	£	£	£	£	£
	£		%	£	£	£	£	£
	£		%	£	£	£	£	£
	£	Bus	%	£	£	£	£	£
	£		%	£	£	£	£	£
	£	Bus	%	£	£	£	£	£
	£		%	£	£	£	£	£
Total	8.1 £ *Total column H*				8.5 £ *Total column K2*	8.6 £ *Total column K3*		8.3 £ *Total column M*

11 **Attributed gains from UK resident trusts where no election has been made for the set off of personal losses** (see page CGN4) *(enter the name of the Trust on Page CG7)* £

12 **Attributed gains from non UK resident trusts where no election has been made for the set off of personal losses** (see page CGN4) *(enter the name of the Trust on Page CG7)* £

Total of attributed gains where no election has been made (total of rows 11 and 12) 8.4 £

Total taxable gains (after allowable losses and taper relief) box 8.3 + box 8.4 £

Copy to box 8.7 on Page CG8 and complete Pages CG4 to CG6 for all U, L and O transactions

	Losses arising
	£
	£
	£
	£
year	8.2 £

continued over

Other shares or securities (U) - further information

Please give details of each transaction of this type of asset in the boxes below. If you have more than two of these transactions to return, please photocopy this Page before completion. (Please also complete Pages CG2 and CG3.)

1st transaction

Description of shares or securities - including name of company, company registration number (if known), number, class and nominal value of shares. Also, if possible, give a history of the shares disposed of, for instance, if there has been a reorganisation or takeover (give details of the original company and shares held in that company)

Tick box if you have already submitted form CG34 ☐

State any connection between you and the person from whom you acquired the asset, or to whom you disposed of the asset (see Notes, page CGN14)

If you have used an estimate or valuation in your capital gains computation but have not submitted form CG34, please enter the date to which the valuation relates, the amount (£) and the reason for the estimate or valuation. Please also attach a copy of any valuation obtained

2nd transaction

Description of shares or securities - including name of company, company registration number (if known), number, class and nominal value of shares. Also, if possible, give a history of the shares disposed of, for instance, if there has been a reorganisation or takeover (give details of the original company and shares held in that company)

Tick box if you have already submitted form CG34 ☐

State any connection between you and the person from whom you acquired the asset, or to whom you disposed of the asset (see Notes, page CGN14)

If you have used an estimate or valuation in your capital gains computation but have not submitted form CG34, please enter the date to which the valuation relates, the amount (£) and the reason for the estimate or valuation. Please also attach a copy of any valuation obtained

BS 12/2002net

Land and property disposals (L) - further information

Please give details of each transaction of this type of asset in the boxes below. If you have more than two of these transactions to return, please photocopy this Page before completion. (Please also complete Pages CG2 and CG3.)

1st transaction

Full address of land/property affected (attach a copy of any plan if this helps identification)

Description of land/property disposed of, including details of your ownership, for example freehold/leasehold and any tenancies affecting your ownership and the date of transaction or any other date for which a valuation has been made.

Tick box if you have already submitted form CG34

State any connection between you and the person from whom you acquired the asset, or to whom you disposed of the asset (see Notes, page CGN14)

If you have used an estimate or valuation in your capital gains computation but have not submitted form CG34, please enter the date to which the valuation relates, the amount (£) and the reason for the estimate or valuation. Please also attach a copy of any valuation obtained.

2nd transaction

Full address of land/property affected (attach a copy of any plan if this helps identification)

Description of land/property disposed of, including details of your ownership, for example freehold/leasehold and any tenancies affecting your ownership and the date of transaction or any other date for which a valuation has been made.

Tick box if you have already submitted form CG34

State any connection between you and the person from whom you acquired the asset, or to whom you disposed of the asset (see Notes, page CGN14)

If you have used an estimate or valuation in your capital gains computation but have not submitted form CG34, please enter the date to which the valuation relates, the amount (£) and the reason for the estimate or valuation. Please also attach a copy of any valuation obtained.

BS 12/2002net TAX RETURN ■ CAPITAL GAINS: PAGE CG5 *continued over*

Other assets (O) - further information

Please give details of any transaction involving any other type of asset in the boxes below. If you have more than two of these transactions to return, please photocopy this Page before completion. (Please also complete Pages CG2 and CG3.)

1st transaction

Full description of the asset (other than shares or land/property) affected and any other information which helps identify the asset.

Tick box if you have already submitted form CG34 ☐

State any connection between you and the person from whom you acquired the asset, or to whom you disposed of the asset (see Notes, page CGN14)

If you have used an estimate or valuation in your capital gains computation but have not submitted form CG34, please enter the date to which the valuation relates, the amount (£) and the reason for the estimate or valuation. Please also attach a copy of any valuation obtained.

2nd transaction

Full description of the asset (other than shares or land/property) affected and any other information which helps identify the asset

Tick box if you have already submitted form CG34 ☐

State any connection between you and the person from whom you acquired the asset, or to whom you disposed of the asset (see Notes, page CGN14)

If you have used an estimate or valuation in your capital gains computation but have not submitted form CG34, please enter the date to which the valuation relates, the amount (£) and the reason for the estimate or valuation. Please also attach a copy of any valuation obtained.

BS 12/2002net

TAX RETURN ■ CAPITAL GAINS: PAGE CG6

Chargeable gains and allowable losses

Once you have completed Page CG1, or Pages CG2 to CG6, fill in this Page.

Have you 'ticked' any row in Column B, 'Tick box if estimate or valuation used' on Pages CG1 or CG2 or in Column C on Page CG2 'Tick box if asset held at 31 March 1982'? **YES** ☐

Have you given details in Column G on Pages CG2 and CG3 of any Capital Gains reliefs claimed or due? **YES** ☐

Are you claiming, and/or using, any clogged losses (see Notes, page CGN11)? **YES** ☐

Enter from Page CG1 or column AA on Page CG2:

- the number of transactions in quoted shares or other securities **box Q**
- the number of transactions in other shares or securities **box U**
- the number of transactions in land and property **box L**
- the number of gains attributed to settlors **box T**
- the number of other transactions **box O**

Total taxable gains (from Page CG1 **or** Page CG3) **8.7** £

Your taxable gains *minus* the annual exempt amount of £7,900 (leave blank if '0' or negative) — box 8.7 *minus* £7,700 — **8.8** £

Additional liability in respect of non-resident or dual resident trusts (see Notes, page CGN6) **8.9** £

Capital losses

(If your loss arose on a transaction with a connected person, see page CGN14, you can only set that loss against gains you make on disposals to that same connected person. See the notes on clogged losses on page CGN11.)

■ ***This year's losses***

- Total (normally from box 8.2 on Page CG3 or box F2 on Page CG1. But, if you have clogged losses, see Notes, page CGN10) **8.10** £
- Used against gains (total of column K1 on Page CG3, or the smaller of boxes F1 and F2 on Page CG1) **8.11** £
- Used against earlier years' gains (generally only available to personal representatives, see Notes, page CGN11) **8.12** £
- Used against income (only losses of the type described on page CGN9 can be used against income) **8.13A** £ amount claimed against income of 2003-04; **8.13B** £ amount claimed against income of 2002-03 — box 8.13A + box 8.13B — **8.13** £
- This year's unused losses — box 8.10 *minus* (boxes 8.11 + 8.12 + 8.13) — **8.14** £

■ ***Summary of earlier years' losses***

- Unused losses of 1996-97 and later years **8.15** £
- Used this year (losses from box 8.15 are used in priority to losses from box 8.18) (column K3 on Page CG3 or box F6 on Page CG1) **8.16** £
- Remaining unused losses of 1996-97 and later years — box 8.15 *minus* box 8.16 — **8.17** £
- Unused losses of 1995-96 and earlier years **8.18** £
- Used this year (losses from box 8.15 are used in priority to losses from box 8.18) (column K3 on Page CG3 or box F6 on Page CG1) — box 8.6 *minus* box 8.16 (or box F6 *minus* box 8.16) — **8.19** £

■ ***Total of unused losses to carry forward***

- Carried forward losses of 1996-97 and later years — box 8.14 + box 8.17 — **8.20** £
- Carried forward losses of 1995-96 and earlier years — box 8.18 *minus* box 8.19 — **8.21** £

BS 12/2002net

Index

See overleaf for information on other
BPP products and how to order

AAT Order

To BPP Professional Education, Aldine Place, London W12 8AW
Tel: 020 8740 2211. Fax: 020 8740 1184
E-mail: Publishing@bpp.com Web:www.bpp.com

Mr/Mrs/Ms (Full name)
Daytime delivery address
Postcode
Daytime Tel E-mail

FOUNDATION (£14.95 except as indicated)	5/03 Texts	5/03 Kits	Special offer	8/03 Passcards	Tapes
Units 1 & 2 Receipts and Payments	☐	☐		Foundation	
Unit 3 Ledger Balances and Initial Trial Balance	☐		Foundation Sage Bookeeping and Excel Spreadsheets CD-ROM free if ordering all Foundation Text and Kits, including Units 21 and 22/23 ☐	£6.95 ☐	£10.00 ☐
Unit 4 Supplying Information for Mgmt Control	☐				
Unit 21 Working with Computers (£9.95) (6/03)	☐				
Unit 22/23 Healthy Workplace/Personal Effectiveness (£9.95)	☐				
Sage and Excel for Foundation (CD-ROM £9.95)	☐				
INTERMEDIATE (£9.95 except as indicated)					
Unit 5 Financial Records and Accounts	☐	☐		£5.95 ☐	£10.00 ☐
Unit 6/7 Costs and Reports (Combined Text £14.95)	☐				
Unit 6 Costs and Revenues		☐		£5.95 ☐	£10.00 ☐
Unit 7 Reports and Returns		☐		£5.95 ☐	
TECHNICIAN (£9.95 except as indicated)					
Unit 8/9 Managing Performance and Controlling Resources	☐	☐		£5.95 ☐	£10.00 ☐
Spreadsheets for Technician (CD-ROM)	☐				
Unit 10 Core Managing Systems and People (£14.95)	☐		Spreadsheets for Technicians CD-ROM free if take Unit 8/9 Text and Kit ☐		
Unit 11 Option Financial Statements (A/c Practice)	☐	☐		£5.95 ☐	£10.00 ☐
Unit 12 Option Financial Statements (Central Govnmt)	☐	☐			
Unit 15 Option Cash Management and Credit Control	☐	☐		£5.95 ☐	
Unit 17 Option Implementing Audit Procedures	☐	☐		£5.95 ☐	
Unit 18 Option Business Tax (FA03)(8/03 Text & Kit)	☐	☐		£5.95 ☐	
Unit 19 Option Personal Tax (FA 03)(8/03 Text & Kit)	☐	☐		£5.95 ☐	
TECHNICIAN 2002 (£9.95)					
Unit 18 Option Business Tax FA02 (8/02 Text & Kit)	☐	☐			
Unit 19 Option Personal Tax FA02 (8/02 Text & Kit)	☐	☐			
SUBTOTAL	£	£	£	£	£

TOTAL FOR PRODUCTS £

POSTAGE & PACKING

	First	Each extra	
Texts/Kits			
UK	£3.00	£3.00	£
Europe*	£6.00	£4.00	£
Rest of world	£20.00	£10.00	£
Passcards			
UK	£2.00	£1.00	£
Europe*	£3.00	£2.00	£
Rest of world	£8.00	£8.00	£
Tapes			
UK	£2.00	£1.00	£
Europe*	£3.00	£2.00	£
Rest of world	£8.00	£8.00	£

TOTAL FOR POSTAGE & PACKING £
(Max £12 Texts/Kits/Passcards - deliveries in UK)

Grand Total (Cheques to *BPP Professional Education*)
I enclose a cheque for (incl. Postage) £
Or charge to Access/Visa/Switch
Card Number
Expiry date Start Date
Issue Number (Switch Only)
Signature

We aim to deliver to all UK addresses inside 5 working days; a signature will be required. Orders to all EU addresses should be delivered within 6 working days. All other orders to overseas addresses should be delivered within 8 working days. * Europe includes the Republic of Ireland and the Channel Islands.

See overleaf for information on other
BPP products and how to order

AAT Order

To BPP Professional Education, Aldine Place, London W12 8AW
Tel: 020 8740 2211. Fax: 020 8740 1184
E-mail: Publishing@bpp.com Web:www.bpp.com

Mr/Mrs/Ms (Full name)

Daytime delivery address

Postcode

Daytime Tel E-mail

OTHER MATERIAL FOR AAT STUDENTS	8/03 Texts	3/03 Text
FOUNDATION (£5.95)		
Basic Mathematics	☐	
INTERMEDIATE (£5.95)		
Basic Bookkeeping (for students exempt from Foundation)	☐	
FOR ALL STUDENTS (£5.95)		
Building Your Portfolio (old standards)		☐
Building Your Portfolio (new standards)	☐	
	£	£

TOTAL FOR PRODUCTS £

POSTAGE & PACKING

	First	Each extra	
Texts/Kits			
UK	£3.00	£3.00	£
Europe*	£6.00	£4.00	£
Rest of world	£20.00	£10.00	£
Passcards			
UK	£2.00	£1.00	£
Europe*	£3.00	£2.00	£
Rest of world	£8.00	£8.00	£
Tapes			
UK	£2.00	£1.00	£
Europe*	£3.00	£2.00	£
Rest of world	£8.00	£8.00	£

TOTAL FOR POSTAGE & PACKING £

(Max £12 Texts/Kits/Passcards - deliveries in UK)

Grand Total (Cheques to *BPP Professional Education*)

I enclose a cheque for (incl. Postage) £

Or charge to Access/Visa/Switch

Card Number

Expiry date Start Date

Issue Number (Switch Only)

Signature

We aim to deliver to all UK addresses inside 5 working days; a signature will be required. Orders to all EU addresses should be delivered within 6 working days. All other orders to overseas addresses should be delivered within 8 working days. * Europe includes the Republic of Ireland and the Channel Islands.

Review Form & Free Prize Draw – Unit 18 Preparing Business Taxation Computations (FA 2003) (8/03)

All original review forms from the entire BPP range, completed with genuine comments, will be entered into one of two draws on 31 January 2004 and 31 July 2004. The names on the first four forms picked out on each occasion will be sent a cheque for £50.

Name: ______________________ **Address:** ______________________

____

____

How have you used this Interactive Text?
(Tick one box only)

☐ Home study (book only)

☐ On a course: college ______________

☐ With 'correspondence' package

☐ Other ______________

Why did you decide to purchase this Interactive Text? *(Tick one box only)*

☐ Have used BPP Texts in the past

☐ Recommendation by friend/colleague

☐ Recommendation by a lecturer at college

☐ Saw advertising

☐ Other ______________

During the past six months do you recall seeing/receiving any of the following?
(Tick as many boxes as are relevant)

☐ Our advertisement in *Accounting Technician* magazine

☐ Our advertisement in *Pass*

☐ Our brochure with a letter through the post

Which (if any) aspects of our advertising do you find useful?
(Tick as many boxes as are relevant)

☐ Prices and publication dates of new editions

☐ Information on Interactive Text content

☐ Facility to order books off-the-page

☐ None of the above

Have you used the companion Assessment Kit for this subject? ☐ **Yes** ☐ **No**

Your ratings, comments and suggestions would be appreciated on the following areas

	Very useful	*Useful*	*Not useful*
Introduction	☐	☐	☐
Chapter contents lists	☐	☐	☐
Examples	☐	☐	☐
Activities and answers	☐	☐	☐
Key learning points	☐	☐	☐
Quick quizzes and answers	☐	☐	☐

	Excellent	*Good*	*Adequate*	*Poor*
Overall opinion of this Text	☐	☐	☐	☐

Do you intend to continue using BPP Interactive Texts/Assessment Kits? ☐ Yes ☐ No

Please note any further comments and suggestions/errors on the reverse of this page.

The BPP author of this edition can be e-mailed at: suedexter@bpp.com

Please return this form to: Janice Ross, BPP Professional Education, FREEPOST, London, W12 8BR

Review Form & Free Prize Draw (continued)

Please note any further comments and suggestions/errors below

Free Prize Draw Rules

1. Closing date for 31 January 2004 draw is 31 December 2003. Closing date for 31 July 2004 draw is 30 June 2004.
2. Restricted to entries with UK and Eire addresses only. BPP employees, their families and business associates are excluded.
3. No purchase necessary. Entry forms are available upon request from BPP Professional Education. No more than one entry per title, per person. Draw restricted to persons aged 16 and over.
4. Winners will be notified by post and receive their cheques not later than 6 weeks after the relevant draw date.
5. The decision of the promoter in all matters is final and binding. No correspondence will be entered into.